PRAIS

PRACTICAL SUSTAINABILITY

"As governments have launched their new green deals to implement the Paris Accord and the UN Agenda 2030, Glickman and Kavanaugh have provided a timely, much-needed, and actionable guide on how to make it happen. In *Practical Sustainability*, a well-researched and science-based handbook, they show in detail how to achieve environmental targets and carbon neutrality through circular commerce and exponential technologies across industries and smart cities. I highly recommend *Practical Sustainability* to everybody who seeks an integrally sustainable, fast road out of current existential crises and who wants to ensure the future of civilization on our beautiful blue planet."

—DR. MARIANA BOZESAN, Europe's Leading Female Investor 2019 and author of *Integral Investing: From Profit to Prosperity*

"*Practical Sustainability* goes deep into the domain of sustainability and returns with a thoughtful and comprehensive framework that can really help asset managers get proactive about this critical topic."

—DEAN HOPKINS, EVP and COO of Oxford Properties

"We are at the dawn of the ESG revolution. Corey Glickman and Jeff Kavanaugh have done the hard job of simplifying a very complex topic and giving enterprise leaders an actionable playbook for a practical sustainability model. For every stakeholder looking at ESG, this is the strategy and playbook you've been looking for."

—R "RAY" WANG, CEO of Constellation Research and two-time bestselling author of *Disrupting Digital Business and Everybody Wants To Rule The World*

"Corey and Jeff weren't joking when they called this book *Practical Sustainability*. It's bursting with helpful frameworks for readers to apply in their own projects to make sustainability really happen. The focus on Smart Spaces fills me with hope for the future: the technologies already here today are going to transform how our offices, factories, homes and more, operate—this work will help us all to accelerate the implementation of the technologies and the sustainable outcomes that the world needs."

—**MATTHEW MARSON**, Global Technology Sector Leader, Arcadis

"There is an urgency to provide next-generation workplaces that are safer, healthier, more collaborative, and more productive. In their book *Practical Sustainability*, Glickman and Kavanaugh present how to deliver resiliency."

—**SCOTT RECHLER**, Chairman and CEO of RXR Realty

"*Practical Sustainability* is required reading for universities, government and community leaders, and students looking to fulfill the promise of smart region initiatives."

—**DIANA BOWMAN**, ASU Associate Dean and Professor and Co-Director of the Center for Smart Cities and Regions (CenSCR)

"Ideas are to human action what steel is to the skyscraper. Corey Glickman and Jeff Kavanaugh expand our practical imagination, inspiring those of us with power to stop the impending ecocide. Read this book and do something!"

—**JOHN SVIOKLA**, Senior Executive and Partner at Manifold Group, a venture holding company

"Smart cities will be a driving force for sustainable, equitable growth for the rest of this century. In their book *Practical Sustainability*, Glickman and Kavanaugh share a model that practitioners and policymakers alike can use to create a more sustainable future."

—**GORDON FELLER**, Founder of Meeting
of the Minds and smart cities leader

"Understanding how to leverage technology in smart spaces is a key success factor. In their book *Practical Sustainability*, Glickman and Kavanaugh provide real-world experience and strategies on the role technology plays in the race to carbon neutrality.

—**SPYROS SAKELLARIADIS**, Global Director of
IoT Business Development at ICONICS

In *Practical Sustainability*, Glickman and Kavanaugh address an important problem: How do leading organizations achieve sustainability targets while staying strong financially? These solutions are not merely a social good, but must serve a purpose that results in profit without harming people, our planet or our future prosperity.

—**RON BOSE** Ph.D., Professor of Information
Technology and Management, Naveen Jindal School
of Management, The University of Texas at Dallas

PRACTICAL SUSTAINABILITY

CIRCULAR COMMERCE, SMARTER SPACES, AND HAPPIER HUMANS

COREY GLICKMAN and
JEFF KAVANAUGH

HOUNDSTOOTH
PRESS

PRACTICAL SUSTAINABILITY
Circular Commerce, Smarter Spaces, and Happier Humans

ISBN 978-1-5445-2744-4 *Hardcover*
      978-1-5445-2742-0 *Paperback*
      978-1-5445-2743-7 *Ebook*

Only within the moment of time
represented by the present century has
one species—humans—acquired significant
power to alter the nature of the world.

—Rachel Carson

CONTENTS

FOREWORD
by DR. MICHAEL M. CROW

For millennia, human beings have taken natural resources and utilized them as instruments for social advancement, raising living standards. In most countries, we have generally moved beyond the poverty, widespread starvation, and lack of representation that characterized the lives of almost all in the pre-industrial era. In doing so, however, we have become increasingly disconnected from nature during our socioeconomic development and divorced from our historical reliance on nature for our well-being.

As a result, we need to undertake conscious, global efforts to improve our stewardship of natural capital—air, water, other natural resources—and to elevate sustainability as a value just as fundamental to modern society as liberty, justice, and equality. These must be efforts to repair and renew our connection to the environment and redefine the search for real-world solutions to meet today's challenges.

When I led the founding of a Global Institute of Sustainability and a School of Sustainability at Arizona State University in 2004,

I was acutely aware of the importance of sustainability to the built environment around ASU. I also sensed a unique opportunity within ASU to create a sustainability research laboratory focused on generating practical solutions, including new mindsets, cultures, and workforce capacities. This importance has only grown in the years since, and those academic institutions must play an important role in promoting and advancing sustainability research.

Sustainability and the role of research and development in it had been part of my life's work since my PhD at Syracuse University in the mid-1980s; my dissertation discussed the balance between market and political authority in R&D systems. Before joining Columbia University, I was intimately involved in R&D at energy laboratories in several roles at Iowa State University, my alma mater. I founded the Earth Institute, a prototype for the sustainability work that ASU carries on today. In these prior roles, I became attentive to the design and the outputs of research organizations—and, often in sustainability, how this research failed to lead to outcomes, just as our society's unmitigated exploitation of the planet has caught up with us and brought us to the brink of catastrophe.

This ineffectiveness is because research is typically seen as the end goal when it is the means to our future. At ASU, our sustainability science is outcome-driven: it leads to building sustainable cities and systems. Just as importantly, like the rest of our research enterprise, it is transdisciplinary—enabling new modes of thinking about critical environmental challenges. We have brought together a variety of interests in support of the sustainability mission. We are producing use-inspired research that can have an immediate impact on the Phoenix metropolitan area and beyond.

The world is experiencing upheaval at an accelerated pace—new technologies, the COVID-19 pandemic, and, behind them all, the climate crisis. These events have prompted a collective rethinking of conventional wisdom and brought about new communication and collaboration patterns. As the impacts of a changing climate become more apparent than before, and we have even less time to act, so too must universities accelerate the pace of their sustainability research. There is a tremendous opportunity—indeed, an imperative—in sustainability to achieve global impact.

Recently, we opened the Julie Ann Wrigley Global Futures Laboratory, a "medical school for the Earth." When we sought partners for the lab and its new smart cities endeavors, it came as no surprise that we found a like-minded soul in Infosys, known for its innovative, science-minded process and commitment to Practical Sustainability.

Practical Sustainability: Circular Commerce, Smarter Spaces, and Happier Humans by Corey Glickman and Jeff Kavanaugh lays out a compelling case and a practical, outcome-based approach to sustainability. These Infosys executives, with contributions from ASU experts, have provided a framework for leaders to understand and act across buildings, supply chains, and the human element.

The importance of buildings in sustainability often goes unnoticed. They are responsible for nearly 40% of annual greenhouse gas emissions, a third of which is generated in the construction process or the generation of building materials—embodied energy. In 2013, we embarked on a significant renovation of Manzanita Hall, a dormitory on ASU's Tempe campus, allowing us to retain all the embodied energy in the original 1967 structure. We have built many new structures using materials with low, embodied energy.

The production of consumer goods is a significant driver of climatic stressors. More than 80% of water withdrawals are connected to these goods, and nearly two-thirds of tropical forest loss is attributable to agriculture. Supply chains are the vital link in this system. A decade ago, we collaborated with the University of Arkansas to create The Sustainability Consortium, a partnership with leading companies and organizations to help them deliver more sustainable products and make their supply chains more resilient to climate risks.

Lastly, sustainability is a problem with an often-ignored *human* dimension. Not only is climate change the result of human actions, but we can also have all the scientific and technological solutions we seek yet lack the political will to use them. At ASU, we have brought together humanities and sustainability scholars to provide critical, ethical, and moral perspectives on the issues we face. Repairing the interface between the natural and human systems cannot be done without a working understanding of the human system.

This framework goes in hand with the ASU ethos of use-inspired research, not done for its own sake but carried out to achieve social impact in our region and the world. The smart spaces initiatives at ASU are essential steps in crafting scalable solutions across the Greater Phoenix Smart Region and beyond. Glickman and Kavanaugh emphasize the importance of continuous innovation, tools and thinking, and sustainability as something to be done now instead of an abstract concept.

This emphasis on action *now* helps Glickman and Kavanaugh propose solutions with immediate application in global settings—technology-enabled but designed for humans—conceived with sustainability embedded at every level. At its best, Practical Sustainability becomes *regenerative*—giving back to the environment instead of taking from and exploiting it, as humans have for so long. Suppose we wish to leave this planet "greater and better and more beautiful than it was transmitted to us" for future generations, in the words of an ancient Athenian oath. In that case, Practical Sustainability is essential in that endeavor.

— DR. MICHAEL M. CROW

PRESIDENT, ARIZONA STATE UNIVERSITY

JULY 2021

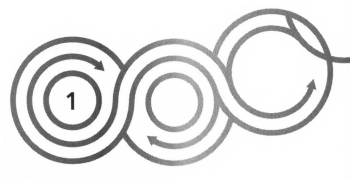

PRACTICAL SUSTAINABILITY MODEL

SUSTAINABILITY, EVOLUTION, AND OPPORTUNITY

BLACK EARTH, ARCHITECTING AMAZONIA

The first Europeans in the Amazon reported people living in the rain forest, villages, and farms ribboned along the river with massive cities in the distance.[1] Two centuries later, these reports were dismissed, believing the Amazon's soils were too poor in nutrients to support large numbers of people, let alone cities and civilizations.[2]

Then modern science changed everything. Researchers created a digital twin of southern Amazonia—a soft copy of the region, allowing them to digitally peel back the jungle canopy and see what's underneath. The result? Traces of a civilization ten million strong, and cities linked with villages, all interconnected by radiating roads in a system of systems.[3]

How did the Amazon support so many people? They used a technology called *terra preta*, an ultra-fertile regenerative super soil,[4] a carbon sink reportedly able to retain up to six times more carbon than normal—extremely useful if you're trying to get to Net-Zero.

Terra preta was considered a natural phenomenon until as late as the 1990s.[5] Then experts became aware that its mix of charcoal, bone, compost, and manure pointed to human origins.[6] The broader implications are shocking—*humans architected Amazonia and helped construct the rain forest*. These were agrarian smart cities, and the technology was the very ground beneath their feet—a regenerative, fertile mix like soil on steroids. If so-called primitive peoples could engineer a sustainable ecosystem, why not us today?

GREEN MOUNTAIN, EDEN IN ASCENSION

In 1836, a young Charles Darwin prepared to leave for Ascension Island. Thirty-four square miles small, Ascension Island sits a thousand miles west of Africa and fourteen hundred miles east of Brazil. On arrival, Darwin looked up and saw 'The Peak,' a mountain rising 2,818 feet into the mist. It was bare, except for a single, solitary tree. This barren biosphere sparked an idea and a vision in Darwin's mind—why not test evolution by introducing new, non-native species of flora and fauna to the island from around the world?[7]

Ascension became a laboratory and an experiment. Darwin's best friend, Joseph Dalton Hooker, arrived on the island and put Darwin's idea into action seven years later. Hooker eventually succeeded his father as director of the Royal Botanical Gardens in Kew,[8] site of the largest and most diverse botanical collection on Earth[9]—and provided the opening for Hooker to pull strings to aid the experiment.

In a public-private partnership with the Royal Navy, Hooker created a green, global supply chain into Kew, and then onto Ascension. First came the trees by the thousands, trapping The Peak's mountain mist, creating a cloud forest saturated in moisture. Then came the birds and the fruit.[10]

In under a century, The Peak was terraformed into a tiny Eden and renamed Green Mountain. What was once species-poor became species-rich. Sparse ferns became a lush forest, and the natural ecological timescales of millennia shrunk down into decades. Ascension's cloud forest, however, is different from every other on Earth—it's artificial, not natural or pristine at all. Like *terra preta* in the Amazon, it's designed and built by humans who hacked evolution.

Over time, humans evolved the Amazon and Ascension into novel, sustainable ecologies. These lessons from the past provide clues to our present. Together, they might even guide our future when we leave this planet.

A CHANGED WORLD

Sustainability is hardly a new concept, as the earlier examples suggest. The Industrial Age distracted humanity through the incredible inventions and gains in efficiency that lifted the standard of living for many millions of people and created the middle class that sustained democracy. Humans saw the Earth mainly as an infinite source of resources, given the much lower population base and energy consumption (one billion people and six terawatt-hours in 1800, compared to nearly eight billion people and 173K TWh in 2019[11,12]). As the twenty-first century gained steam, a new awareness took hold about Earth's finite resources and fragile ecosystem.

Then events in 2020 threatened us with a new Dark Age. A "known-unknown," the COVID-19 pandemic opened our eyes to the fact that we were sorely unprepared for its threat. The pandemic brought entire industries to a halt. Global supply chains stretched to the breaking point; millions were unemployed within weeks, and buildings were left uninhabited. As a society, we believed that becoming digital meant controlling our future, yet we must also respect the natural part of our existence and ability to thrive. COVID gave us a preview of the potential consequences we all face when unable to adapt, improvise, and overcome.

At the same time, people saw the possibility of the planet healing itself during this time of pause, with a brief drop in emissions coupled with businesses and workers adopting the new norm.[13] Our response to COVID highlighted the absolute necessity for resilience, along with the urgency of climate change and its corrective possibilities. Then the world came together to develop and distribute vaccines that set in motion a return to more in-person social and business activities. In our return to the new norm, we also accelerated our efforts to battle climate change and the threat to our economic well-being and very existence.

Taken together, the events of the past decade have accelerated the need for businesses and buildings to do more—they need to become symbols of the era, of progress. Where once it was commerce and grand structures, enterprises now need to reflect and convey a message to stakeholders, including shareholders, employees, customers, partners, and society.

In the preface to his 2021 book, *Stakeholder Capitalism: A Global Economy that Works for Progress, People and Planet*, Klaus Schwab recalls the first call from Beijing about COVID-19. He describes it as "an AC/BC moment when attention shifted from the time before COVID-19 to the reality that set in *after* COVID-19."[14]

Professor Schwab mentioned how "one thing has changed in the interim period between 'BC' and 'AC'...a greater understanding among the population, business leaders, and government that creating a better world would require working together."[15]

Together with heightened expectations, all this change has coincided with technologies such as Internet of Things (IoT), artificial intelligence, and machine learning reaching a tipping point in functionality, price point, and adoption. Digital tech has crossed the chasm, and leaders have difficulty envisioning the potential combined impact of these converging exponential technologies.

For instance, the market rapidly adopted cloud computing in the past decade, aggregating large amounts of data from disparate sources, and applied highly scalable computing power. Sensors have changed the market, driven by a combination of smartphones and intelligence at the edge. Consumer devices like iPads and smartphones have a depth-finding laser scanner, which was unimaginable until recently. These sensors are not only proliferating, but they're also extremely lightweight, very low power, and inexpensive.

NEW REQUIREMENTS, NEW SOLUTIONS

While the pandemic significantly accelerated change, it was hardly the only trend, and in fact, several underlying trends were already in motion.

The most powerful and profitable companies have demonstrated a clear path to a carbon-neutral future, with a steady stream of new commitments. Sustainability efforts are sustainable only if leaders take a science-based approach and intertwine them with the operating model, company culture, and bottom line. At Infosys, we found that environmental, social, and governance (ESG) efforts are best developed organically, with an eye toward measurable change rather than checking boxes. The emergence of exponential technologies and new mindsets allows companies to chase these lofty goals practically without dragging down the financials. The virtuous cycle need not be a cost center.

To a great degree, the elements needed to pursue sustainability are already in place; it's just that companies have not yet unlocked their full potential. Five overarching trends have raised sustainability to be on the boardroom agenda simultaneously and a priority for first-line employees, and here is why:

1. **Environment:** Sustainability is now on the boardroom agenda with an emphasis on reducing the carbon footprint and reduced waste. Buildings generate 40% of all greenhouse gas emissions (GHG) and are the most prominent factor to meet United Nations and Paris Agreement goals.[16]

Figure 1.1. **Megatrends Affecting Sustainability**
Source: Infosys Knowledge Institute

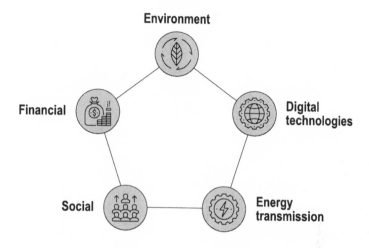

2. **Digital technologies:** At the same time, there has been a convergence of exponential technologies like cloud, AI, ML, data, Internet of Things, and computational power. The possibilities seem endless, but applying all this tech to buildings and supply chains is still evolving.

3. **Energy transmission:** Power purchase agreements (PPAs) manage energy assets, provide low carbon power, heating and cooling, and campus mobility driven by intelligent digital platforms. Integrated Energy-as-a-Service enables campuses and cities to use energy more efficiently and optimize supply and demand across multiple users and assets.

4. **Social:** Society expects organizations to aid their people's development and provide meaningful opportunities for

all employees—and even their communities—through diversity, inclusion, and accessibility.

5. **Financial:** From counting coins to constraining carbon, finance takes a holistic approach, analyzing ESG and traditional financial performance in a unified view. Auditing and portfolio management have expanded to include sustainability in risk management and credit ratings.

The sustainability discussion can no longer be one of high-minded, impractical theories addressing aspirational goals targeted for 2050. Nor can sustainability be a series of tactical, low-impact activities that comply with regulations and signal virtue but do not make a real difference. At Infosys, we have experienced this during our ten-year journey to carbon neutrality and delivered social initiatives at scale in our communities. This activity-outcome gap led us to envision and develop a new, evolved sustainability model for the stakeholder capitalism era.

THE CASE FOR *PRACTICAL* SUSTAINABILITY

NAVIGATING THE SUSTAINABILITY MAZE

This book is for optimistic yet clear-eyed practitioners on sustainability concepts that are practical: grounded in science, acknowledged by human behavior, and focused on outcomes. We define Practical Sustainability as continuous environmental, social, and governance innovation based on science, human-centric technology, and regenerative thinking. It is urgent, focused on outcomes, and something to be done now instead of viewed as an abstract concept.

The authors wrote this book based on Infosys' experience in our sustainability journey, client portfolios of similar work, and primary research from the Infosys Knowledge Institute. For context, Infosys is a global technology and engineering services firm founded in 1981. It operates fifty million square feet of its buildings, across eighteen campuses and offices in fifty countries, with 270,000 full-time employees.

In the past decade, Infosys' own experience provided an abundance of data points as to what works and what does not. How do we know Practical Sustainability works? Through intelligent automation, Infosys reduced carbon emissions by 9.3% year over year for ten years (helping us become carbon neutral) and reduced water consumption by 60%. We also reduced per capita energy usage by 55% ($225M in energy savings) and certified twenty-seven million square feet as the highest-rated green buildings. We also eliminated single-use plastics and achieved 100% recycling of plastic waste across operations. At the same time, we increased our employee count to 270,000, more than 160% growth since 2008, yet only 20% growth in energy usage.[17] Equally important, Practical Sustainability improved employee productivity and experience measured through efficient desk and room-booking services and improved visitor satisfaction-rate experience from site entry to exit.

Our social initiatives matched these environmental results, where Infosys also invested heavily of its time, talent, and treasure to help the communities and countries in which it operates. Sixty thousand libraries were refurbished, a daily hot midday meal was provided for one million students (to keep them in school), and thousands of schools and millions of students were assisted with computer science education. The common theme across initiatives was to apply our expertise to solve a business or technical problem with social impact in a quantifiable way. That is the essence of Practical Sustainability—to use business expertise through the lens of ESG and hold initiatives to a science-based, financially sound standard.

Infosys has also helped numerous companies start or continue their journeys to Practical Sustainability. However, this book is not about Infosys—the authors' primary goal is to provide insights and recommendations to assist individuals, companies, and governments in improving sustainable practices, reducing energy costs, and enhancing user experience. While Practical Sustainability is a fresh approach to a significant business trend, it is also much more—the more of these ideas that are shared and implemented, the better for all.

As we progressed on our journey and served clients in the practical aspects of sustainability, a fundamental question emerged:

How do leading organizations use circular commerce and smart spaces to achieve sustainability targets while staying strong financially?

It is hard enough to be profitable through disruption—how on Earth can a company also meet environmental targets, support social goals, and demonstrate good governance? Others were asking the same question because we saw Practical Sustainability emerge as top of mind in discussions with our clients and industry analysts as they explored these programs. Along the way, we delivered solutions for individual buildings, campuses, multi-tenant facilities, stadiums, airports, and various public infrastructures—across all program phases, from concept through delivery and operations.

The research for this book incorporates and extends earlier Infosys research, tracking the progress of Global 2000 companies. It also includes our ten-year journey and interviews with executives of leading companies that provide technology and services in the ESG ecosystem.

Over the last few years, we surveyed these stakeholders and analyzed findings to understand trends, develop insights, and provide recommendations. There are few playbooks set yet for the still-emerging technology wave in sustainability. We offer this book as a guide and recommend a consultative approach with a robust partner ecosystem and consortium-supported innovation.

FRAMING THE SUSTAINABILITY PROBLEM

Even though companies generally share common sustainability goals, wide variability exists within industry verticals, regions, and regulatory jurisdictions. Consider the difference between a building used for pharmaceutical discovery, one for manufacturing, and a building used as a hospital. All three are part of the healthcare value chain, but each has unique needs for utilizing space. Further, consider the building requirements for sustainability. Although all are interested in security and employee safety, one may emphasize invention, another autonomous production system, and the third could focus on knowledge access for doctors and relaxation for patients.

While corporate social responsibility has evolved into broader sustainability, building construction and operation buildings have changed little in the past thirty years.[18] New digital and technology-aided strategies will drive the change necessary to meet environmental and social targets. A good starting point is a digital roadmap that considers ESG capabilities and typically includes IoT technology investments.

The process of solving a problem begins with the ability to ask the right questions. With that in mind, let's start with the following questions:

- How to measure and reduce carbon emissions?
- How to ensure physical security, safety, and comfort?
- How to increase productivity and unleash creativity?
- How to calculate baseline operational costs?
- How to build resiliency against unforeseen events?

After asking the right questions, identify the metrics required for success. Then test the feasibility of the technology, desirability of the experience, and viability of the business model. Our experience indicates that practitioners can expect to see:

- Up to one year to yield results.
- Twenty-five percent annualized return on investment in three to five years.
- Investment returns in one to two years to retrofit existing space to optimize energy use.
- Four percent productivity improvement with revenue growth.

A baseline provides a starting point for the journey and a source of truth to manage expectations for what one can achieve over time.

SUSTAINABILITY ELEMENTS

Organizations drive continuous improvement through adaptation. It will not be the largest or fastest companies that will succeed, but those that continuously adapt to change successfully. Understanding human (and corporate) impact on the environment influences that adaption. An evolving perceived responsibility also affects enterprise adaption to society and an expanding regulatory compliance burden at local, national, and global levels.

Value chains have changed. We now see the potential to digitize our built environment beyond just the "hearts and lungs" of a physical structure or supply chain. Consumption rapidly evolved from focusing on convenience and disposable use to a new, progressive view based on sustainable practices and reusable goods. Employee expectations have moved from getting a paycheck to having a purpose. Enterprise expectations on safety are now juxtaposed with individual rights concerning privacy.

IT systems are the levers and plumbing of the digital economy. The connection of physical and digital systems will create new challenges and opportunities. It will proliferate the concept of digital democratization, putting much of IT directly into the hands of system users.

Decision-making has changed. We now see the potential to add an integrated digital brain that makes decisions with feedback loops to learn and self-heal. Of course, the COVID-19 pandemic accelerated and intensified change.[19] We see this manifested in five areas, and Table 1.1 shows the transition in thinking across these sustainability operating elements.

Table 1.1. **Evolution of Practical Sustainability Elements**
Source: Infosys Knowledge Institute

Element	Traditional (from)	Practical sustainability (to)
Organization	Physical workplace Shareholder CSR Full-time employees Compliance	Anytime, anywhere workplace Stakeholder ESG Gig economy workforce Change agent
Value chains	Extraction Global sourcing Offline, periodic analysis Black box resources Self-reported, targets	Circularity Proximity to source Connected, instant simulation Resource visibility Supplier-reported, indexes
People	Performance Generic training Physical security Diversity	Fulfillment Personalized learning Holistic wellness Inclusion
IT systems	Corporate tech support Point solutions Dumb endpoints Guarded data Privacy considered	Digital democratization Systems design Smart connected Data transparency Privacy prioritized
Decisions	Dumb endpoints Policy execution Profitable Reactive Analyze everything	Smart connected Influencer Sustainable Predictive Identify anomalies

CSR = corporate social responsibility; ESG = environmental, social, and governance

Organizations have traditionally focused on arranging resources and product (service) delivery to optimize shareholder value. While financial strength is still table stakes in the C-suite, environment, social, and governance requirements add additional complexity and constraints. Further, the market pace of change requires enterprises to evolve rapidly while addressing these other requirements. Resilience has replaced ROI as the persistent narrative, with climate-induced environmental disasters and severe weather, along with ransomware attacks on power grids, connectivity services, businesses, and supply chains.

Value chains for decades focused on efficiency and getting the right product to the right place, at the right time, at the lowest cost, across a global network of raw materials, factories, and transportation channels. Essentially, it was a one-way trip from extraction to the consumer. But now, enterprises must consider a bigger picture: carbon footprint and product provenance, labor practices involved, and reuse of packaging and even the product itself when its useful life is complete. While these concepts are not new, stakeholder expectations have ratcheted higher, and technology advances enable rapid response that was not possible previously.

People have long been vital to enterprise success, but organizations often treated employees and partners as tactical resources. Now people and their talent are ascendant, with employees—not just customers—commanding significant influence. Further, their expectations and priorities have changed about sustainability. They want the good feeling that their employer prioritizes carbon neutrality and social initiatives along with a personalized experience that helps them be productive and learn.[20,21]

IT systems are the levers of the digital economy—the actions that sense input, process data, and initiate response. Like other functions, IT leaders traditionally focused on performance and cost-effectiveness. For example, cloud computing took off due to significant business benefits and lower costs. However, enterprise leaders also need to consider the carbon footprint for all those data centers that support their companies. Despite the remarkable new digital technologies, companies still struggle to respond operationally due to legacy systems, lack of integration, or adoption.

Decisions are the triggers of the digital economy, and they have the power to move markets. While insights engines are on the rise, the additional complexity of environmental, social, and governance requirements demands more from these systems. Deterministic rules engines have accelerated decision-making, but more is needed. The explosion of data and the ESG lens of stakeholder capitalism require new ways to set goals, identify metrics, capture data, and apply cognitive artificial intelligence to add judgment while minimizing destructive bias.

THE PRACTICAL SUSTAINABILITY CONSTRUCT

Practical Sustainability projects are complex because they combine physical attributes with exponential technologies such as IoT. We make them more so through heightened expectations in an age when we compare buildings to other aspects of our life, like autonomous vehicles and Amazon shopping. The adoption of technology and social change has been a laggard in building and real estate, but buildings are physical places and can't just reside in cyberspace form. Furthermore, brownfield conversions will heavily outnumber greenfield building opportunities, and each project will come with its unique challenges.

The real estate industry is transforming how they work while transforming the buildings they create. Real estate owners are now digital service providers whose customers have high expectations. If they fail to deliver, users may choose to avoid the experience altogether and set up shop wherever there is a Wi-Fi hotspot. Technical talent is now as crucial as traditional architects to design and deliver building functionality. In the past, architects were relied upon to include innovative materials and processes in their designs. Today, the pressure is even higher, as the digital world is cross-functional and multi-disciplinary, not an individual or small design team that passes blueprints to construction structural engineers. Digital twins and data scientists have replaced drawings and foam core models.

Integrated architecture and technology strategy are each required in the building design phase. Digital tools and methods are essential to how we think and live and are no longer an afterthought in how we interact in our spaces. Furthermore, our buildings and spaces will become the largest connected network of assets and data on our planet, orbiting the Earth and beyond. Imagine building an orbiting space station or high-tech submarine and the technology, resources, and metrics needed to make it happen cost-effectively.

Our leaders face intense pressure to survive and grow, and they need new models to address the challenges. Taken together, the five sustainability elements described above are pillars that support the Practical Sustainability approach. Each element has a core theme: regenerative future, circular commerce, human experience, system of systems, and digital twin. These themes operate as a combination of natural (physical) and digital, at a scale of one or many. Figure 1.2 shows the Practical Sustainability framework.

Figure 1.2. **Practical Sustainability Framework**
Source: Infosys Knowledge Institute

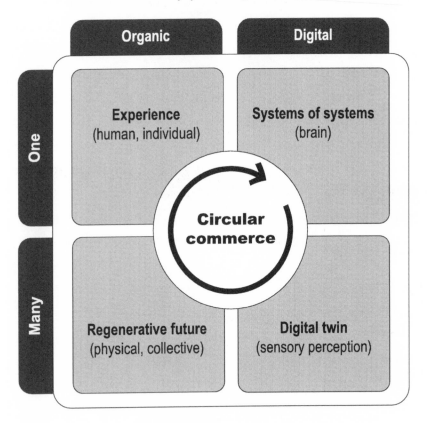

These five themes offer guidance on how to change perspective and view Practical Sustainability as a competitive differentiator, not a commodity to be optimized or regulated to drive compliance. Table 1.2 summarizes the Practical Sustainability themes, along with the key ideas for each theme. Let's review each theme in more detail.

Table 1.2. **Practical Sustainability Themes**

Source: Infosys Knowledge Institute

Element	Theme	Key ideas
Organization	Regenerative future	True ESG with social and governance Decarbonization as quantified priority Formal carbon offset strategy Digital strategy that enables Scope 1, 2, 3 goals Prioritized triple bottom line: people, planet, profits
Value chains	Circular commerce	Circular supply chains Predictive product life cycle management Traceable, ethical product provenance Digital finance with velocity and trust Low carbon energy
People	The human experience	Delight by delivering technology for good Environment, health, and safety management Socially progressive activism Diversity and inclusion as talent engine Measurable quantified outcomes
IT systems	System of systems	Systems design to tame complexity Convergence of cloud + connectivity + IoT Synchronized tech-driven operating model Security and data privacy by design
Decisions	Digital twin	Contextual and spatial data relationships Single pane of glass Historic modeling, real-time status, and future cast simulation Enhanced asset valuation Quantifiable science-based targets

ESG = environmental, social, and governance; IoT = internet of things

REGENERATIVE FUTURE

The first theme is **regenerative future**. Sustainable ecosystems address and elevate environmental, social, and governance considerations to equal footing with financial returns. Environmental metrics can be financial performance drivers. Spending on buildings is only second to costs invested in workforce resources, and buildings generate significant emissions through construction and operation.

Before COVID-19, organizations underutilized 40% of their space.[22] This efficiency gap has increased even more as the world rethinks how to safely and securely office people in our spaces.

Beyond the allure of cost reduction, smart spaces have already shown evidence of improved resource usage and dramatically improved KPIs in energy, carbon, water, and waste. For example, environmental initiatives in our Infosys campus network drove $225 million in energy savings. Energy savings have been reinvested to fund top-line initiatives like employee experience. Further, smart spaces are potent means to pursue decarbonization, develop a formal, carbon-offset strategy, and implement a digital approach that enables sustainability goals.

However, it is not enough to be sustainable. A regenerative mindset is needed to overcome the cumulative burden of past decisions, practices, and infrastructure. The responsibility for new sustainability initiatives, whether new greenfield or retrofit brownfield, extends beyond the organization. Enterprises now evaluate their own sustainability goals and those of their partners and supply chain. Companies and local and national governments have joined the Environmental, Social, and Governance (ESG) movement. This trend includes adopting the seventeen United Nations Sustainable Development Goals (SDGs) and Global Reporting Initiative (GRI) standards, forming Healthy Buildings Indexes,[23,24] and developing ESG policy playbooks. They realize that green practices go hand in hand with wellness, which becomes core to Practical Sustainability. An added incentive is that the ESG investment index of environmentally and socially responsible public firms has begun to outperform peers that lack ESG maturity.[25] Local government is vital to make ESG successful, as buildings are a tangible, stationary asset, and regulations and codes have a distinctly local scope. A paradox of these smart spaces and social initiatives is that companies have local physical presence but are often global in reach. As they choose their goals and standards, these may not align with local or national government standards, or global agreements like the Paris environmental accords.[26]

Sustainable ecosystems are needed to ensure livable cities, where people choose to work, live, and raise their families. Cities will become regenerative through public and private partnerships, seeking to create a strong sense of community and a tax base that attracts and retains businesses, attracting and serving a growing population.

CIRCULAR COMMERCE

The second operating theme is **circular commerce**, which refers to shifts in traditional business models to enable materials and products to be reused and remain in the economy for as long as possible, reducing waste and regenerating natural systems.

Manufacturing generally converts raw materials to components and finished goods, culminating in a customer purchase. Recycling is typically a compliance afterthought, and with products not designed for resource recovery, it wastes many potentially reusable components. This unidirectional model is unsustainable because many vital resources are nonrenewable, extraction can be environmentally damaging, and access to diminishing deposits drives global conflict. Even with potential off-world sources of mined materials, waste and cost will remain a problem.

Circular commerce shifts business and operating models toward products with longer service life and that can be more completely recycled. It seeks to use policy and education to encourage the intentional redesign of products and services for extended use and recirculation of components for the most prolonged viable period. This transition requires a broad combination of business model, technology, and social innovation. For example, in addition to shifting the manufacturing model, financial and consumer habits may also need to adjust. The traditional notion of "better, faster, cheaper" may not capture the full scope today. A sustainable product may require more cost or time to produce in exchange for a significantly longer service life. Products may shift, such as office furniture leases instead of sales, with the lessor reupholstering the furniture after a set time and avoiding the need to discard and produce new updated furniture.

HUMAN EXPERIENCE

The third theme is **human experience**. Each company and each person have the innate drive to achieve success as they define it. If one can find joy in their daily activities, they become content, productive, and display general wellness and inclusivity. Practical Sustainability helps people do more and have better experiences.

Smart spaces sense, adapt, and amplify our experience when we enter a workplace or attend a sporting event. Living, thinking buildings, and spaces are connected through IoT endpoints and sensors, powered by data, and amplified through artificial and machine-learning technologies. They surround us with capabilities and processes that are both intuitive and serendipitous. Imagine a seamless interface where you are inside of a digital experience and connected globally to millions of others interacting in the same fashion. If it sounds like The Force of Star Wars' mythology, this is not far off.

Space optimization is central to maximize the human experience. Use cases range from health, security, privacy, occupancy tracking, and operations optimization, creating a healthy and safe environment for its users. Each of these cases contributes to developing a state of wellness and productivity.[27]

At the time of writing, the world is coming out of a global pandemic known as COVID-19, moving toward normalcy as vaccinations proliferate and restrictions ease. As every company, community, and country grapples with safely enabling people to return to places of work and social interaction, Practical Sustainability is a means to create a new normal state of being. This challenge is at the top of every elected leader's agenda, and at the time of writing, the authors were working with real estate executives to reopen New York City using smart-space strategies.[28]

SYSTEM OF SYSTEMS

The fourth operating theme is **system of systems**. Buildings and value chains are complex, with many disparate components of technology, data, experiences, and policies. The convergence of cloud, connectivity, and IoT decreases cost and drives the potential for a better experience. The challenge is to move from systems theory to reality.

Buildings have significant, complex problems because each one is an interconnected system of systems. Applied systems design addresses this complexity by combining a design-led approach with a systems-thinking mindset. It structures physical and digital architecture, modules, interfaces, and data, based on problem type and context to establish an ecosystem solution that adapts to real-world requirements.[29]

Leading practitioners have redefined space and network-asset valuation through integration into our physical spaces. More productive spaces with personalized experiences that improve our safety and well-being command a premium fee in the market. They also create a halo effect for everything and everyone in the network. For Practical Sustainability, networks consist of spaces, buildings, logistics, IoT devices, data, and users. The utility of large networks, particularly social ones, scales exponentially with the size of the network. When leaders apply sustainability principles to systems design, a comprehensive view emerges to measure, analyze, and respond. This applied, system-design perspective will redefine how we value our real estate assets, spaces, and supply and distribution networks.

DIGITAL TWIN

The fifth and final operating theme is **digital twin**. Digital twins are digital manifestations of data interacting with the physical world, giving us a deep understanding of spatial relationships in context. Put more simply, they allow us to observe, model, and interact with our system of systems in an intelligent space or supply chain network in a meaningful and practical manner. We can process the massive amounts of data generated from buildings by collecting data from sensors, IoT devices, apps, and other third-party sources. Further, digital twins make data actionable through visualizations and dashboards that create a "single pane of glass" view.

The digital twin interacts with data in a 2D or 3D model, using building and asset data to analyze past performance, manage operations, and optimize future scenarios. For example, an owner may want to examine historical data patterns to understand if an occupancy-use-case result matches what the space initially planned to support. Recent studies show that offices underutilize 40% of space, wasting space and cost.[30] We can also monitor real-time data when output exceeds performance metrics, with alerts and exception messages when controlling thresholds. Digital twins use analytics to move from schedule-based to condition-based services. Lastly, we can futurecast (simulate) scenarios to make strategic decisions and improve plans. Digital twins are the definitive risk management tool.

SMART SPACES AND CITIES

Making a space smart means making people more productive in a connected, sustainable, accessible, and secure environment. The challenge is to put these ideas into action. Buildings and spaces can use design practices that merge physical structure with location and optimize productivity and energy efficiency for users. These benefits are realized through smart technologies and thoughtful policies, and addressing pain points in areas, such as ingress and egress.

Distinct models apply across the major building types: enterprise offices and campuses designed for employee service and experience. Commercial office space mitigates the impact of urbanization for two-thirds of the population who will live in cities, following principles like ultra-high efficiency buildings, year-round venues, and flexible retail space. Manufacturing is all about Industry 4.0 and smart, connected equipment and increasing efficiency.

Smart cities are the supersized public-private manifestation of smart spaces, and they hold the key to sustainability as the percentage of urban dwellers rises. Tech-savvy digital natives demand more from their government, and academic institutions like Arizona State University play a vital role in research and experimentation for smart-city solutions. As private companies deliver the technology, connectivity, and handling of urban data, a new era of regulation and trust will be essential to protect the rights of citizens and maintain the solvency of good government.

JOURNEY TO PRACTICAL SUSTAINABILITY

The Practical Sustainability themes indicate where to focus and what to do differently. The question then becomes, what are the outcomes and how to achieve them? This section provides an overview of the journey to practical, sustainable results. See Figure 1.3 for the six-stage journey to Practical Sustainability.

The first stage is a **sustainability plan**, including metrics selection, data, and science-based targets initiatives. Once in place, enterprises determine how to collect that data for monitoring, compliance, operational purposes, and planning. Sustainable development requires a systematic approach and considers contributions to intergenerational asset well-being, plus the trade-offs and interactions.

Figure 1.3. **Journey to Practical Sustainability**
Source: Infosys Knowledge Institute

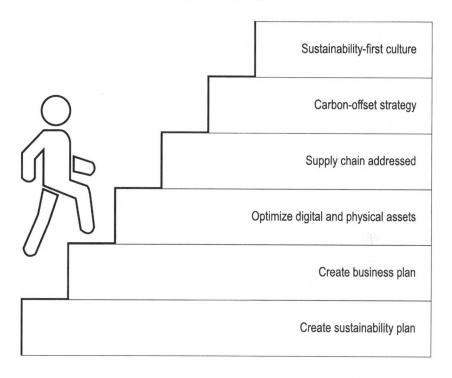

The next stage is the **business plan**, which requires a sustainability plan in place to be effective. They intersect with and accelerate each other. Traditional growth areas still apply: market penetration, product development, market expansion, and diversification. However, leaders view each growth area through the lens of sustainability criteria, such as carbon footprint, regulatory requirements, market demands, and policy-driven investments.

Digital and physical assets support the sustainability plan in parallel with service delivery. Physical assets may be easier to understand than digital. While digital agendas have been prevalent for a few years, the sustainability overlap with digital is less understood than physical assets and systems.[31] This asset-based view starts with buildings and rolling stock with the addition of tech-laden smart spaces. The digital aspect significantly increases a building's worth and potential, which also requires new asset valuation approaches.

The next stage is **supply chains**, which present wide-ranging complexity, and the extent of detail to include in the enterprise ESG footprint. The value-delivery system incorporates the asset base, whether conversion of raw materials into finished product culminating in point of sale, or service-intensive offerings delivered through a combination of office-based and remote work. Beyond traditional financial return on assets, the buildings and supply chain need robust measurement for GHG emissions and carbon offsets as part of a formal enterprise strategy.

The next stage is **offset strategy**, which is quickly becoming a crucial aspect of financial institution portfolios.[32] Offset strategy includes investments, carbon trading, green-bond issuance, and corporate social responsibility. Corporate social responsibility (CSR) is essential to meet the social impact component of ESG. Talent is the link between corporate social responsibility and the bottom line. With the acute shortage of digital talent, talent strategies in recruitment, skills (re)development, and retention are potent drivers of financial returns. Further, authentic community outreach goes beyond the veneer of corporate branding to nurture meaningful local and global relationships, which increase resilience, grow loyalty in good times, and overcome future adverse events.

The final stage is **sustainability-first culture**, where sustainability becomes a native part of corporate, customer, and employee strategies. Beyond the cliché, a sustainability culture converts vague, noble purpose and regulatory compliance into Practical Sustainability. It provides a North Star and compass to guide decision-making at all levels. In a world of fractured and evolving interests, a sustainability-first culture is a unifying force.

GUIDE TO THE REST OF THE BOOK

The following eight chapters explore each of the five Practical Sustainability themes. The chapters also cover how to apply them. We will share a rich mix of examples from companies that get it right, as well as cautionary tales. We highlight experiences from our Practical Sustainability journey at Infosys and weave in findings from our primary research conducted over the last few years.

The Regenerative Future chapter covers how sustainability concepts have moved beyond efficient energy consumption to include other factors and create a virtuous cycle. The Circular Commerce chapter examines the transition from extraction to reusability and the intertwined relationship of a physical product, data, and finance. In the Human Experience chapter, we look at the human element and how experience has become a primary consideration for diverse stakeholders, such as customers, employees, facilities professionals, and even citizens. In the chapter on System of Systems, we cover how building complexity has evolved to require applied systems design to conceive and manage individual structures, campuses, and geographically dispersed networks of buildings. The next chapter shows how Digital Twins replicate the physical world of structures and occupants digitally to understand previous results, manage current activity, and simulate the future.

The best ideas are not valuable unless they see the light of day. The Smart Spaces chapter discusses how the built world integrates the Practical Sustainability elements and themes into a modern, high-value adaptation of the millennia-old concept of buildings. This chapter also includes a perspective on smart cities, emerging as the most critical path to addressing environmental and social challenges. The Implementation chapter addresses the design, deployment, and adoption of Practical Sustainability themes. It provides useful, proven frameworks and tools to build smart spaces and introduces new roles and responsibilities for each actor in the complex web of real estate owners, enterprise occupants, government bodies, and the technology industry supporting this area.

The epilogue, Metamorphosis, brings all these ideas together in the context of the daunting yet exciting future for our planet and society—a supersized manifestation of science-based, human-centric sustainability. In addition to generating returns for shareholders, leaders must also operate with heightened focus on environment, society, and governance for citizens, customers, and employees.

While new technology often grabs the limelight, we emphasize practical, proven approaches to understanding this momentous period in the history of buildings and commerce. This book chronicles the sustainability journey from efficiency to experience, from building to ecosystem, and consumption to regeneration.

Enterprises will still perform the essential functions of commerce; buildings will continue to provide shelter; and supply chains will literally deliver the goods. But if Practical Sustainability appears to imply a much broader responsibility, that's because it does. The market has placed greater responsibility on enterprises and provided more significant opportunity through the simultaneous convergence of tech and timing. In the next chapter, we will explore sustainability and the practical approach needed to enable it.

RECAP

- Today's buildings and supply chains have not kept up with the explosion of exponential technology. Companies have not uniformly addressed the potential impacts of convergent, exponential technologies in their dynamic and complex nature when it comes to building a sustainable future.

- The Practical Sustainability framework has five themes: regenerative future, circular commerce, human experience, system of systems, and digital twin.

- The complexity of the built world requires a system of systems model and partner ecosystem to operate and innovate. Applied systems design has emerged to address building challenges across technology, experiences, policies, and sustainability.

- Sustainability efforts are sustainable only if leaders take a science-based approach and embed them into the operating model.

- As private companies deliver the technology, connectivity, and the handling of urban data, a new era of regulation and trust will be essential to protect the rights of citizens and maintain the solvency of good government.

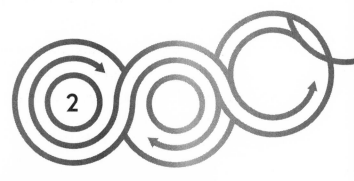

REGENERATIVE FUTURE

ESG (RE)DEFINED

LAND OF THE THUNDER DRAGON

Thanks to storms rolling in from the Himalayas, *Bhutan* means "Land of the Thunder Dragon." This tiny kingdom tucked between China, India, and Tibet was closed to the outside world until 1974.[1] Bhutan has no KFCs, McDonald's, or Burger Kings;[2] tobacco is frowned upon;[3] traffic lights are nonexistent;[4] and television only arrived in 1990.[5]

Bhutan takes the subject of happiness *very* seriously—so seriously that in 1998, the prime minister introduced the Gross National Happiness Index to the United Nations, which formally adopted the concept in 2011,[6] declaring happiness a fundamental human goal.[7] Bhutan's leaders believe Gross National Happiness is a worthier measure of progress than GDP.[8] It's hardwired into Article 9 of the nation's constitution, declaring, "The State shall strive to promote those conditions that will enable the pursuit of Gross National Happiness."[9]

Based on its four pillars of sustainable development, cultural preservation, good governance, and a healthy environment, the emphasis on Gross National Happiness has helped make Bhutan the only carbon-negative country on Earth. This emphasis is thanks to the country's constitution also requiring at least 60% of the country to be covered by forest—the lush, green canopy acting as a national carbon sink.[10]

Bhutan has a saying, "We don't inherit this planet from our fore-fathers; we borrow it from our children." While the country provides an admirable template for human experience, it also suggests how to protect the environment. In corporate terms, the Land of the Thunder Dragon is a case study in ESG, and a model to move from extraction to sustainability and from sustainability to regeneration.

BEYOND THE BASICS

We define sustainability for our practical purpose as Environmental, Social, and Governance, commonly referred to as ESG as a broad term. Those three letters are now commonplace in the corporate and governmental vernacular, and a surprising number of organizations have quantified and applied the concepts to improve environmental metrics tangibly. For example, in 2018, the US emitted 0.24 kilograms of carbon dioxide for every dollar of gross national product, down from 0.81 kilograms in 1990.[11] Britain and Japan have shown similar declines. There is still much more work to do, and future improvements will be harder to realize. Another challenge is that because ESG goals often align closely with personal values, individuals may rush forward without a traditional business case. What appears to be a solid moral argument—say, decrease GHG emissions—stops people from building a case and understanding how to drive real improvement. This groundwork is critical to accelerating adoption and appealing to the head as well as the heart of those you wish to reach.

Enterprises are now viewed through the ESG lens to measure performance, forecast results, and evaluate suitability for investment.[12] However, ESG metrics can be confusing, as they are not a single line item and are in three distinct categories. Leaders need to look at each area on its own merits to address overall sustainability objectives.

- **Environmental** addresses emissions, energy use, biodiversity, waste, pollution, and resource depletion. This category is the sweet spot for global logistics, supply chains, and buildings. This book addresses environmental aspects directly, particularly decarbonization.

- **Social** includes all things people: employee relations, local communities, privacy, security, working conditions, health, safety, diversity, inclusion, consumer protection, and even animal welfare. As physical structures, buildings have a unique link to the local community and the experience of all who enter its doors. Smart spaces energize this relationship and extend it into the community and even employee homes, as remote work becomes an accepted dimension in the notion of spaces.

- **Governance** includes management structure, board diversity, political lobbying, donations, executive compensation, and anti-bribery and corruption. On the surface, governance appears straightforward—essentially, do the right thing. While that may be true in some areas, companies contextualize governance practices for situation, culture, and geography. Buildings represent the physical dimension of work and influence leaders and workers through office layout and human interactions.

THE ABCS OF ESG

There are numerous ways to measure sustainability: a veritable alphabet soup of standards (ESG, GRI, GRESB, CDP, and UN SDGs). Depending on the context and counterparty, some standards matter more than others. If it's Black Rock as financial manager, corporate purpose is critical.[13] If working with tangible assets, Global Real Estate Sustainability Benchmark (GRESB) matters.[14] If concerned with emissions, Carbon Disclosure Project (CDP) will be necessary.[15] While each has individual merit, they also need to relate to each other in an overarching framework.

Beyond reducing confusion for companies to adopt, a unified framework enables multiple companies to partner as an ecosystem for more significant impact.

Companies are motivated to improve ESG scores, at least to comply with sustainability requirements. Ideally, measurement should be quantitative in decarbonization. However, the full scope of ESG, particularly social impact, is often qualitative, and companies need to apply additional measures like proxies for talent hiring, development, and retention.

REGULATION AND MATERIALITY

Companies currently determine what material is in their ESG reporting; without clear, consistent standards from regulatory bodies, it is difficult for asset managers to assess how companies perform in ESG on an absolute basis and relative to peers. Buildings are the single most significant impact factor to materiality investments and are subject to regulation from multiple authorities. Smart spaces have been underutilized, yet they are vital to understanding ESG execution and reporting disclosures. The emergence of smart spaces has created uncertainty for asset owners as to how they should address it.

The corporate and investment community tracked materiality disclosure well before signing the Paris Agreement in 2016. This history suggests that decisions based on more than just profit and loss are mainstay strategies; now, disclosure must also focus on how companies perform on ESG measures relative to their peers. How are buildings reported? Does an intelligent building impact an ESG rating? Smart spaces technology optimizes building systems and operations—such as energy, lighting, air quality, water, waste, and occupancy usage—to improve the environmental footprint.[16] Smart spaces help an organization manage and measure social aspects of ESG for its occupants through enabling safe, inclusive, and productive environments to personalize experiences for individual and workgroup well-being. Companies address governance by creating a space where organization ESG data can be collected and reported as quantifiable and autonomous.

Sustainability Accounting Standards Board (SASB) is the leading body that connects businesses and investors on the financial impacts of sustainability. SASB designed sustainability accounting standards to help public corporations disclose financial material information to investors in a cost-effective and decision-useful format. However, SASB reports that two-thirds of disclosures do not contain performance metrics, and over 50% of submitted disclosures use generic reports of limited value.[17] This shortfall is due to ESG reporting that is driven by unstructured and unregulated data, making it challenging to comply on topics like climate, diversity, and gender pay. A materiality matrix is an effective method to align vision to measurable action and reporting.[18] The matrix maps ESG objectives by their influence on stakeholder behavior or opinion along one axis and impact on sustainable business performance on the other, over a period, which is sequenced by priority. As an example, the adjacent figure shows the materiality matrix used by Infosys in 2020.

A materiality matrix communicates a company's commitment and planning to ESG, especially when included in external reporting. It provides a valuable North Star to measure progress on investments and actions.

Smart spaces support SASB's goal for transparent, inclusive, and rigorous standards-setting in materiality reporting. Smart spaces' ability to provide quantifiable data on the buildings we occupy makes them a focus area for companies and investors. As an added benefit, facilities are already subject to reporting transparency enforced by regulatory statutes—a place where other ESG components do not yet have universal clarity. These existing standards make buildings an immediate solution to drive sustainability and quickly mitigate risk in ESG reporting.

Figure 2.1. **ESG Materiality Matrix**

Source: Infosys Knowledge Institute

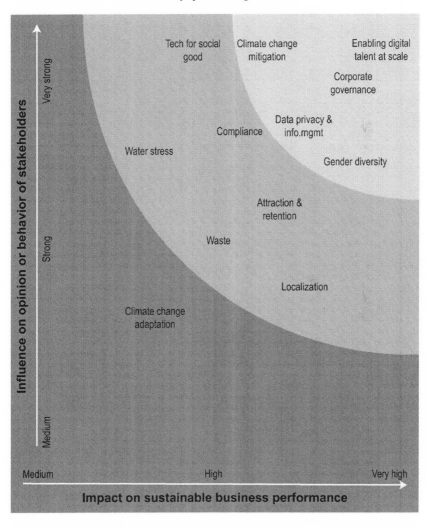

THE RISE OF ROI IN ENVIRONMENTAL, SOCIAL, AND GOVERNANCE

Contrary to popular belief, cash and their accountant's green eye-shade has not been green's limit for investors. For several years, investors have evaluated companies based on ESG practices beyond standard traditional financial performance metrics. ESG-based investing has experienced significant growth—global sustainability investment represents over $30 trillion, up 68% since 2014.[19] According to Barron's 100 Most Sustainable Companies, more than half of the one hundred outperform the market[20]—illustrating that ESG practices may correlate to better financial performance. However, the next era in ESG investing demands proof of these higher returns. For example, Japan's Government Pension Fund ($1.6 trillion) backed away from ESG investing when the relative returns dipped,[21] putting retirees—another valuable actor in their stakeholder capitalism—in financial harm's way.

Investors increasingly expect companies to have mature environmental, social, and governance (ESG) practices and provide the data to prove it. Companies need to consolidate their ESG data and convert it to an actionable improvement roadmap. A prominent feature of these roadmaps is smart space investments, including initiatives like the Internet of Things to optimize buildings for comfort, emissions, and cost reduction.

Seventy-two percent of global organizations say their prime business goal for smart buildings is to reduce facilities and operations costs, and 66% name energy management as the primary driver for their smart space investments.[22] Energy cost-savings is an easily quantifiable metric and traditionally provides a good return on investment. Organizations need apparent successes to gain stake-holder buy-in and approval. Beyond measurable metrics, the ROI can be impressive: Forrester, a leading analyst firm, found that companies implementing IoT-enabled sensors and intelligent devices realize energy savings of up to 70% in three years.[23]

Yet, companies miss out on smart spaces' much more significant opportunities by focusing solely on energy savings. Our research, and from other firms', suggests that user experience will overtake energy savings as the primary focus for smart space projects. If you consider the industry standard 3/30/300 model, this is not surprising.[24] Tenants spend roughly $3 on utilities, $30 on rent, and $300 on employee-related expenses every year for each square foot of space. By the logic of this model, employee experience is two orders of magnitude more impactful than energy, and investments for employees can generate much higher returns than investments in energy savings. Chapter 4 addresses the area of human factors and experience. We will begin with how the triple bottom line (TBL) helps companies widen their focus beyond the single bottom line (SBL).

TRIPLE BOTTOM LINE

THE TRIPLE BOTTOM LINE DEFINED

The famed sustainability champion, John Elkington, introduced the concept of the "triple bottom line" in 1994. The following year, this concept crystallized into the 3Ps—the idea that instead of one corporate bottom line, there should be three: people, planet, and profits. Businesses that focus on profits only, disregarding people and the

Earth, do not cover the total cost of doing business. This limited perspective fails to measure a company's financial, social, and environmental performance over time.[25]

Figure 2.2. **Triple Bottom Line**
Source: John Elkington

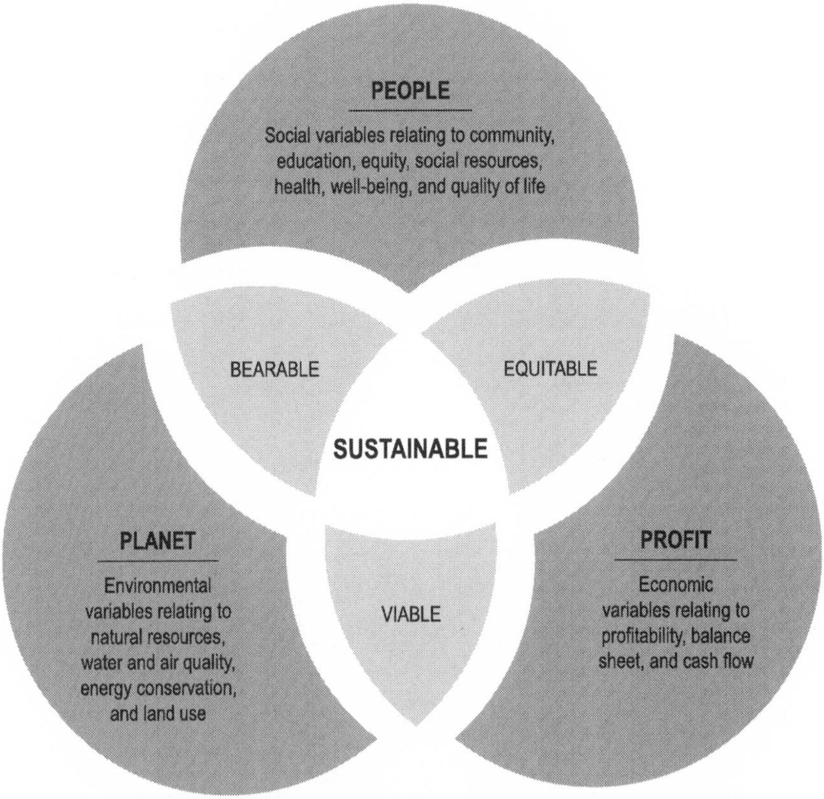

PEOPLE
Social variables relating to community, education, equity, social resources, health, well-being, and quality of life

BEARABLE   EQUITABLE

SUSTAINABLE

PLANET
Environmental variables relating to natural resources, water and air quality, energy conservation, and land use

VIABLE

PROFIT
Economic variables relating to profitability, balance sheet, and cash flow

The corporate world has acknowledged the criticality of social and environmental responsibility using the triple bottom line (TBL) accounting method. However, the TBL methodology is challenging due to the difficulty of measuring social and environmental impact.

Businesses gravitate to understandable quantitative metrics over qualitative ones, constraining newer concepts like environmental and social accounting.

THE SINGLE BOTTOM LINE SUSTAINABILITY PARADIGM

The triple bottom line, corporate social responsibility (CSR), and the investment of carbon offset projects are closely linked. TBL provides a more holistic view of a company's performance than the traditional single bottom line. However, TBL positions sustainability first as an ethical stance for business and second as a mechanism of value and growth opportunities, and this causes friction among stakeholders. TBL has been around since 1994. Although many prominent companies, including Shell, who was the first adopter, have made this part of their corporate culture, the world has yet to see a significant impact from the TBL nearly forty years later. On the twenty-fifth anniversary of its inception, founder John Elkington published a controversial "product recall" for the TBL movement, citing that it had "failed to bury the single bottom line paradigm" due to its "proliferation of potential solutions, providing businesses with an alibi for inaction."[26]

Mr. Elkington, at that time, redefined the triple bottom line categories to *people*, *planet*, and *prosperity*—the three new P's.

- **People.** Addresses stakeholders, including employees, customers, supply chain, communities, future generations, and customers. CSR is an obligation for organizations to be accountable to meet the needs of their stakeholders.

- **Planet.** Businesses that adjust their business models to support the environment gain strong motivation for change based on consumer and employee sentiment when selecting products and services.

- **Prosperity.** The objective for all human beings is to have prosperous and fulfilling lives, and economic, social, and technological progress should occur in harmony with nature at an equitable level across society.

He observed that an organization focused only on profit—ignoring people and the Earth—cannot account for the total cost of doing business and thus will not succeed long term. The model also more accurately reflects the UN Sustainable Development Goals (SDGs) by replacing profit with prosperity. The seventeen SDGs were created to address the diverse environmental, people, and economic opportunities, and include providing safe working conditions, equitable living wages, and compassionate leadership for communities in need.[27]

As the market seeks to deliver on ESG, there is also now a Single Bottom Line Sustainability (SBLS) methodology that creates a new so-called single bottom line, guided by environmental, social, and governance values. The adjacent figure shows the single bottom line sustainability methodology.

SBLS offers an alternative approach to corporate social responsibility and triple bottom line in that it focuses on value creation through promotion, design, and implementation of sustainability strategies. This focus on value enables quantifiable measurements for sustainability agendas and has gained advocates from large corporations such as DuPont, Ford, BHP Billiton, and SC Johnson.

Figure 2.3. **Single Bottom Line Sustainability (SBLS) Methodology**
Source: Reed, Gilding, and Hogarth, Infosys Knowledge Institute

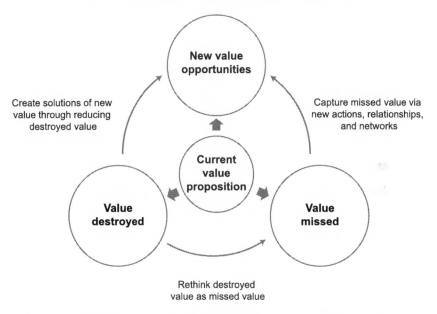

REGENERATION: TRIPLE BOTTOM LINE 2.0

The strategy to evolve capitalism around TBL has two dimensions. First, technology captures people, planet, and prosperity outcomes and integrates them into measurable scorecards and the enterprising resource planning (ERP) systems used by our company. For example, at Infosys, we created a data collection and reporting platform called Infosys Ecowatch, built on the Microsoft Dynamics platform and hosted on the Azure cloud, to track and measure ESG and climate-action project activities. This application uses a triple bottom line, standard tool-based strategy with quantifiable attributes.

Second, consider deploying conscious capitalism—a business philosophy developed by John Mackey, co-founder and CEO of Whole Foods Market, and professor Raj Sisodia, who wrote a book on the concept.[28] They founded Conscious Capitalism, Inc., a firm that commits to TBL by extending the lines of impact across the larger ecosystem, reflecting stakeholders, investors, customers, employees, vendors, and the environment. Profound possibilities emerge for the ecosystem to align scopes 1, 2, and 3 and the associated complexities. In this challenge, where the traditional single bottom line does not work well, the door of opportunity opens for TBL enhanced by these two strategies.

We have discussed a few frameworks that share attributes, and we advocate different measurement methods and proof of value. Each has the right intentions, yet after thirty years, the authors can recommend only what we have seen work—that our company, Infosys, achieved carbon neutrality in ten years, which is thirty years ahead of the Paris Agreement timeline of 2050. Our formula was one of Practical Sustainability—a combination of strategy, technology, and social fairness backed by quantifiable scientific principles, delivered as a "tech for good" digital transformation agenda. Our firm set ambitious science-based targets, switched to renewable energy sources, optimized our operations, made our buildings smart spaces, promoted diversity and inclusiveness in our workforce, and created offsets by investing in the betterment of local communities.

PATH TO SUSTAINABILITY

Sustainability matters because resources are finite—not just physical assets like a building or even inputs like energy or water. This also applies to human talent, budgets, and time.

While digital transformation and overcoming disruption are challenging enough on their own, adding the additional threshold of sustainability criteria requires bold thinking and action. To illustrate the complexity, consider a large European consumer goods firm. They must report by several different standards: GRI, CDP, and a Dow Jones sustainability index. Then they must determine science-based targets and how they will achieve these targets by 2030 or earlier. They communicate these requirements to thousands of suppliers worldwide and collect all this data on an ongoing basis. They need to align it to operational and transformation initiatives, all while meeting financial targets. Finally, they are required to provide an auditable trail, likely supported by blockchain technology, to verify that all these activities and transactions took place. Little wonder that sustainability is on both the boardroom and project room agenda.

China-based Ping An Group is the world's largest insurer and in June 2020, it created the CN-ESG Smart Rating System, which provides a suite of smart ESG investment tools with a variety of China-specific features.[29] Ping An's CN-ESG System has four dimensions: Environmental €, Social (S), Governance (G), and Business (B), which allows companies to analyze through General Indicators, Industry Matrix, and Public Opinion modules. The system is powered by artificial intelligence (AI) technologies and automated data collection. It seeks to overcome the challenge of manual data collection.[30]

Developing nations need a longer runway to reach sustainability targets. Max Jarrett, Africa Programme Manager of the International Energy Agency, emphasizes the need for a global perspective as cities in Africa pursue their growth agenda. This pragmatic view may mean a delayed phase-out of fossil fuels while aggressively developing clean energy sources with much-needed affordable financing from the developed countries.[31]

ENHANCED ASSET VALUATION AND MANAGEMENT

A PHYGITAL WORLD

We live in a world where physical objects interact with digital objects, where human experience involves blending the physical and digital to produce new environments that interact with occupants. Digital technologies play an important role by empowering users to generate, contextualize, and communicate insights from physical world data to improve efficiency and ensure that assets are better serviced and maintained.

First-line workers are responsible for maintaining building structures and systems, such as HVAC, elevators, and safety. While they have traditionally not benefitted from digital tools as much as information workers, that is changing rapidly with advanced modeling and the advent of 5G. The correct information at the right time, delivered in the right way to make decisions in the field, is a critical requirement for first-line workers. From building chiller systems to large oil rigs, digital replicas enable first-line workers to improve inspections, manage maintenance operations, and decrease downtime through rapid and collaborative decision-making.

Architecture and visualization also help first-line workers predict and adapt to change before it happens, through remote guidance and seeing what a worker sees in the field to identify the problem. Contextualized visual information and data can significantly improve a technician's service KPIs and an operator's asset uptime.

TECHNOLOGY EVOLUTION IN BUILDING LIFESPAN

Real estate development teams design and construct buildings, while commercial real estate firms operate them. These phases use different workers, which cause knowledge and data flow-through problems. For example, design and construction firms may use external architects and consultants, while real estate companies might use internal operators like CBRE. These two categories have different mindsets, technologies, and approaches to information management.

Contractors and architects rely on project management applications to track the status of activities, personnel availability, timesheet management, and invoicing. The emphasis is on the timely execution of construction tasks, not archival for post-construction analysis. Architects and contractors have their tools to enter data during the construction phase, and the modeling software varies and is typically incompatible. As a result, there is no easy way to use the data in a unified model for construction data management.

The other challenge is integrating architecture and design data with other tools like ERP due to proprietary data formats. This constraint is compounded during testing and commissioning when IT administrators store data in contractor systems. This multiparty activity creates data collection gaps and siloed data. Data management inconsistency drives a lack of portability and coherent data structure.

CRADLE TO GRAVE ASSET MANAGEMENT

The Information Age was slow to reach the built world, including the operation, maintenance, and repair of individual physical assets. There were isolated exceptions: in 1970 NASA used pairing technology to save Apollo 13 astronauts through remote connectivity, even though they were physically a hundred thousand miles away.[32] However, the impetus for building asset management arose after digital technologies began to model physical products of increasing complexity (think jet engines). Technology progressed and enhanced a broad spectrum of applications, from monitoring the health of oil field well pads to training surgeons. These systems have evolved to manage collections of complex physical-digital assets like buildings to observe and maintain complex smart spaces, as illustrated in Figure 2.4.

Data and information integrate physical assets to report the state of the environment, and dashboards observe performance, analytics, and predictive scenarios to manage physical building performance.

Facilities leaders typically manage maintenance, service, and warranty using multiple systems, which result in data fragmentation and inefficient processes. Traditional asset management emphasizes efficient task management and exhibits slow decision-making. Various systems store data with no single view, which reduces an asset's useful life and total value created throughout the life cycle.

Figure 2.4. **Digital Management of Physical Assets**
Source: Infosys Knowledge Institute

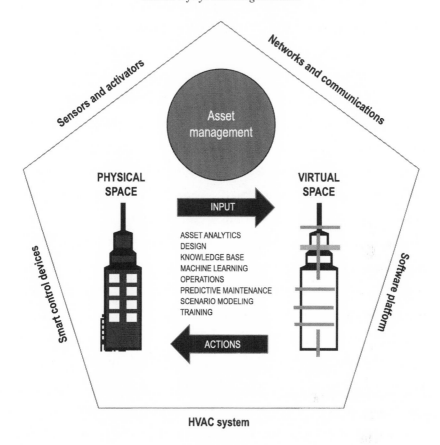

HVAC system

Digital asset management practices offer an ability to centralize all data during asset commissioning, operations, maintenance, and retirement. This centralization allows performance simulation during the commissioning phase. It also enables better decision-making for asset maintenance through condition-based monitoring instead of interval-based maintenance. Digital-based asset management mirrors the asset life cycle for a variety of decisions related to its useful life.

REALIZING ESG VALUE

Knowing what an asset is worth and what determines that value is a prerequisite for intelligent decision-making, whether choosing building investments or deciding on the right sale price. The premise of valuation is reasonable estimates of value for most assets, and that the same fundamental principles determine the values of all asset types.

Asset valuation is a function of acquisition date, initial cost, useful life, residual value estimate, and it directly impacts ESG metrics and value realization. The impact of depreciation and renovation work is also material. In some cases, sentiment (landmark building) drives building valuation or competition due to scarcity. Tenant attraction is another valuation factor, as companies seek office spaces that will help them attract talent in a competitive market.

However, expected cash flow generated over useful asset life is still the primary factor determining asset valuation.[33] Efficiency increases cash flow, and sensors that maintain comfort and wellness for occupants also lower operating costs.[34] Standard data models and system integration streamline the onboarding or offloading, reducing transaction costs and driving higher valuations. ESG metrics improvement also translates to better financials, demonstrates to executives that IT investment delivers financial value, and contributes to asset valuation.[35] See Figure 2.5 for an example of an asset valuation model.

Figure 2.5. Infosys Asset Valuation Model

Source: Infosys Knowledge Institute

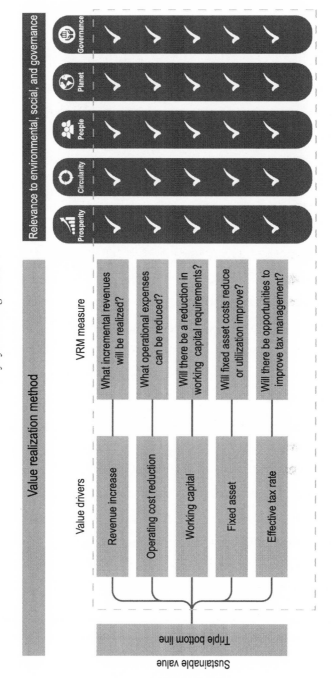

THE DECARBONIZATION IMPERATIVE

DEFINING SCOPES 1, 2, AND 3 EMISSIONS

Understanding how carbon emissions are defined and monitored is the first step to carbon footprint reduction. Scope 1, 2, and 3 goals delineate direct and indirect emissions sources as defined for greenhouse gas (GHG) auditing and reporting. Scopes 1 and 2 are carefully described in this standard to ensure that two or more companies will not account for emissions in the same scope. Scope 1 is the direct GHG emissions from sources owned or controlled by the company, except for biomass-generated emissions. Scope 2 accounts for GHG emissions from the generation of purchased electricity consumed by a company. Scope 3 is an optional reporting category that allows for treatment of all other indirect emissions, such as extraction and production of purchased materials, transportation of purchased fuels, and use of products and services.[36]

Smart spaces play an outsized role in economic impact modeling to drive long-term decarbonization benefits. They do require near-term investment to transition energy technology to renewable energy and more efficient, building energy usage. This investment delivers benefits to the overall economy and includes infrastructure rebuild for commercial, industrial, and consumers. It produces next-generation energy, air quality, and construction technologies, which create positive, local, economic impact.[37]

FROM LEAN TO CLEAN

The relationship between *lean* and *clean* can drive resource productivity gains and significant positive environmental benefit. However, this is not a journey without friction. Lean manufacturing is the systematic elimination of waste in an organization's operations, including reductions in liability, management costs, waste management costs, material input costs, and avoided pollution control equipment.[38] Lean supports sustainability principles through reduction, even avoidance, of waste. But lean traditionally removes all non-value-added activities, and companies may not identify decarbonization and other environmental activities as value-added activity. In other words, a strictly lean implementation may not improve environmental performance. The relationship between lean and clean needs to be formalized into a framework that includes continuous improvement and a scorecard to drive operational and environmental benefits.

EMISSIONS: THE DARK SIDE OF BUILDINGS

Buildings are a significant emissions offender,[39] yet less than 1% are net-zero carbon today.[40] Building emissions result from embodied carbon of a building, the activities involved to create a building, operational carbon emissions, and actions to occupy and maintain a building, including associated infrastructure and transportation activities.[41]

Leadership in Energy and Environmental Design (LEED) is the most widely used green building rating system globally.[42] LEED-certified green buildings optimize water consumption, solid waste, transportation, and amenities. They produce 50% fewer greenhouse gas emissions than conventionally constructed buildings.[43] Carbon-emission reduction, also known as decarbonization, is the path to achieving carbon neutrality's strategic goal. This objective is daunting, and even the most sustainability-minded companies typically indicate a carbon-neutral date a decade in the future, with a significant portion achieved through purchased carbon offsets (think forests or solar energy).

Companies can achieve decarbonization through both greenfield build and brownfield retrofit. There is an organic path to carbon-neutral, and the first step is to reduce or eliminate carbon and emissions from current operations and the supply chain. The unremovable remainder then needs to be addressed through a four-part offset strategy.

For example, Infosys actively pursued carbon neutrality from 2008 and achieved this milestone in 2020 by focusing on decarbonization.[44] The strategy included carbon-footprint reduction across global operations, transition to renewable energy, and carbon offset through corporate social responsibility programs. These programs helped more than 100,000 families in local communities reduce carbon emissions by using cattle dung methane cooking biogas instead of wood. This achievement is noteworthy, as the offset was actual carbon reduction, not simply purchasing credits.

There are four recommended steps in a carbon-offset strategy, listed in the adjacent figure.

1. **Offset strategy:** The first step in the offset process starts with an operations benchmark to assess carbon footprint and offset demand projections required for Scope 1 and 2 emissions. Then the company needs to set an internal carbon price. This amount is the cost assigned to each ton of carbon used for business, investment decisions, and business operations.

Figure 2.6. **Decarbonization: Carbon and Emissions Offset Strategy**

Source: Infosys Knowledge Institute

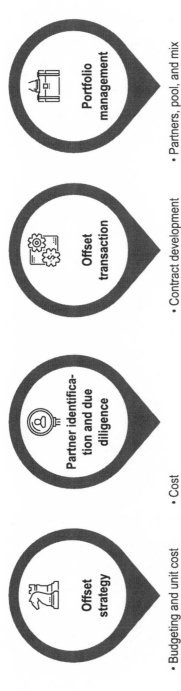

Offset strategy
- Budgeting and unit cost
- Carbon footprint assessment and review
- Contract sourcing
- Offset attributes
- Offset demand projections
- Offset registry
- Partner ecosystem
- Strategic interests alignment

Partner identification and due diligence
- Cost
- Experience and offset knowledge
- Financial standing
- Implementation capability
- Legal status
- Market reputation
- Project concept and methodology
- Risks

Offset transaction
- Contract development
- Cost
- Delivery timing
- Delivery volumes
- Financing model, forward or spot purchase contract
- Partner and project due diligence

Portfolio management
- Partners, pool, and mix
- Portfolio offset approach
- Portfolio planning and design
- Project portfolio management
- Transaction interrelationships

2. **Partner identification and due diligence:** The second step
    is partner identification and due diligence to address the
    scope 3 supply chain carbon footprint. Businesses now
    require that their suppliers have good ESG practices in
    place, as this impacts their decarbonization metrics.

3. **Offset transaction:** The third step is to initiate offset
    transactions, including partner and project due diligence,
    contracts, and financing. Infosys achieved its offsets solely
    through CSR strategies. However, in many cases, businesses
    may need to use funding that may include green bonds and/
    or direct selling or trading of offsets in the marketplace, in
    combination with their CSR projects.

4. **Portfolio management:** The final step is portfolio manage-
    ment of the offset strategy to leverage opportunities and
    optimize impact as the decarbonization program matures.

Accomplishing sustainability in a building setting is more than
just net-zero emissions agendas. It also acknowledges the economic,
social, racial, and class-based dimensions of our environmental
challenges. Further, it encompasses quality of life, work productivity,
and how humans engage with the environment.

REDUCE CARBON EMISSIONS

Supply chains that incorporate sustainable circular loop practices
produce less carbon and less waste, which increases product use,

reuse, and longevity. The hard part is establishing standards across the entire tier of suppliers that make up the value chain. Start by assessing each contributor to baseline their maturity level and then articulate the goals and metrics to achieve. Define the transformation benefits and create certification mechanisms to confirm the change needed. Integrate these approaches with other initiatives, such as Industry 4.0 programs, and establish a lean-to-clean operating model. Learn from lessons of smart spaces initiatives with certification programs, including LEEDS, Energy Star, Passive House, and the Living Building Challenge. However, the current level of voluntary pledges is not accountable enough. This means architects, technologists, construction firms, structural engineers, and real estate owners must engage more actively with business stakeholders and policymakers to reduce carbon emissions. These actions include courses on energy-efficient design, increased use of low-carbon materials, and building code updates. Policy and accountability are needed at all government and business auditing levels to eliminate so-called greenwashing and thus institute real change. Buildings present an opportunity for quantifiable positive impact on sustainability—driven by design, technology, and policy. Companies are developing strategies with decarbonization in mind. These strategies address climate risk and the impact it will have on their assets and supply chains. They also evaluate carbon risk, the impact on their investments, and returns due to climate-change policies.

Carbon capture (and storage) is another method to reduce greenhouse gases. Carbon capture mitigates the adverse impact of large-scale emissions sources, including coal and gas-fired power generation, natural gas processing, and fertilizer production. Carbon capture also diminishes negative effects from the manufacture of industrial materials, such as cement, iron, steel, pulp, and paper. According to investment house Morgan Stanley, the rising demand to decarbonize offers one of the most significant ESG investment opportunities in the market. However, carbon capture and storage require substantial investment, including subsidies, tax credits, or other forms of government support to scale the capability.[45]

Companies create internal carbon pricing to set a monetary value on their emissions and use this figure to evaluate investments and risk mitigation strategies.[46] Carbon prices are expected to rise because of anticipated price-implied regulation, taxation, cap, and trade.[47] In addition, companies will feel the burden of increased scopes 2 and 3 accountability and need to protect themselves against more risk scenarios.

Carbon pricing integrates carbon economics with company operations, identifying a monetary value per ton of carbon emittance. Price setting varies by industry, country, and company objectives. The carbon price enables companies to decide capital investments, manage financial and regulatory issues, create a strategy to mitigate risks and recognize investment opportunities. Companies that choose not to set internal carbon pricing are at risk. Even if they self-rate as low-carbon producers, regulators may challenge reported scope 2 or 3 results for trading partner interactions. This is also true if a workforce commutes to a corporate office workspace. They are all calculated as part of their actual carbon footprint.

THE VIRTUOUS CYCLE OF REGENERATION

CONVERTING CARBON PROBLEMS INTO SUSTAINABLE SOLUTIONS

The energy transition from fossil fuels to net-zero carbon sources is critical to reducing greenhouse gas emissions. The decarbonization flywheel figure illustrates a framework to address our buildings, residences, transportation, electricity, and industry decarbonization needs.

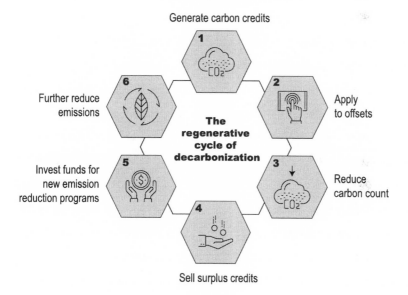

Figure 2.7. **Regenerative Cycle of Decarbonization**
Source: Infosys Knowledge Institute

The decarbonization flywheel becomes a virtuous cycle as credits generated reduce carbon through offsets creation, which lowers costs and produces surplus credits. These credits, in turn, become a funding source for new investments to reduce emissions further and restarts the cycle of generating carbon credits.

Carbon offsetting is a mechanism to neutralize the carbon footprint through emission reduction programs that capture or avoid carbon emissions.[48] Companies can purchase carbon credits, a permit that a company then holds, allowing it to emit a mass equal to one ton of CO_2 (or GHG) per one credit. Some companies create projects that generate carbon credits, while others find it more practical to participate in another organization's project due to a lack of internal resources or capabilities. These projects also benefit the UN SDGs.

Carbon offsetting is a quick way to address an enterprise's carbon footprint, but it does not solve its operations, services, and products to become more sustainable. The more practical approach is to first reduce emissions before engaging in a carbon-offsetting program. Second, thoroughly investigate and verify that the project is credible and not a greenwashing scheme.

A clear view of the current ESG state reveals decarbonization risks and opportunities by tracking new indicators of climate change. These indicators are absolute carbon emissions, carbon intensity, emissions reduction targets, carbon earnings at risk, and climate-change revenues. These indicators provide historical performance, status, and simulation of options and outcomes. While each company has a unique set of data and correlating strategies, there will be a standard set of regulatory benchmarks and voluntary metrics to establish targets and measure performance.

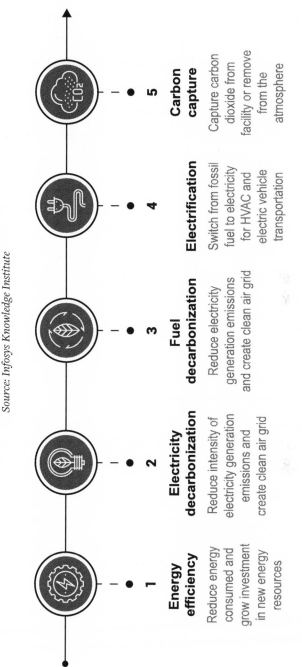

Figure 2.8. Practical Decarbonization Model
Source: Infosys Knowledge Institute

1

Energy efficiency

Reduce energy consumed and grow investment in new energy resources

2

Electricity decarbonization

Reduce intensity of electricity generation emissions and create clean air grid

3

Fuel decarbonization

Reduce electricity generation emissions and create clean air grid

4

Electrification

Switch from fossil fuel to electricity for HVAC and electric vehicle transportation

5

Carbon capture

Capture carbon dioxide from facility or remove from the atmosphere

PRACTICAL DECARBONIZATION AND EMISSIONS GOALS

Smart spaces deployment, coupled with industrial process and transportation efficiencies, decreases energy and resource consumption, which reduces decarbonization. While the regenerative cycle in Figure 2.7 highlights offsets and credits, a practical decarbonization model emphasizes a structural shift to electricity-based energy, as shown in Figure 2.8.

ESG assessments use this model with the following five factors to diagnose issues, identify opportunity, and develop the plan.

1. **Energy efficiency:** Reduce energy consumed and grow investment in new energy resources.
2. **Electricity decarbonization:** Reduce electricity generation emissions intensity and create a clean-air grid.
3. **Fuel decarbonization:** Reduce fossil fuel emissions via electric and biomass source replacement.
4. **Electrification:** Switch from fossil fuel to electricity for building HVAC and EV transportation.
5. **Carbon capture:** Capture CO_2 from a facility or remove it from the atmosphere.

ROLE OF DIGITAL STRATEGY

Enterprises are under pressure to adopt sustainable practices, and they tend to use ERP applications for sustainability initiatives and reporting. Track-and-trace capability is crucial for clean energy infrastructure transformation. Existing IoT and cloud systems report on smart space operations, such as building management systems, energy, and user experience data. Digital transformation benefits extend beyond the enterprise, integrating data with supplier systems to optimize the transparency and efficiency of sustainability applications. Sustainability should be added to the corporate balanced scorecard and include ESG investment and lending. Embedding sustainability into ERP systems demonstrates that companies put forward their best efforts and not simply greenwash to seek consumer loyalty. Product management on digital transformation projects should include sustainability criteria. The dominant ecosystem player may mandate additional levels of reporting and compliance to hold trading partners accountable to ESG standards.

Decarbonization will also have a dominant impact on social and cultural aspects of civic policy through the transfer to clean, carbon-free energy.[49] New agreements will complement policy updates on how electricity markets will operate. Since regional electricity markets operate under federal oversight, decarbonization of the electricity provider's service reform could be embedded. On the other hand, if decarbonization policy controls the regional population it serves, there may be incremental benefits due to greater flexibility and innovation at the edge.

DIVERSITY AND INCLUSION AS A TALENT ENGINE

Analysis has shown that executive teams in the top quartile for gender diversity are 25% more likely to deliver above-average profitability, with diversity and inclusion a factor to build a sustainability-first workforce culture. Antidiscrimination and anti-harassment policies apply to everyone in a company, and companies that become UN Global Compact (UNGC) signatories agree to support the protection and elevation of human rights by following the labor guidelines outlined in the UNGC.[50]

THE POWER OF PRINCIPLE 6

Discrimination in employment means treating people differently or less favorably because of characteristics not related to their merit or inherent job requirements. In national law, these characteristics commonly include race, color, sex, religion, political opinion, national extraction, social origin, age, disability, HIV/AIDS status, trade union membership, and sexual orientation. The UN Global Compact Ten Principles draw a critical line in the sand, connecting the philosophical with the practical.[51] Principle 6 allows companies to consider grounds where discrimination in employment and occupation may occur.[52]

Discrimination can arise in a variety of work-related activities. These include access to employment, occupations, promotions, training, and vocational guidance. Moreover, it can occur in the terms and conditions of work, like recruiting, pay, holidays, and benefits.

In many countries, additional emerging workplace discrimination issues include age, HIV status, and sexual orientation. It is also important to realize that discrimination at work can be a problem anywhere, whether in rural agriculture or high technology cities.

Discrimination can take many forms when gaining access to employment and treating employees once they are at work. It may be direct, when laws or practices explicitly cite a reason, such as sex or race to deny equal opportunity. More commonly, however, discrimination is indirect and arises where rules or practices appear neutral but lead to exclusions. This indirect discrimination often exists informally in attitudes and practices, which, if unchallenged, can perpetuate in organizations. Discrimination may, in certain instances, also have cultural roots that require more specific approaches.

PEOPLE-CENTRIC ENVIRONMENT

From a business perspective, discrimination does not make sense. It leads to social tensions that are potentially disruptive to the business environment within the company and in society. A company that uses discriminatory practices in employment denies itself access to talent from a wider pool of workers and those skills and competencies. The hurt and resentment generated by discrimination affect individual and team performance in the company.

Increasingly, candidates assess companies based on their workplaces' social and ethical policies. Discriminatory practices result in missed opportunities to develop skills and infrastructure to strengthen competitiveness in the national and global economy. Finally, discrimination isolates an employer from the wider community and can damage a company's reputation, potentially affecting profits and share value.

On the positive side, diversity and inclusion in the workplace can produce positive outcomes for businesses, individuals, and societies. For business, it improves productivity, is a source of innovation, facilitates better risk management, and enhances customer and partner satisfaction. As far back as 2013, the *Harvard Business Review* cites that "employees at these companies are 45% likelier to report that their firm's market share grew over the previous year and 70% likelier to report that the firm captured a new market."

THE DIVERSITY BONUS AND RADICAL INNOVATION

Modern psychology recognizes the phenomenon of *cognitive elaboration*, the ability to share, challenge, and expand thinking. Diverse teams are more likely to deliver this with research identifying a "diversity bonus," where companies with diverse management are more likely to introduce new product innovations than are those with homogeneous senior teams. Gender diversity also positively relates to radical innovation. In effect, diversity may generate an organizational dynamic more conducive to new solutions and radical innovation.

Diversity councils can champion business-led diversity across geographies and business units. Diversity goals increase leader contribution when they are part of the corporate scorecard. Diversity councils comprise members from business and enabler functions, and periodic reviews enable teams to increase their effectiveness and measure quantifiable outcomes.

INTERDEPENDENCE: HARMONIZING THE FIELD OF VIEW

THE INTERDEPENDENCE IMPERATIVE

The world is one humanity that faces common, wicked challenges. The default progress measure is typically economic health for countries and individuals, yet this is a flawed metric in scope and scale.[53] Disruption occurs when we no longer control the value chain where we seek the benefits, or we become socially conscious of our actions to generate change. Trouble also arises when societal need outweighs government structure or when natural disaster strikes. We are taught at a young age that all life is interconnected and dependent on a biodiverse environment. We learn of social interactions through family and religious institutions. We realize that citizen participation is the only means to ensure the idea of a government that serves the population justly. Those values need to be re-shared and possibly relearned as adults, so they become part of the triple-bottom-line model.

VALUE CHAIN

The triple bottom line of people, planet, and prosperity shows us how to use sustainable business operations to drive positive results. Profitability is not a contradiction with these strategic objectives, but it is the monetary catalyst for businesses, employees, and our health and well-being to prosper. Public-private partnerships (PPPs) are essential in complex sustainable development. They bring together skillsets from the private sector and resources at scale from the public sector. These partnerships provide capital access, greater outcome certainty, off-balance-sheet borrowing, innovation, and risk transfer. See the adjacent figure for an overview of the public-private partnership ecosystem.

Sustainable technology companies play a significant role in PPPs. Cooperative risk sharing and mutual support occur where innovation by private enterprises and investors push our public institutions to act with speed and scale. A great example is space flight. For over seventy years, the world considered space flight so challenging and complex that only a government could create and manage the institutions to make it a reality. Over the past decade, private programs such as SpaceX have accelerated globally, with governments now incorporating these companies into their programs as partners that share risk and reward.

Figure 2.9. **Interdependence: Public-Private Partnership Ecosystem**
Source: Infosys Knowledge Institute

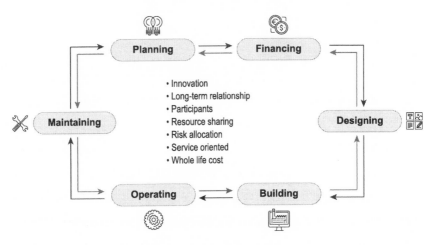

SOCIAL

Communities seek to provide for the present without sacrificing the future. Smart spaces can provide infrastructure, just governance, well-being, social equality, productivity, and economic stability—all in a sustainable manner. Companies and ESG investors recognize that a growing number of consumers select products based on a company's ESG performance.[54] Customers expect sustainable products and services, and they are willing to pay a premium to companies that share their values. Even with technology and automation of smart spaces, companies that attract and retain the best talent will determine the winners in the age of sustainability. Employees see companies with strong ESG agendas as desirable places to build careers, work hard to drive results, and make a real impact. They also actively recruit like-minded talent, which is crucial, because as we approach the 2030 mid-term ESG goals, approximately two-thirds of the world's workforce will be millennial and Gen Z talent.[55]

GOVERNANCE: RATIONALIZING THE GEO DILEMMA

Geographic jurisdiction and corporate governance are prominent topics when it comes to sustainability. Perceived value and benefits influenced the announcement of the Paris Agreement in 2016 and how governments and companies chose to apply policies at corporate, local, national, and global levels. Successful programs require public and private partnerships and essential decisions on metrics and how data is collected and verified. For example, if a government-regulated energy company is responsible for decarbonization, data tracking and funding will be standardized and dependable. However, having private companies deliver decarbonization could create a more robust engine for innovation and ESG investment portfolios. Leaders should experiment to find the optimal mix of governance and innovation.

Many employees are global and part of a multinational corporation. Decisions that determine citizen wealth, health, and benefits often do not come from their government but from the citizen and their employer. As such, employees who are vested in their company's ESG plans become the flag bearers of that firm's sustainability culture. We are well-equipped to succeed.

Each of us must acknowledge the significant sustainability challenges we now face together on a global scale. At the same time, the authors believe that humanity is better prepared than ever with technology, knowledge, and understanding how to combine the two. We can create a future where the three types of interdependence—value chain, social, and just governance—exist in proper balance. We may feel things have always been as they are in our lifetime, yet we date our current technology impact on the Earth's environment back to 1790, or 230 years ago.[56] The economic miracles of industrialization are the cumulative result of this period. Yet, unfortunately, so is the environmental burden, especially the carbon footprint. With a shared sense of purpose, experts have declared a thirty-year window of opportunity through 2050 to create a solution ecosystem. This ecosystem includes environmental, social, and governance components and seeks to not only avert potential disaster, but propel humanity to a better life for all. We individually possess the tools to make progress, but interdependence will bring together complementary capabilities to achieve Practical Sustainability objectives.

Social interdependence is when the outcomes of individuals are affected by their own and others' actions. It creates positive impact when people receive fair and humane consideration at the micro (product and process) and macro (ecosystem and economy) levels. Governance interdependence serves the interests of all stakeholders by leading through core values and fact-based decision-making. The authors believe in this future because we have participated in this journey as part of a leading technology company and are now in our second year as net-zero carbon neutral. Our journey took place over ten years of implementation—we know it is possible, can be profitable, and have witnessed the positive power of its ethical impact.

RECAP

- ESG materiality prioritizes the sustainability agenda. To create a materiality matrix, map ESG objectives by their influence on stakeholder behavior or opinion along one axis and impact on sustainable business performance on the other, over time and sequenced by priority.

- The practical approach to carbon reduction is to first reduce emissions, then pursue a carbon-offsetting program. Carbon offsetting is a quick way to address an enterprise's carbon footprint, but it does not overcome the fundamental issues in operations, services, and products to become more sustainable.

- Smart spaces are foundational to sustainability because buildings account for nearly 40% of all GHG emissions,[57] with less than 1% net-zero carbon at the time of this writing.[58]

- Supply chains that incorporate sustainable circular-loop practices produce less carbon and less waste. The hard part is establishing standards across the entire tier of suppliers that make up the value chain.

- Analysis has shown that executive teams in the top quartile for gender diversity are 25% more likely to deliver above-average profitability, with diversity and inclusion a factor to build a sustainability-first workforce culture.

- Public-private partnerships (PPPs) are essential in complex, sustainable development. They bring together skillsets usually residing in the private sector and resources at scale in the public sector.

CIRCULAR
COMMERCE

CIRCULAR SUPPLY CHAINS

THE GARBAGE PEOPLE

The Great Pyramid in Egypt is the last remaining wonder of the ancient world. Perhaps the most recognizable building on Earth, its gleaming white limestone covering was so bright in the sun that it hurt the eyes. In 1303, Cairo was hit by a massive earthquake, shaking some of the limestone loose and crashing it to the ground.[1] In 1356, local leaders repurposed the limestone to build the Citadel and mosques in old Cairo. Five hundred years later, locals used even more pyramid limestone to create the Alabaster Mosque.[2] Depending on your perspective, these were either monumental acts of historical vandalism or simply intelligent recycling.

Manshiyat Nasser lies on the edge of modern Cairo. A slum

known as "Garbage City," it is home to 265,000 people living below the poverty line.[3] The people living there are the Zabbaleen—literally the "garbage people"—landless peasants who migrated to Cairo in the 1940s.[4] The Zabbaleen support themselves by collecting trash door-to-door and, over the course of seven decades, have developed a finely tuned system that leads the world in recycling.

Despite being some of the poorest, most marginalized people on Earth, the Zabbaleen created a circular supply chain with recycling rates of 85%[5]—greatly exceeding Germany's 56 percent so-called global best.[6] In 1990, the government insisted the Zabbaleen finally replace their donkey carts with trucks. This modernization not only freed their children to go to school but spawned a trading, finance, and manufacturing system of systems from Aswan to Alexandria.[7]

In a megacity of twenty million people, the Zabbaleen designed and created a flourishing, green, financially viable circular economy. These remarkable people understand that materials matter and that product life cycle management and circular supply chains are essential to Practical Sustainability. For the Zabbaleen, it's a matter of survival.

For an enterprise, success in the age of sustainability depends upon creating customer-valued products and services through the most efficient means possible. Success also requires meeting regulatory guidelines, safety standards, and environmentally sound practices. An organization continuously reinvents itself by renewing its existing products and services and creating new ones. Manufacturing systems convert raw materials into finished goods, utilizing finite natural resources like water, air, and energy. Enterprises convert human talent, information, and digital technology into services valued by customers. At their end of life, products should convert to reusable materials and components, recycled with minimal waste and environmental impact. In the middle of it all are buildings—the places we spend 90,000 hours at work over a lifetime[8]—offices, factories that produce goods, warehouses where products are stored, and storefronts where consumers shop (when not online). These buildings are central to living, and they also need to be practical, sustainable, and intelligent.

A ONE-WAY STREET TO RUIN

Companies that integrate smart spaces into their value chains increase sustainable practices and flexibility across these complex networks. Current commercial models are unidirectional systems for efficiency and convenience, encouraging material and labor flow from source to the end consumer. While traditional commerce has driven revenue at the micro-level and gross domestic product at the macro, this approach has become unsustainable, with waste disposal the final destination for many goods. Companies with linear source-to-consumption models struggle to create circular flows of sourced goods, sold products, and packaging. In the linear model, companies continuously take resources from a finite source to make products that never return to that source and instead end up in landfills or oceans as waste. For example, consider the single-serve coffee makers and coffee pods many of us enjoy each morning. We cannot recycle the pods without great personal effort to cut apart the plastic from the foil top, scoop out coffee grounds, dispose of them, and thoroughly clean all the pieces before placing them in a recycling bin.[9] When the coffeemaker finally breaks, either mechanically or digitally, we discard it and buy a new one since we cannot source the parts or the service to repair it. This steep recycling hurdle is an example of value leakage in two dimensions:

1. Biological leakage of nutrients in the coffee grounds not returned to the biosphere due to inaccessibility or possible contaminations.

2. Technical leakage of the brewing machine, resulting in the loss of energy, materials, and labor required to manufacture it.

An estimated seventy-five million homes brew single-use pods every day, with billions of plastic pods dumped in landfills.[10] This problem is not one of necessity but of not applying known innovations in technology and marketing to consumer behavior. Companies that create solutions to eliminate this cycle of waste and share their story with socially aware consumers will strengthen branding and increase market share.

THE EMERGING NATURE OF INTEGRATED COMMERCE

Digital platforms that integrate e-commerce and supply chains increase profit margin compared to their peers. However, their sustainability measures will be questionable unless they also integrate circularity into their model. Circular commerce is the fire break that decouples economic growth from material consumption, shifting from linear models of industrial growth to ones with social benefits and service-oriented systems. Circular commerce relies on three principles:

1. Design out waste and pollution.

2. Keep products and materials in use.

3. Regenerate natural systems.

Principles of "better, faster, cheaper" and "take, make, dispose" drive traditional models of linear commerce.[11] At first glance, supply chains that shift to sustainable models with longer lifespans seem less operationally and financially attractive. However, *restoration* creates value within circular commerce, replacing end-of-life, waste-generating models. Products designed from inception for cyclical disassembly and reuse are more economically, socially, and environmentally beneficial. The building construction industry is exploring the concept of Design for Disassembly (DfD). Building concrete can be reused for future buildings, reducing cost, demolition, and landfill usage.[12]

THE GLOBAL SWITCH FROM UNIDIRECTIONAL TO CIRCULAR

In the linear model, there is a constant strain on supply to match demand. As a result, disruptions due to resource scarcity at any point in the supply chain tend to have severe consequences in our modern global economy.

A circular economy grounded in sustainable practices redesigns products, services, and their broader systems to promote the circulation of resource value for the most prolonged period possible. The primary benefit of shifting to the circular economy model is eliminating waste and one-time resource usage. This conservation mitigates the negatives of linear commerce, while it also presents economic opportunities and builds long-term resilience. A circular economy is regenerative in nature, circulating products and materials that eliminate waste and pollution. The continuous flow of technical and biological materials through the value circle is illustrated below.[13]

Figure 3.1. **The Circular Economy: An Industrial System That Is Restorative by Design**
Source: Ellen MacArthur Foundation

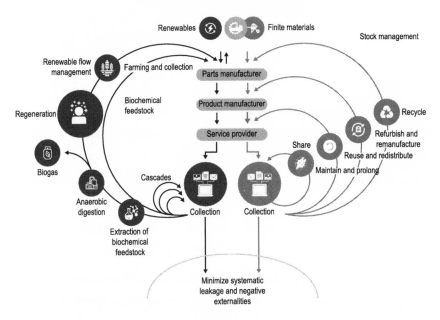

- **Inner loops:** Maintain product integrity at a higher percentage rather than completely separating it for refurbishment, remanufacturing, or recycling.

- **Circle longer:** Design for longevity to delay the need to make additional investments or purchases.

- **Create cascaded uses:** Utilize materials, products, and infrastructure from one value chain in adjacent value chains. This reuse reduces the cost of new materials, energy, labor, and capital.

Use non-toxic, pure, high-quality feedstock from regenerative sources. Reduce the costs to remove toxic or polluting particles by not using them in your product designs. Maintain and restore essential ecosystem services, like using vegetable-based dyes instead of synthetic ones in the textile industry.

PREDICTIVE PRODUCT LIFE CYCLE MANAGEMENT

Companies can apply the value strategies to innovate and evolve to more practical, sustainable business models. They start by identifying circular principles relevant to their business, and then they define the value strategy that activates them, and finally the required technical or social innovation needed to achieve the results. The good news is that the digitalization of many businesses has already created the foundation and ability to deliver predictive product life cycles at scale. These foundational benefits emerged due to the availability of high-speed connectivity, ubiquitous cloud services, and edge computing.

PRODUCT DESIGN

Product design underpins the successful transition to circular commerce. The design of a product dictates its longevity, repair, maintenance, upgradability, and even ease of recycling. Equally important is the choice of materials to deliver optimum performance, adherence to circular goals, and profitability. Recycled material usage is possible only with product quality; otherwise, consumers won't purchase the product in the first place. In the traditional linear scenario, high-quality materials increase landed cost and lower-unit sales volume due to longer product life. However, once the shift to

Figure 3.2. **Predictive Product Life Cycle Management (PLM)**

Source: Infosys Knowledge Institute

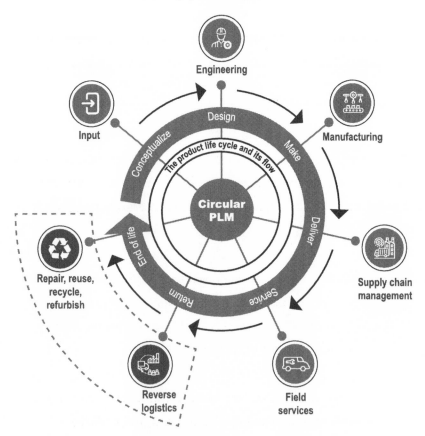

circularity occurs, the same product now designed for reuse and recycling generates value numerous times through reuse, compensating for the increased cost.

An everyday example is the introduction of refillable ink cartridges for consumer printing. While pay-per-print models existed in business-to-business (B2B), companies have also implemented pay-per-print models in business-to-consumer (B2C). This model enables printer manufacturers to design and build printers with more prolonged use in mind so they rely more heavily on ink sales than hardware. This business model uses predictive product lifecycle management (PLM) to optimize manufacturing and circularity design principles. As shown in Figure 3.2, this optimized model, in turn, streamlines production for minimal waste and maximum reuse and recycling.

MANUFACTURING AND LOGISTICS

Manufacturing and distribution are where companies convert strategies and design into physical goods and productive activities. Manufacturing and logistics achieve circularity goals through the following five approaches:

1. **Increased efficiency:** While most companies use efficiency initiatives to reduce cost and increase profitability, the reduced material consumption is an additional positive outcome.

2. **Optimized point of manufacture:** Located within smart spaces, new methods like 3D printing and additive

manufacturing consume less material and produce less waste. They also enable manufacturing in a distributed network, reducing transportation requirements. For example, 3D-printed models of spare parts can be sent on demand to customers or printed locally.

3. **Increased adoption of remanufactured parts and components:** Industries like automotive, aerospace, and discrete manufacturing already remanufacture parts from old products, to the extent proportional to the cost of the product (think aircraft engines). End-of-life products yield complex and highly durable components, recovered for reuse in remanufacturing or repair.

4. **Reduced and reusable packaging:** Before the advent of single-use plastics, goods transport usually occurred in reusable packaging made of wood, metal, or glass. Consumerization, small packaging, and cheap plastics led the move away from these traditional practices. However, recent consumer preferences and a shift to service models present an opportunity to revisit previous methods of reusable packaging.

5. **Industrial symbiosis:** This is the process in which industrial waste and by-products become the raw materials for another. While already an active practice, this concept is typically applied only in specific cases—like the waste from ethanol plants as an ingredient in farm animal feed—rather

than on a broader basis and global scale. New product life cycle feedback loops are needed, so the waste of one party becomes a resource for another.[14]

SERVICE AND END OF LIFE

Product use and end of life is the final stage of predictive product life cycle management, and, depending on the product, multiple methods and strategies exist to achieve circular objectives. These include:

- **Product repair services.** Abundant, affordable products have conditioned modern-day consumers to dispose of products as soon as a fault occurs. While preference plays a role, so does economics, as repairs can be difficult and more expensive than simply buying a replacement product. On the other hand, there is a growing movement to repair goods instead of replace them. Nearly two-thirds of Europeans say they would rather repair their products than buy new ones.[15] The "right to repair" movement is gaining ground with government support, forcing manufacturers to improve the ability of older products to be repaired instead of forced obsolescence. There are substantial gains possible in electronics alone. The world produced a record 53.6 million metric tons of electronic waste in 2019, with only 17.4% recycled.[16] Hundreds of repair cafes and workshops have sprung up across Europe, and the authors expect this trend to continue for sustainability as well as to conserve the limited supply of rare earth minerals that are part of high-value electronics.

- **Product reuse.** Product reuse and secondhand commerce represent a significant opportunity to reduce waste and retain product value.[17] In the developing world, economic motives drive this practice. However, product reuse has regained popularity in the developed world due to waste management guidelines and more conscious consumers.

- **Product as a service.** The service is product performance instead of the product itself, and this business model is rapidly gaining momentum as a shift from single (capital) expense to recurring (operational) cost. As the economics catch up to sustainability, this will permeate all manufacturing, technology, and even service delivery sectors. An example is Amazon's Elastic Compute Cloud (EC2) on-demand service, in which you can use your credit card online to get instant access for the duration of your need. A similar service model is vehicle-as-a-service in the automotive industry, where users do not own a vehicle but subscribe to it and pay to use the car only when needed.[18]

- **Reverse collection and recycle.** When products reach their end of life, reverse collection networks are critical to close the material loop. Extracting reusable components to remanufacture and recycle raw material generates significant savings and reduces waste and handling costs. Electric vehicles (EVs) are a $46 trillion market opportunity between now and 2050.[19] EV makers have a chance to design for sustainability, not pursue it as an afterthought.

Neodymium and dysprosium are rare metals used to make magnets for EV electric motors, and vehicle batteries require lithium and cobalt (also rare). Extraction is expensive and environmentally damaging, and financial models should consider these costs and risks. Circularity in the automotive industry could reduce carbon emissions up to 75% and resource consumption up to 80% per passenger kilometer by 2030, according to the Circular Cars Initiative.[20] Unlike internal combustion engine vehicles, the EV market is new. This small base provides the opportunity to introduce circularity from the start.

Recycling is also important. Predictions indicate lithium-ion battery demand from EVs will rise sharply, from 269 GWh in 2021 to 2.6 TWh per year by 2030 and 4.5 TWh by 2035.[21] While less than 5% of these batteries are recycled currently, 262,000 tons will need to be recycled by 2022 as they are considered hazardous waste.[22] Batteries can have a second life through reuse for home-power storage, as they retain 50–70% of their capacity for up to a decade after their initial lifespan.[23]

SUSTAINABLE SUPPLY CHAINS = HIGH-VALUE SUPPLY CHAINS

The classic supply chain converts raw materials into finished goods by transporting and adding value at each stage of the conversion cycle, also known as a value chain. These value chains are massive for large corporations that exercise direct control over many internal units and external trading partners, and even smaller firms that operate through their networks. Circularity drives operational efficiency and cost savings but requires more than logistics efficiency.[24] Sustainable supply chain goals have been the corporate kindling for new ideas and methods to improve energy consumption, packaging, and logistics costs. Sustainability ideas permeate the entire manufacturing process, from sourcing raw materials to manufacturing and distribution processes, usage, and product recyclability. The tech industry has shown how reclaiming materials from old products, reducing packaging, and recycling materials are tangible steps to becoming more sustainable. In the process, they have benefited from more efficient operations, lower costs, and have created revenue opportunities in subscriptions and product returns management. As a result, supply chain sustainability has evolved from fad to perennial business opportunity.

The impact of sustainable supply chains extends beyond economics due to their social and environmental impact. Supply chains need to be legally compliant in the geographies in which they operate—across source, manufacture, transport, storage, and consumption.

BLOOD IN OUR POCKETS: TRANSFORMING THE SUPPLY CHAIN

Companies can optimize supply chain environmental impact by comparing their demands on natural resources—such as water, energy, and minerals—to the value added to their products. Large supply chains should not abuse dominant market position to indiscriminately hoard these resources and leave little for less-influential supply chains. Our indispensable smartphones and laptops depend upon precious natural resources, commonly described as conflict resources. Child labor in fighting zones mine these rare earth minerals to fund prolonged conflicts—the financial trail of tears masked through opaque supply chains.[25] Each supply chain member should align with goals to increase sustainably sourced resources, reduce energy footprint, and reduce resource consumption.

Driving this transformation across supply chains is a gradual process, and impacts will be seen only over time, emphasizing the need to act now. First, organizations must map their existing value chain to provide visibility, map relationships, and encourage measurement—then engage with stakeholders to set expectations and plan improvement programs with clear and relevant measures. The dominant supply chain partner should take a leadership role, as it influences progress by building and executing sustainability programs across its ecosystem.

PROVENANCE AND CONSUMPTION

MATERIALS MATTER

The raw materials needed to create products, whether metal alloys or digital code, must come from somewhere, and virgin forests, farmland, and mines come to mind as physical headwaters. However, secondary resources also play an increasing role in accessing raw materials, such as recycled electronic products and biological recovery of natural resources. Sustainable strategies reduce natural resource consumption while producing and processing raw materials. Sustainable materials management (SMM) is a higher-productivity approach to use and reuse materials across their lives.[26] Sustainably designed products require fewer materials, lower toxicity, and easier dissembling for recycling or reuse. Recycled material adoption is a worthy goal, yet it increases complexity in product flow and supply constraints—like the need to have a steady supply of recycled products. Raw materials companies feel the impact as the economy moves toward less consumption and greater reuse. In their traditional business models, less material used means less revenue. Therefore, companies should innovate into material-as-a-service models where revenue is generated not by selling material but through the performance of the materials. One example is car engine lubricants rented by the consumer instead of a single-use purchase. Used motor oil doesn't degrade; it simply gets dirty. If properly drained and filtered, it can be re-refined using less energy than refining base stock crude oil. One gallon of used motor oil produces two and a half quarts of lubricating oil, which requires forty-two gallons of crude oil to make.[27]

THE LAST MILE

Product consumption is the amount of a good or service used and often results in less availability afterward. Labor and energy are required to manufacture, transport, store, merchandise, and ultimately dispose of the product. Smartphone procurement is an example of a mass-consumer product customized to user preferences. The smartphone value chain has various players: communications service provider, handset manufacturer, user interface code, service package, connectivity services, and third-party apps.

When we replace our phones, carriers incent the consumer to send the phones back to the service provider through leasing programs during upgrade to a newer device. We intend to give back our old phone during an upgrade, yet the reality is an estimated 75% simply collect dust in drawers.[28] According to the EPA, consumers recycle less than 20% of unwanted cell phones each year.[29]

The phones that recycling firms collect enjoy second lives, often in corporate environments, at little or no cost. There is an opportunity for merchandisers to create consumer-marketing programs to lease refurbished phones, thereby highlighting environmental benefits and cost savings. Manufacturers recycle phones that they cannot reuse for their rare earth metal and chip components because the material is expensive to source and is in short supply. The global market for refurbished smartphones reached just over 137 million units in 2019.[30] Analytics' firm, IDC, predicts an 11.2% compound annual growth rate for refurbished smartphones by 2024 and $65 billion for secondhand devices in the same timeframe.[31] Slowly but surely, consumers are changing their behavior.

SERVITIZATION

The move from linear products to circular, intelligent, connected, long-lasting product-service systems also affects how we view consumption. Instead of low-cost and disposable, we view products as sustainable and a service. Manufacturers need to shift from product to service orientation. Servitization enables manufacturers to leverage their core product strengths by providing a suite of services like maintenance and fleet logistics through subscription-based models that deliver value to customers and manufacturers.

Rolls-Royce's "Power by the Hour" for aircraft engine operations is the oldest and best-known of these services. The trademark service provides a complete engine and accessory replacement service on a fixed-cost-per-flying-hour basis.[32] This arrangement aligns the interests of the manufacturer and operator, which only pays for engines that perform well. Automotive and industrial equipment sectors are rapidly moving to this model,[33] aided by the advances in connectivity from IoT, cloud, and network bandwidth. Beyond business benefits, the net effect is longer-lasting core assets and reduced material consumption, energy to produce it, and transportation to move it to the point of purchase and consumption.

BLOCKCHAIN TO THE RESCUE

Blockchain technology supports circularity through traceable supply chains, like in our smartphone scenario, with its ability to provide trust in a distributed database of transactions.[34] There are challenges, the first being how to establish trust. The blockchain incentivizes external providers to verify proof of work (mining). As blocks move down the chain, the amount of mathematical and computational effort supplied would be insurmountable to replicate, providing a decentralized ledger as proof. For example, cryptocurrency blockchains also establish trust via proof of stake, committing a held amount of the cryptocurrency to a pool where the consensus of a plurality—value chain influencers—determines truth. Linking blockchain technology with physical assets presents new issues, like establishing truth when objects tracked are physical goods outside the chain. One possibility is to associate cryptocurrency and use proof of stake with transaction fees to fund awards to businesses that stake their inventory and provide a means for companies to recapture some of those fees as revenue from otherwise idle inventory. More development is needed to create a workable model.

Supply chain ledgers are challenging because they represent physical products existing outside the digital chain, introducing weakness since the chain may be impenetrable, but serial numbers on physical products are not. Fraud may also appear in the genesis of product tracking as unscrupulous actors launder products through shell companies before linking, to hide their true nature.[35] Additional concerns arise for products or materials that are of lower value or interchangeable, while the model works better for manufactured goods that are individually serializable. To start, consider a solutions network that includes centralized organizations, blockchains, and other undeveloped systems to track circularity.[36]

Significantly more exploration of models is needed to establish how a blockchain could suit this need. However, the technology's promise and ability to provide an immutable, traceable record fits the use case exceptionally well. There are strong incentives as demands for advanced logistical capabilities increase and global supply chains become more complex, with demand for goods rising in developing economies.

LOW-CARBON ENERGY

THE SHIFT TO PROSUMPTION

The energy and utilities industries are moving aggressively to green energy and sustainability. Energy companies are evolving their core business of producing hydrocarbons to renewable energy generation.

Rooftop solar and small windmills have disrupted the utility industry, as electricity consumers have become "prosumers," mitigating or net contributing energy to the grid. For example, Infosys has partnered with global energy and utility firms to develop a smart-grid-energy transition platform that delivers electrification through renewables. Beyond generating economic returns, Infosys' green energy generation and usage reduce carbon intensity and provide another lever to achieve net-zero sustainability targets.[37]

Figure 3.3. **Infosys Green Energy Use**
Source: Infosys Knowledge Institute

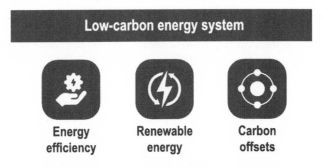

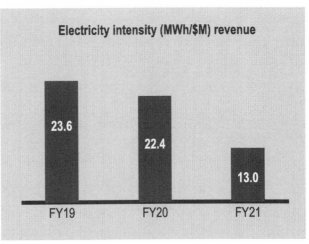

Distributed energy resources like rooftop solar, wind, EVs, and storage have challenged utilities to operate the grid reliably.[38] The intermittent nature of these resources creates grid operational issues related to system reliability, power quality, and power availability. Combined with historic disruptive weather, such as freezes, heat waves, hurricanes, and forest fires, the need for careful asset monitoring is greater than ever. Utilities have developed distributed energy resource management systems to analyze historical and real-time data to integrate, manage, and control resources and electric demand. Intelligence derived from these systems is then applied to synchronize energy transmission and distribution systems. These insights provide distribution system operators with network visibility and control to maintain system reliability and power quality.[39]

ADVANCED DISTRIBUTION, THE SMARTER GRID

Advanced distribution management systems (ADMS) provide a shared network model and a common user experience for all roles required to monitor, control, and secure the operation of electric distribution networks. It guides distribution operators during storm-related outage restoration activities, optimizes network asset utilization, and manages the integration of distributed energy resources. ADMS integrates with geographic information systems and the enterprise systems mentioned above. Distributed energy resource systems are challenging and complex to implement and can take several years based on requirements and utility customer base, with New York-based utility Con Edison being a good example.[40]

Global energy users are developing energy transition offerings to create the next generation power grid. These frameworks emphasize distributed energy resources and acknowledge the accelerating convergence of energy and mobility. Beyond the big picture, grid modeling aids detailed network planning and optimization. Frameworks align with NIST Smart Grid IEEE Architecture standards and are executed with new, tech-savvy industry partners to create a sustainable, utility-grid ecosystem. This new approach will increase renewables, technology upgrades, modern regulatory requirements, and resilience for disaster recovery.[41]

THE NOT-SO-GRACEFUL AGING OF INFRASTRUCTURE

Aging infrastructure adversely impacts the economy and the environment. The 2020 California wildfires started by faulty Pacific Gas and Electric transmission lines, causing the evacuation of 100,000 people, highlight this reality.[42] Beyond the investment needed to upgrade buildings and other energy infrastructures, robotics is part of the solution. Robots have many uses in the energy sector, for the dull, dirty, and dangerous jobs like cleaning transmission lines across hundreds of miles of rough terrain. Utilities face a significant problem of aging infrastructure and huge transmission power losses. To put this in perspective, the US has an installed conductor base of 400,000 miles with a power loss of $25 billion annually and requiring 25% replacement of the installed conductor base by 2030.[43] In addition, power lines heat up due to the transmission of power and exposure to solar heating. This excessive heat causes the conductors to sag and increases the risk of forest fires due to vegetation intrusions.[44] To address this problem, innovative autonomous robots clean and coat the overhead conductors with proprietary material. This coating solution increased carrying capacity by 25% while reducing power losses and conductor sag by 25%.[45]

Robots have many uses in the energy sector where labor is arduous, and environments are often harsh and remote. For the Infosys solar power plant in Hyderabad, India, robots clean solar panels, which improves productivity and reduces losses in solar power generation. Additionally, IoT and AI technologies monitor and improve the performance of the solar power plant. This state-of-the-art installation can generate twelve million units (kWh) annually and has helped Infosys completely offset electricity consumption at the large Hyderabad campus. In fact, the plant generates a surplus of electricity.[46]

Traditionally, the building industry had many manual operations and used devices with older technologies and data systems. Manual processes, such as spreadsheets and handwritten notes, hamper the ability to accurately track data to measure quality, efficiency, and safety. This tracking issue leads to errors on the job site by contractors, subcontractors, materials suppliers, and inspectors. Multiple systems require significantly more operations time than single data sources and digitalization.

Beyond performance, manual processes and devices also increase the possibility of error. Operator understanding, not AI algorithms, traditionally drove operations of lighting and climate-control systems. Experienced operators had rules of thumb and good judgment, yet human and data silos isolated knowledge among groups. This segregation of relevant data and insights is insufficient to succeed in a complex, rapidly changing world that demands better efficiency and sustainability.

Smart spaces deploy a command center that centrally manages the operation of buildings through remote monitoring and feedback. This centralized approach leads to increased quality, efficient supply chains, materials conservation, equipment uptime, and employee productivity.

The smart, connected approach converts brownfield physical spaces into low-energy footprint facilities, enhanced with digital experiences. Smart energy solutions build on this foundation with smart grid and renewables, architecture reference blueprints, and partnerships with technology, hardware, and service providers.

An Infosys manufacturing client created a central building management command center to manage resource efficiency. They realized 15% energy savings, plus a 20% reduction in IT support costs. The command center continuously monitored energy flow, and its data-driven approach avoided 1,700 million kWh of energy consumption over eight years. This initiative reduced energy costs of $185 million and 1.5 million tons of carbon emissions. In 2018, the company reduced per capita electricity consumption by 53%, compared to the 2008 baseline.

Most energy consumption occurs in buildings and efficient design matters.[47] Whether gleaming new buildings or deep-green retrofits, operational excellence through intelligent automation is crucial to achieving energy efficiency.

DIGITAL FINANCE WITH VELOCITY AND TRUST

NEW ECONOMICS AND END OF THE ONE-TIME SALE

The transition to circular business models creates significant financial opportunity with companies needing to diversify from a focus on one-time sales to drive top-line revenue.[48] Auto manufacturers have mastered the art of financing for vehicle purchases, leasing, and services, such as repair and warranty. With supply-chain digitalization, they are now addressing intellectual property to license EV platforms, 3D printed parts, and software onto standardized components. These innovations provide opportunities to adopt new business models, and leaders need to think about stable, recurring revenue instead of emphasizing a large initial sale (see Figure 3.4).

Figure 3.4. **Sustainable Finance**

Source: United Nations

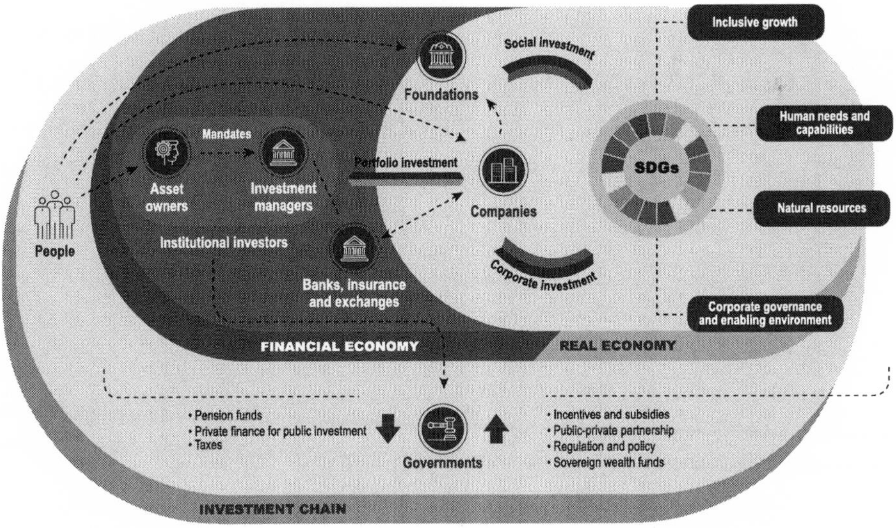

While this could mean leasing and subscription, there are other ways to achieve this goal. Auto manufacturers can sell upgrades, so consumers swap out the dashboard for new functionality in the same vehicle. Another option is a renewal plan where, instead of vehicle trade-in, after five years, the customer brings it to an authorized refurbisher for a comprehensive refresh based on foundational and cosmetic changes. This model is especially relevant for electric cars, where main vehicle components are long-lasting, but newer technology and batteries will still drive trade-ins. This trend is a fundamental shift from the traditional, disposable, planned obsolescence approach in auto sales and even from the quality focus for lower total cost of ownership. The past is again a precedent here, as a similar trend occurred with large appliances in the mid-twentieth century. Products become more expensive but longer-lasting (and more functional), emphasizing repair over replacement.[49]

Financing and leasing keep products affordable and increase customer choice while also driving new revenue opportunities. There will be an increased emphasis on consumer financing and a transition to leasing models if products are expensive but intended for long-term use. As raw material costs rise, better recycling and reuse programs encourage customers to return products at the end of their life cycles. Money plays a role in changing behaviors by offsetting some of the increased cost through rebates, as is done for car batteries, bottles, and other products.

COMMERCE AS AN ESG CATALYST

While the previous chapter sections cover product life-cycle stages individually, there is also value in how they come together. When designing a product, the energy required to form and transport it is an important consideration. In food, there is an argument to move from dairy to plant-based products because of the perceived environmental impact by cows. From almond milk to Beyond Meat, these ideas generate significant investment interest as sustainability-friendly, high-growth markets. However, total sustainability impact should shape product evaluations. While almond milk comes from sustainable plant protein, the product requires seventeen times more water than dairy milk.[50] While Beyond Meat has a much lower carbon footprint than traditional meat, its packaging is not compostable, and its reporting lacks transparency.[51] Other farm-to-table factors include responsible farming practices, fair labor usage, local manufacturing, and reusable (recyclable) packaging. These market innovation examples are attractive to consumers and investors, yet they also require comprehensive sustainability measures and transparency in reporting.

CIRCULARITY FINANCIAL CREDITS

Green bonds, also called climate bonds, are a financial product used to fund sustainability, with the proceeds or asset-linked bonds to underwrite green projects. ESG investors and supply-chain participants have increased demand for this financial instrument.

A significant challenge in this area is how to value raw-material recovery versus extraction, beyond prices rising as easily accessible resources deplete. Investors have financed waste management projects and assets in the green bond market since 2015.[52] Dealing with waste generation and raw material extraction, along with CO_2

emission reduction, requires significant investment to improve management infrastructure and processes. This investment capital flows from the issuance of green bonds; according to Japan's Ministry of Environment, allocations to waste management totaled $6.8 billion in December 2019.[53]

Investors and suppliers identify opportunities using voluntary sustainability practices known as the Green Bond Principles,[54] which include:

1. Use of proceeds
2. Process for project evaluation and selection
3. Management of proceeds
4. Reporting

The scope covers sustainable waste management, renewable energy, energy-efficient smart spaces, clean transportation, and sustainable land use. As more global financial institutions and government entities enter this growing market, providing capital to fund projects, regulatory standards are required to reduce the risk of greenwashing, as the market expects green bond issuers to use their proceeds to deliver results.

INVESTOR ANALYSIS: FROM GROWTH TO RESPONSIBILITY

The markets, not just regulatory bodies, will drive sustainability adoption. For a comprehensive view, investors need to look at sources of revenue, not just amount, as part of ESG analysis and financial health. Savvy investors can derive total relevant income from product sales, repair services, support, upgrades, recycling, and reuse loops.

This green accounting evolution also means executives will shift strategies from a perpetual focus on growth (implies more consumption) to profitability (implies responsible usage). Analysts will devalue companies that rely on frequent customer replacement of otherwise durable products, so-called planned obsolescence. Sustainable product development will not just be virtue signaling to investors. Hard economic trends will also drive longer-lasting products: rising material prices, increased consumer preference for circular models, and regulatory policy.[55]

Investment analysis should include supply chain disruption and material reliance. If a company produces a product that relies on rare earth minerals and cannot recycle them, this implies increased risk. As companies increase financed purchases of their products, this requires partnerships with lenders to underwrite customer financing plans or securitize to offer financing to cover the cost of goods sold. Financing may become an essential constraint to a circular economy. With higher material prices and fewer overall sales, financing becomes a lifeline to capture more profits per sale and maintain long-term viability.

Circularity will become a distinct dimension of ESG analysis when evaluating investments.[56] This dimension is especially relevant for products where a fully circular model is not feasible, like recyclable packaging in consumer food retail. Valuation will also discourage trading one environmental problem for another, like replacing carbon pollution with nonrecyclable solar panels or waste-producing batteries.

RECAP

- For an enterprise, success in the age of sustainability depends upon creating customer-valued products and services through the most efficient means possible. Success also requires meeting regulatory guidelines, safety standards, and environmentally sound practices.

- Traditional linear practices are not sustainable: materials, components, and products lose value and are not available for reuse; they often result in landfills, oceans, or incineration.

- Circularity is an age-old yet thoroughly modern concept that creates high-performance, eco-friendly, cost-effective, and reusable products across the supply chain. The primary benefit of shifting to the circular economy model is eliminating waste and one-time resource usage.

- Manufacturers need to shift from product to service orientation. Servitization enables manufacturers to leverage their core product strengths by providing a suite of services and solutions that deliver value for both the customers and the manufacturers.

- Facilities that are smart spaces energy systems present a significant opportunity to lower carbon emissions and consumption overall. These systems gather and analyze data in real-time, improving energy efficiency while reducing energy consumption, emissions, and enhancing resilience.

HUMAN EXPERIENCE

DELIGHT BY DELIVERING TECHNOLOGY FOR GOOD

EDGES, ARISTOTLE, AND *EUDAIMONIA*

Over two thousand years ago, Aristotle said, "Happiness depends upon ourselves."[1] *Eudaimonia*—the Greek word for "happiness" or "human flourishing"—links the individual to the group, the concept that individual and group well-being are interdependent.[2]

Humans spend 90% of their time in buildings,[3] with 68% predicted to live in urban spaces by 2050.[4] These spaces drive our productivity, health, and happiness. The new fields of cognitive architecture and neuro-architecture help us understand what makes us human, shape how we interact with the built environment, and improve our quality of life.

Our brains have one hundred billion neurons—about the same number of stars in the Milky Way.[5] Those one hundred billion nerve cells spark more than one hundred trillion connections, pulsing information around the skull at 250 miles an hour.[6] The neuron forest in our heads filters every quantum of human experience through this biological smart space.

Research into the relationship between human experience and the built environment goes back to the 1960s. However, analysis of the human mind's role in this is far more recent—only a couple of decades old. We learned from research published in 2015 that when it comes to people and the built environment,[7] five simple principles influence human thinking:

1. Edges matter
2. Patterns matter
3. Shapes carry weight
4. Storytelling is key
5. Nature is our context

It is this understanding of human needs that will deliver technology for the common good: sustainability, productivity, well-being, and inclusion—in other words, our collective *eudaimonia*.

FROM FEELING GREEN TO FULFILLING EXPERIENCE

People's priorities have changed for the spaces in which they work, live, and interact. The pandemic rapidly moved expectations from comfort and in-person efficiency to safety and remote productivity. Behavior evolved from compliant acceptance to purposeful fulfillment through our social and work interactions with people and technology.

Traditional buildings address human needs: office buildings for work, education, and utilities; grocery stores and restaurants provide food; hospitals deliver healthcare; religious institutions serve the faithful and care for the disenfranchised. Similarly, one can see how smart spaces enable these traditional buildings to offer higher value as they augment human performance and capabilities. Just as the computer, internet, and smartphone improved our lives, data, computation, and connectivity energize smart spaces—the physical merging with the digital to enhance human potential further.

Our daily interactions with smart spaces reinforce this phenomenon of enhanced human performance. An everyday example is free coffee shop Wi-Fi, making the physical space smarter for visitors and owners. Visitors can drink coffee and work or recreate on mobile devices. The shop owner uses the network to monitor their electricity, HVAC, air quality, and people counting for social distancing. Healthy spaces drive productivity, and a smart space is more valuable to the owner and enriching to the user.

EXPERIENCE ACROSS THE STAKEHOLDER SPECTRUM

Smart spaces fulfill the needs of multiple stakeholders: owners, facility managers, tenants, and visitors.

Owners

With a vested interest, owners are responsible for ensuring a safe and secure building. In the after-COVID era, the rules have changed, and they start literally at the entry gate. Traditional access control revolved around identity management to allow authorized access and emergency egress. Smart buildings now require specialized equipment to accommodate new functions, such as counting and body temperature checks. Owners have new accountability for business continuity and tenant safety.

Facility Managers

Facility managers inspect, maintain, and repair building systems, and manage operations and regulatory compliance. They ensure imaging cameras and all manner of sensors and analytics work with building management systems to keep people safe upon entry and throughout their day.

Figure 4.1. **Smart Space Participants**
Source: Infosys Knowledge Institute

Employees (Tenants)

Tenants are the primary day-to-day building users. They may have strict security measures with stadiums, hospitals, and government buildings as prime examples of access needs that reflect each building's unique purpose. In most cases, tenant employees are the majority, but temporary workers, maintenance staff, and delivery personnel also work on-premise.

Customers (Visitors)

Everything that makes a good tenant experience also contributes to a good customer or visitor experience. Personalization systems need to be available to them as well. This availability includes ready access to company amenities, such as Wi-Fi and wayfinding tools that support people with disabilities.

FROM SINGULAR TRANSACTION TO HOLISTIC EXPERIENCE

When was the last time you went to a hospital for an overnight admission? The experience is typically frustrating, fraught with repeated information requests, culminating with anxiety upon waking up in the hospital room, and all the while feeling vulnerable. Smart patient room offerings overcome these issues, serving patient needs with enhanced amenities and accelerated recovery to improve the broader experience into a more satisfying, less-stressful journey. The smart patient room illustrates the human experience in smart spaces because the experience is central to the patient's journey.

The service blueprint design method aims to understand what is first involved from a human perspective, and then what technology is needed to deliver the solution.[8] In the following diagram, these aspects are shown in the labels on the left, with durations shown across the top. The diagram is just one page from over a dozen that visualize the relationships between different service components of a smart, patient-room experience. The patient can control room attributes, such as lighting, ventilation, and temperature. A valuable visualization outcome is awareness of technology dependencies that affect the physical world.

Figure 4.2 illustrates the hospital service experience from the patient's perspective.

A COMFORTABLE TRUTH: TECH SERVES HUMANS

The service blueprint designs the experience around the patient, aided through the interaction artifact (typically a mobile device) shown at the top of the figure. At this point, the patient has already onboarded with the software and has obtained proper authentication for their location (room and bed) as shown in the bottom left at "Support Processes."

The actions and system responses are comprised of four steps in this patient's journey, which require people, technologies, and time to succeed. The primary goal is to enable the patient to be comfortable and feel in control. The first step is when the patient opens the application. If the person cannot do this themselves, staff or family can assist. Second, the patient can adjust the comfort section of the app to adjust room temperature. This second step triggers the back-stage actions below the "line of visibility" as seen in Figure 4.2. The system interacts with the building management system to retrieve the current temperature and any existing setpoints. Technology is essential to the successful smart-patient room, but the user and their goals shape its role. The third step occurs when the patient tells the system their desired room temperature. The final step is that the patient receives feedback from the system, accepting their input.

Figure 4.2. **Patient Services Blueprint**
Source: Infosys Knowledge Institute

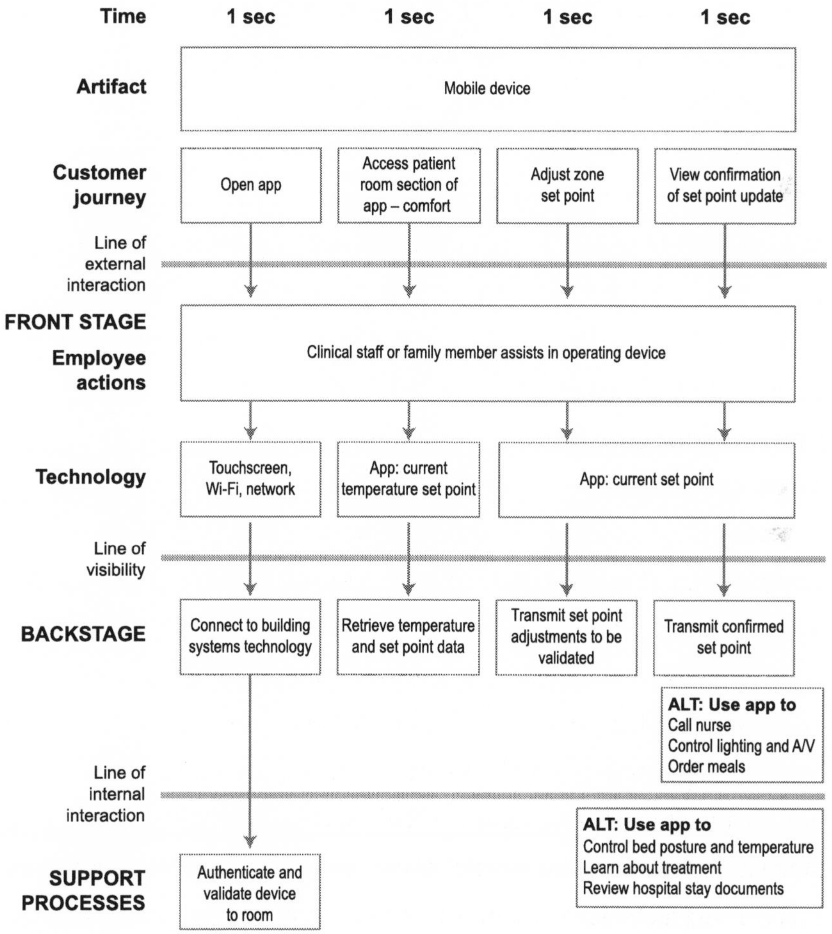

Time	1 sec	1 sec	1 sec	1 sec
Artifact	Mobile device			
Customer journey	Open app	Access patient room section of app – comfort	Adjust zone set point	View confirmation of set point update
Line of external interaction				
FRONT STAGE **Employee actions**	Clinical staff or family member assists in operating device			
Technology	Touchscreen, Wi-Fi, network	App: current temperature set point	App: current set point	
Line of visibility				
BACKSTAGE	Connect to building systems technology	Retrieve temperature and set point data	Transmit set point adjustments to be validated	Transmit confirmed set point
			ALT: Use app to Call nurse Control lighting and A/V Order meals	
Line of internal interaction			**ALT: Use app to** Control bed posture and temperature Learn about treatment Review hospital stay documents	
SUPPORT PROCESSES	Authenticate and validate device to room			

All of this typically happens in under five seconds. Additional alternatives ("ALT"; see the bottom right of Figure 4.2) for the app include calling the nurse, providing entertainment, and learning about a treatment plan for their discharge.

This service blueprint then forms the foundation for creating prototypes and further discovery to find experience gaps before deploying anything in the high-stakes environment of healthcare. It highlights the patient's line of visibility, a highly relevant concept when designing or retrofitting smart spaces.

Smart spaces create holistic human experiences, but there can be a downside if designers prioritize efficiency over empathy. The young Frank Lloyd Wright worked for Louis Sullivan, the Chicago-based architect who coined "form follows function."[9] Lloyd Wright later qualified this sentiment, commenting, "Form follows function—that has been misunderstood. Form and function should be one, joined in a spiritual union."[10] This spiritual union is sometimes in conflict. The air-conditioning system in the Infosys Bangalore campus originally shut off at 5:00 p.m., even if people were still working. For facility managers, this improved efficiency, but for after-hours employees, this created an uncomfortable experience. Once this issue became known, it was modified through sensor recognition and user requests to extend comfort-system hours.

LIVING, SENSING, THINKING BUILDINGS AND SUPPLY CHAINS

Smart spaces are both a physical and digital manifestation, enabling buildings to become connected systems that surround us with capabilities and processes that are both intuitive and serendipitous. At

Infosys, we harnessed the power of smart spaces at our sprawling Mysore education campus in India, with its footprint of 120 buildings and twelve million square feet. The amenities include office space, multiple food courts, housing, training rooms, and recreation centers that accommodate 20,000 people simultaneously. We used a human-centered design process followed by integrating sensors with various technologies supporting training content, physical security, and entertainment. Infosys deployed smart card access, parking management, and store kiosks to deliver comfortable and convenient experiences. These intelligent tools allow many employees to learn effectively and for leaders to incorporate feedback and improve the learning process continuously.

HUMAN FACTORS DESIGN

THE EVOLUTION AND SCIENCE OF HUMAN FACTORS

Human factors is the science of design with human characteristics in mind, exploring the application of the psychological and physiological to engineer new products, systems, and processes.[11] Human factors originally grew out of the military's need to design equipment for diverse people, reflecting World War II's complex weaponry and military vehicles development.

This application of human factors remains a cornerstone of smart spaces design and success. The cockpit of a fighter jet is a classic smart space. Aviation accidents attributed to pilot error were an early area of human factors research. Paul Fitts, Jr., and Alphonse Chapanis conducted studies on pilot error. They discovered a substantial decrease in pilot error when the aircraft design included the person as part of the system.[12]

Human behavior models constitute a significant output from human-factors engineering. The Boyd Observe-Orient-Decide-Act (OODA) model (1976, USAF Colonel John Boyd) integrates incoming information streams with weighting that accounts for human genetics, culture, and prior experience, even in rapidly compressed time to make highly informed decisions. While Boyd focused on battlefield strategy, this dynamic framework also overcomes uncertainty in nonmilitary domains, such as business.[13]

Figure 4.3. **Boyd's Observe-Orient-Decide-Act (OODA) Loop**
Source: John Boyd

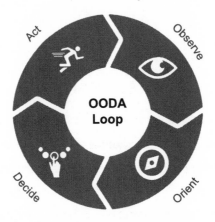

Multiple feedback loops from decisions, actions, and new observations are used in an OODA loop to tie cognition to action, providing a general description of how a system designed to perform some function operates.[14]

The OODA loop breaks down the decision cycle into four parts:

1. **Observation:** Listen, view, and research, while collecting data and information.

2. **Orientation:** Form a mental perspective using analysis and synthesis. Analysis breaks down data into components that allow for deductions that lead to understanding. Synthesis takes (sometimes unrelated) components and recombines them to form a new whole.

3. **Decision:** Determine a course of action based on the current mental perspective.

4. **Action:** Resultant activity informed by the decisions.

BETTER DECISIONS THROUGH HUMAN FACTORS

Smart spaces utilize a building management system with multiple sensors across various building system types, incorporating feedback loops for fault detection to maintain the desired environment. The Boyd Cycle influenced the crucial use of feedback loops.

On March 28, 1979, the US experienced its worst commercial nuclear accident at Three Mile Island near Harrisburg, Pennsylvania, when a relief valve malfunctioned, and nuclear reactor coolant escaped into the atmosphere. System complications quickly compounded when human plant operators failed to recognize coolant loss due to inadequate OODA training and human factors, misreading a system indicator.[15] Ultimately, their actions released even more significant amounts of coolant into the atmosphere while also increasing the probability of a complete reactor meltdown. This accident rallied anti-nuclear activists, created new government regulatory oversight, and spurred the decline of the nuclear power industry in the US. This example shows the importance of human experience for safety, not just comfort, in smart building design.

EIGHTY-TWO STAIRS AND THE DESIGN OF EVERYDAY THINGS

The Americans with Disabilities Act (ADA) created the impetus for accessible and inclusive design. In 1990, activists and legislators fought to ensure forty million disabled US citizens equal rights and access. On March 12, 1990, sixty activists left their canes and wheelchairs behind and crawled up the eighty-two stairs that led to the US Capitol Building. This symbol of democracy was not accessible to the disabled at the time.[16] The event, which became known as The Capitol Crawl, generated visibility and public outrage, and shortly after that, US Congress passed the ADA.

Combined, those eighty-two stairs, public sentiment, and the ADA forever changed how the built world was designed and constructed in the US. Previously, architects designed buildings based on a confusing combination of state and local laws and codes. People were the last consideration, and rarely did disabilities enter the discussion. Disabled people's lives revolved largely around finding accessible routes, buildings, and services. The ADA forced architects and builders to change direction and consider human capabilities in the built world.

Design for accessibility became the new reality. Although some architects thought new ADA regulations would negatively affect building quality, buildings became more usable and accessible for everyone. The Fulton Center is a lower Manhattan transit center and retail space; it highlights this new building characteristic and its benefits. The train lines and shops, wider lanes, elevator accessibility, and improved signage make this busy New York center both ADA-compliant and a smartly designed space that enhances the experience of 300,000 transit passengers daily.[17] Greater accessibility for one becomes more accessibility for all.

Creating Experiences to Remove Friction

Some of the most beautiful buildings fail to deliver beyond aesthetics. Design that unduly emphasizes aesthetics can lead to functional challenges. Despite Frank Lloyd Wright's accent on the spiritual union of form and function, even he was guilty of this. Wright was known for his ability to create buildings in harmony with nature. Yet even a great mind like Wright's sometimes put aesthetics at odds with function.

Affleck House in Bloomfield Hills, Michigan,[18] exemplified Lloyd Wright's Usonian style, blending perfectly with the surrounding landscape; even today, it attracts visitors from around the world. However, this home has a functional challenge. To reach the laundry room, Affleck House requires occupants to either crawl through a narrow four-foot-tall hallway or carry the laundry outside and reenter from an exterior door—even in winter! While a beautiful home, Lloyd Wright favored aesthetics over function, and the result was friction in the experience.

While the inaccessible laundry room may seem an exaggerated example, this type of friction is not uncommon in the built world. People are traditionally an afterthought in building design. In the words of Chris Okamoto, architect and design leader at Infosys, "Buildings and space for the longest time have been built considering budget, form, regulations, and function, with people typically being last, if a thought at all."

Adaptable for Personalization

Smart spaces and supply networks recast the once-rigid boundaries of structures, flows, and behavior. They adapt to individual and team needs, elevating a new, human-centered era of personalization.

When Infosys designed our flagship office in Indianapolis, we avoided the traditional approach of large images of our global headquarters adorning the walls or conveying hierarchical authority through larger workspaces for senior staff. Instead, the new design approach for our Indianapolis office placed people at the center.

We created differentiated office experiences for employees and guests. Our design team interviewed stakeholders who would use the office: executives, sales leaders, billable consultants, and support staff. The designers observed how people used the office, understood stakeholder behaviors, and designed the space to reflect their needs. Five smart space design principles (see Figure 4.4) drove this new office approach: functional, flexible, fluid, flat, and familiar.[19]

First, the office needed to be **functional** for people. As a workplace, the designers wanted every aspect of the space to serve a useful function. There was no wasted wall area on superfluous art pieces or extravagant furniture. Instead, designers focused on essential requirements, like comfortable seats, suitable work surfaces, high-speed internet, multi-use rooms, natural light, and a large kitchen area.

Second, designers made sure the office was **flexible** to changes in day-to-day and individual needs. Furniture was easily moveable,

Figure 4.4. **Smart Spaces Design Principles**
Source: Infosys Knowledge Institute

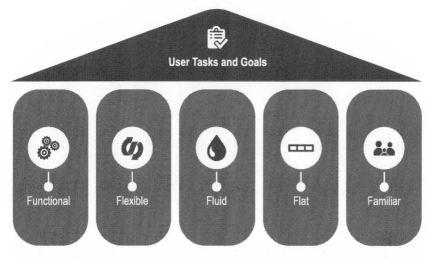

power outlets were highly mobile, and whiteboards were on wheels to create portable makeshift walls. The space flexed in response to the needs of each person and activity.

Third, the space was **fluid**. People chose their desk location, and those who typically worked in the office took priority. There were no reserved seats, and the layout changed based on events that day and who was in the office.

Fourth, the office was **flat**. There was no emphasis on job titles, and the office coordinator assigned workspaces based on need, not hierarchy.

Finally, the designers wanted the Indianapolis office to become a second home—**familiar**. The designers wanted the new office to be where people wanted to come and stay, not depart as soon as allowed. They created an inviting kitchen with shared spaces that were open to all. One of the few permanent office fixtures was a long bar-height table people used as a social place for coffee, meals, or chats with coworkers.

We created an office that was "for the people and by the people." The design did not stop once the office opened, as minor refinements frequently occur as employees provide input about their needs. The office is continually evolving to give employees better experiences. Once we implemented these principles in Indianapolis, we reused them for other offices as well. Table 4.1 highlights the benefits and indicators related to the improved employee experience.

Table 4.1. **Smart Spaces Experience Benefits**
Source: *Infosys Knowledge Institute*

Experience	Indicators
Enhanced comfort	• Control lighting, temperature, and airflow
Control of environment	• Minimize tools and technology friction • Configure project space
Increased confidence and satisfaction	• Maximize employee retention • Increase regard for facilities team through surveys • Employee engagement
Ease of collaboration	• Locate people with opt-in occupancy presence tools • Increase in-person and remote ad hoc conversation • Improve data transfer via 5G

When buildings adapt to people's needs, making technology literally recede into the ceiling and walls, they enable occupants to focus on their work and creativity, driving productivity and a better experience.

ENVIRONMENTAL, HEALTH, AND SAFETY MANAGEMENT

THE EVOLUTION OF EHS

Environment, Health, and Safety (EHS) are the regulations and processes to maintain the health and safety of employees and the public, while protecting the environment from hazardous impacts in the workplace. Work practices include safety requirements that make it easier to initiate, train, and track compliance. Integrated EHS is part of operations and a company's safety culture. EHS has evolved from a compliance-reporting function to a suite of powerful tools:

- **Product, process, and environmental**: Compliance, including audit, inspections, quality management, reporting, greenhouse gas emissions, and hazardous waste.
- **Health and safety**: Incident management, safety policies and procedures, safety culture, safety training, contractor safety, ergonomics, risk and hazard management, industrial hygiene, incident management, and occupational health.
- **Operations management**: Asset management and equipment maintenance, document management, and change management.

EHS has evolved through regulatory compliance requirements, operational changes, corporate reputation protection, accident avoidance, worker well-being, and process standardization. Post-COVID, companies add dedicated sustainability practices to make their offerings more competitive. These offerings include product life-cycle assessment, circular economy, ESG risk reporting, responsible sourcing and consumption, traceability, and product stewardship.

Health

When occupants suffer from health and comfort issues directly attributed to their time spent in a building, it is called sick building syndrome. It manifests in the form of headache or irritation of the eye, throat, or stomach.[20]

Smart buildings optimize EHS performance and streamline facility operations through sensors, Wi-Fi, video, and HVAC systems. Control centers measure air quality and ventilation, occupancy, and temperature, creating a heat map of healthy occupation zones. They also measure and provide alerts to potentially hazardous scenarios. A demand control ventilation technique incorporates CO_2 level detectors with other environmental controls, promotes energy efficiency, and enhances building health and safety.[21] This method includes the detection of potential overuse of chemical cleaning agents within building environments.

With all this collected data, individual privacy needs consideration, and communications and policy must ensure transparency and focus on benefits and compliance, avoiding a clandestine observation tool. Behavioral change and adoption occur when we see healthy spaces outcomes and benefits. Building managers equipped with robust systems can improve worker productivity, healthcare costs, and comfort. These benefits attract and retain employees and maximize a building's purpose, use, and longevity.

Safety

Intelligent buildings enable a safe and secure environment through situation awareness and alerts. They use analytics and control center dashboards powered by IoT, unified video surveillance, and building systems. Real-time and historical data insights provide situational intelligence to identify risks and calculate the best course of action to minimize dangerous situations.

Safe experiences in buildings through security and access control are among the highest value services to users. Cloud technology provides convenience, scalability, and minimal intervention. Infrastructure-monitoring technologies identify system failures and deliver automated maintenance services that minimize operational downtime while physically and digitally safe structures.

Workplace IoT, cameras, and connectivity have proliferated, and they can interact with and control our environments. Yet cybersecurity and privacy also become essential considerations for deployment.

Reporting

ESG reporting is quickly becoming a significant component of corporate board member performance and compensation. Required reporting includes environment, health, and safety management solutions. Smart space technologies automate reporting disclosure to meet EHS principles and industry protocols like Building Wellness Index (BWI), providing senior executives with required auditing data in a timely manner.

Smart spaces use operational control in conjunction with governance and operating protocols. A risk-management committee reviews climate-related risks and opportunities to track the progress of climate-action commitments and the required budgets to miti-gate and build resilience against disruptions. Risk management and CSR committees typically assess and oversee climate-action activi-ties as part of their quarterly meetings.

At an operational level, the sustainability leader drives projects to achieve goals related to climate action. These goals cascade to managers who look after project identification, implementation, and monitoring. Managers collaborate with central and local EHS facilities teams to ensure that objectives drive EHS-related climate action both top-down as well as bottom-up.

Automated data input, along with integration into the ERP sys-tem of record, provides regulatory compliance transparency.

SMART AUTOMATION DELIVERS CREATIVITY

FROM SCIENTIFIC TO HUMANISTIC PRODUCTIVITY

Hyper-productivity is a high-performing state, defined for smart spaces as productivity where people can do much more, in ways they prefer. A smart space aligns with how a person chooses to work, much like how a good tool fits the hand. Productive and creative workforces excel in an environment that promotes wellness, com-fort, and safety, supported by connectivity, efficiency, and tech-nology. This desired state applies to all workplace types: corporate headquarters, research facilities, and factory floors.

An Infosys employee survey found that workplace design directly influenced worker productivity.[22] Over 60% of respondents reported that personal workspace layout improved their ability to complete tasks. Fifty percent of respondents mentioned that the flexibility of their workspace increased their productivity. Beyond workplace design, employees also wanted more technology to enable better productivity. Ninety-one percent of employees surveyed believed that Wi-Fi across all workspaces would increase their productivity.

RENEWED EMPHASIS ON HUMAN WELL-BEING

In a landmark 1943 paper titled "A Theory of Human Motivation,"[23] American psychologist Abraham Maslow theorized that a hierarchy of psychological needs undergirds human decision-making. In his initial paper and a subsequent 1954 book titled Motivation and Personality,[24] Maslow proposed that five core needs form the basis for human behavioral motivation.

Most people have an innate drive to succeed and self-actualize, according to Maslow. If they find joy in their daily activities, they become content, productive, and exhibit general wellness. Modern space planning seeks to find that joy, while still managing construction and operating expense, and drives the objective of maximizing the human experience across actors. Use cases range from health, security, privacy, occupancy tracking, and operations optimization. Each of these cases can create conditions that contribute to a state of wellness.

Today, nearly eighty years after Maslow, the average person spends 90,000 hours at work over their career,[25] literally a third of their life during their working years. Given that significant amount of time, workplaces must support human well-being. Smart spaces promote human well-being in a similar way that the Maslow schema describes the human condition. See Figure 4.5, which maps Maslow's hierarchy to smart spaces.

Figure 4.5. **Maslow's Hierarchy of Needs Mapped to Smart Spaces**
Source: Abraham H. Maslow

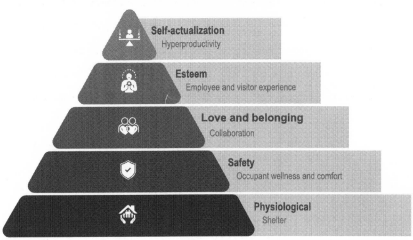

The base level of Maslow's hierarchy describes shelter as how buildings provide protection and safety. Beyond this foundation, clean air, thermal comfort, and pro-health work policies enable workers to apply their skills freely as they feel safe. Contactless entry using palm recognition is another example of intelligent buildings making security and access easier and safer. Reduced technology hurdles, lessened frustration, and increased connectivity also remove factors harmful to mental health, opening the door to wellness.

If not designed properly, even well-intended technologies like guest Wi-Fi and conference room audio-video connectors erode confidence and satisfaction. At the next level of the hierarchy, workers master their environment and tools, promoting enhanced self-esteem. Owners and building designers who embrace smart spaces also encourage the goal of self-actualization, the kind of human fulfillment that enables hyper-productivity.

This renewed emphasis is seen in the WELL Building Standard that codifies these higher-level concepts,[26] exemplifying how smart spaces promote the human experience. The individual's health contributes to the whole organization, and the WELL Institute considerations span buildings, people, and policies. For example, the WELL Building Standard actively discourages people from taking red-eye overnight flights and losing valuable sleep.

Figure 4.6. **WELL Building Standard Concepts**
Source: International WELL Buidling Institute

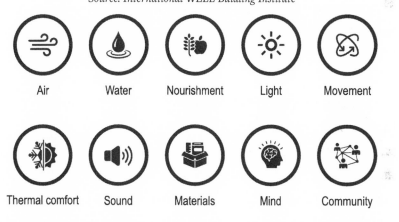

| Air | Water | Nourishment | Light | Movement |

| Thermal comfort | Sound | Materials | Mind | Community |

Modern buildings are a complex collection of systems, much like a computer has its components. Sensors, lighting, plumbing, electrical, HVAC, networking, and fire and safety systems create an intelligent approach to support occupants. Computers have operating systems that make them intelligent. Similarly, smart space technology makes the building and its people smart. Technology becomes an extension of the people who inhabit and manage buildings. At its best, tech just works and becomes invisible, where the IT recedes into the walls or exists on the periphery, like IoT sensors and other ambient technology. The challenge is to achieve both quantitative (energy costs) and qualitative (wellness) metrics. To do so, convert qualitative measures to quantitative ones where possible, through the collection of data generated by the smart space—like environmental variable influence on satisfaction.

DATA PRIVACY—FRICTION MATTERS

Privacy by design is the approach to embed privacy as core functionality into the design and architecture stage of business processes, applications, products, and technologies.[27] Existing policies and regulations alone cannot fully protect privacy. Introducing privacy as the default case for design of processes and IT systems is necessary to implement privacy protection for consumers, businesses, citizens, and governments.

Privacy by design (PbD) relies on seven foundational concepts to mitigate privacy risks and achieve data privacy compliance:[28]

- **Proactive, not reactive, and preventive, not remedial:** PbD supports proactive identification of privacy-risk events in advance and taking necessary preventive steps, rather than being reactive and implementing corrective measures after an event occurs.
- **Privacy as the default setting:** PbD requires privacy to be the default mode of operation while building organization

processes and systems. A data subject should require no specific action to ensure personal data privacy.

- **Privacy embedded into design:** Privacy should be a core functionality, starting from any system's design and architecture stage, not added as an afterthought at a later stage.
- **Positive-sum, not zero-sum:** PbD believes that business functionality and data privacy are equally important. This emphasis means there is no need for trade-offs and accommodates all interests and objectives with a positive-sum mindset.
- **End-to-end security:** PbD supports end-to-end security of personal data across the entire information life cycle.
- **Visibility and transparency:** PbD supports complete transparency and visibility to all stakeholders.
- **Respect for user privacy:** PbD offers data subject measures like privacy defaults and appropriate notifications to keep privacy centered on the user.

For sustainability, the balance among metrics identification and data capturing, storing, and reporting is crucial. Sometimes it's controversial and introduces a necessary form of friction. Data ranges from scientific to social and governance at a global scale, utilizing quantitative and qualitative data, as well as required and voluntary, depending on circumstances and location. There is a risk that if a supplier reports in full detail the consumption and reuse of specific materials, a competitor could potentially reverse engineer a proprietary industrial secret. It is a delicate balance—this interaction friction—between transparency and the protection of an individual's rights. While this issue requires more detail to develop workable answers, smart spaces are a viable and integral component to capture data, provide it for analysis, and navigate policies in a responsible and impactful manner.

Smart spaces are large complex systems powered by exponential technologies producing vast amounts of data. In 2015, intelligent buildings collected 7.8 zettabytes of data globally.[29] They generate this enormous volume of data through both physical and digital components and systems of the building and its users. Through applied systems design, we can successfully navigate the many complexities in the formation of smart spaces. We can leverage the data for insights through observation, predictive analytics, and automation. Whether it is new or retrofitted green building construction, there is a strong case of financial and sustainability ROI.

LEVEL UP

A perennial building function has been to provide safety from the elements. Smart spaces have augmented that with modern fire suppression and more inventive features, such as sophisticated audio detection systems for a dreaded workplace shooting. These are ways intelligent buildings now protect human safety. What is the next level for smart spaces?

As machine learning (ML) and artificial intelligence (AI) continue to advance, building management systems (BMS) will become more sentient. This benevolent AI-powered system will be concerned for people, which is the opposite of HAL and Skynet in popular films. We will automate what computers do best and provide people more time and space to do what they do best, which are creative activities that involve understanding other people. AI and ML can be used in project design and build phases to tackle the most wicked problems.

Operationally, future smart spaces will deliver higher-order Maslow levels. While fulfilling the base of physiological and safety, smart spaces will progress up the hierarchy to self-actualization. The most challenging problem areas aligned with the UN SDGs will be solved as smart spaces free up creativity through AI and ML. Consider how enterprises focus on big problems in the energy and food chains and the most prominent example of 2020: US Department of Defense Operation Warp Speed to develop COVID-19 vaccines.[30] People working on challenging problems need cognitive freedom. Smart spaces will be a core means to improve the human condition moving forward through both creativity and hyper-productivity. Smart spaces will be a living extension of the people, sensing occupant needs, and adapting conditions on their behalf. This sensing agility is the hallmark of what Infosys calls a Live Enterprise, where successful organizations fulfill lower-level requirements to unleash hyper-productivity and creativity as a competitive edge.[31]

RECAP

- People expect organizations to provide spaces that embrace wellness, inclusivity, safety, and privacy. Space planning addresses human experience through occupancy use cases and centralized data systems for efficient operations.

- Smart spaces create holistic human experiences, but there is a downside if efficiency takes priority over empathy. The service blueprint analyzes activities to benefit users. This method shows the human perspective and then the technology needed to deliver the solution.

- Workspaces must evolve and adapt to be resilient. Design them to include space configuration, hybrid-located workforces, and systems that drive safety and productivity.

- Convert qualitative measures to quantitative ones where possible, through the collection of data generated by the smart space, like environmental variable influence on satisfaction.

- As people realize their innate drive to self-actualize, they become content, productive, and have general well-being. Smart spaces align with how a person prefers to work, like how a good tool fits the hand.

SYSTEM OF SYSTEMS

OBSERVATION AS CATALYST

FIRST CONTACT: OCTOBER 29, 1969

There were two moon shots in 1969. The first was in July when Neil Armstrong and Buzz Aldrin walked the Sea of Tranquillity.[1] At the same time, Leonard Kleinrock and Charley Kline were pursuing their own metaphorical moon shot—one perhaps even more far-reaching than NASA's.

ARPANET began life as a US military Cold War fix after President Dwight D. Eisenhower formed the Advanced Research Projects Agency (ARPA) in 1958.[2] In 1964, the RAND Corporation published a paper called "On Distributed Communications" that proposed a decentralized and distributed communication system smart enough to survive a nuclear attack.[3]

Kleinrock and Kline were two UCLA academics who ran with the RAND proposal. At 10:30 p.m. on October 29, 1969, they made first contact—a computer at UCLA talking to another at the Stanford Research Institute. The message was only two letters long—'l' and 'o' (the connection crashed before the word "login" got through)— but it changed our world forever. With that first message, the ARPA Network, or ARPANET, was born and would evolve into today's internet.[4]

ARPANET broke the mold, linking the physical with the digital, a system of systems that operate on the edge and thrive without a center. This network became the genesis of exponential convergence and connectivity, resilience, security, and privacy by design—the epitome of a synchronized tech-driven operating model.

It was, as they say, one small step, one giant leap.

SUPERPOSITIONING, OR SCHRÖDINGER'S ROBOTIC CAT

Erwin Schrödinger was a Nobel Prize-winning physicist in the 1930s who conducted experiments focused on quantum theory. Operating in the space where physics and philosophy overlap, Schrödinger contemplated the question, "How do we really know if something is taking place?" Best remembered for his Schrödinger's Cat thought experiment, the goal was to understand if an object could exist in multiple states at once and, by extension, demonstrate that not every question has a binary yes or no answer.[5]

In Schrödinger's experiment, the alternatives were not yes or no, but alive or dead, and a theoretical box contained a cat and a radioactive substance with equal probability to decay (or not). If the substance decayed, it would trigger release of poison that would kill the cat. An outside viewer had no way to observe if the cat was alive or dead unless they opened the box. Further, the act of opening the box could itself cause the decay and trigger the poison. As long as the box was closed, then the cat could be considered both alive and dead within the bounds of uncertainty in the thought experiment parameters. This concept is called *superposition*,[6] which means that multiple states coexist. The only way to validate the current state is through observation, but observation itself has consequences that may disturb or change the current state.

Like Schrödinger's cat, we humans now exist in a dual state. Our superposition is the coexistence of traditional objectives amidst socio-technical transformation. Traditional objectives are enterprise profit, personal consumption, and local presence, while socio-technical transformation is social prosperity, environmental conservation, and global perspective. The triple bottom line of people, planet, and prosperity is a way to view the allegorical box; observation allows us to understand what is happening in a complex system, which provides guidance to improve or optimize it.

OBSERVE, CONTEXTUALIZE, IMPROVE

Observation allows us to understand what leads to a change or outcome, which demystifies the unknown and reduces uncertainty. For Schrödinger, the technology did not exist to observe the cat inside the box, but technology advancement has dramatically improved observation. Sophisticated intelligent devices and computers monitor a space and its many environmental parameters. Extending Schrödinger's thought experiment, at Infosys we created our own "cat in a box" scenario to illustrate how current technology enables greater observation in buildings. Meet ERWIN, Schrödinger's robotic cat.

Figure 5.1. **Smart Space Command Center**
Source: Infosys Knowledge Institute

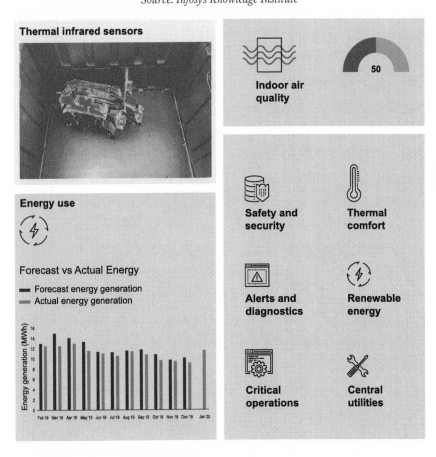

ERWIN the cat is an IoT device equipped with sensors to measure air circulation inside its box. ERWIN's box is equipped with sensors to measure temperature and humidity, sensors that capture oxygen and carbon dioxide levels, and cameras for thermal imaging. ERWIN and its box exemplify the observation enabled by smart spaces, viewing an asset across three time horizons: historical, real-time, and future.

In effect, the cat exists across three states at the same time—superposition. This multistate existence is relevant for sustainability because it shows what caused a problem, what actions to take, and its consequences. The experience changes as the box's conditions change, and whether those changes are related to a problem in a specific system. In smart spaces and quantum physics, observation is the first step to solve a problem.

INTERCONNECTEDNESS OF SYSTEMS

Systems thinking in circular supply chains is an example of Practical Sustainability. Supply chains are complex systems involving raw material, product manufacturing, and logistics. Circularity helps supply chains reduce waste, increase longevity of use, and design for reuse and recycle at the end of life. Systems thinking organizes the many components and creates sustainable operations that can be measured and used to simulate scenarios, such as energy usage and production output.

The human body is an integrated collection of different systems that keep us alive and manage complex biological functions. Likewise, buildings are an interconnected system of systems. A system design mindset across multiple disciplines should drive the approach to sustainability problems in buildings. Sustainability addresses tangible goods yet is also influenced by abstract concepts like philosophy, sociology, political science, and economics.

Technical disciplines like computer science, materials, and civil engineering also affect sustainability.

Even a single metric like carbon emissions reduction requires a comprehensive viewpoint across multiple systems. The facilities manager may be responsible for achieving this but cannot do so alone. Renewable power sources, such as solar installations, need to follow building codes, which may vary across jurisdictions and tie into local power districts. Regulatory aspects constitute a significant part of the emissions equation where businesses rely on Purchase Power Agreements (PPAs). An intelligent HVAC system requires both the CIO and CTO perspectives to ensure that technology meets information technology and operational technology standards. Additionally, HR leaders can launch a communications campaign to motivate their employees to commute using public transportation. In other words, a single metric manifests itself in multiple ways, each one touching different teams and systems. The complex set of actors and actions requires various systems to provide the data and processes to support the business need.

Decarbonization is a wicked problem because it exists at the intersection of systems. While humans can control some systems like building thermal comfort, others like weather are beyond human control. A practical approach is to apply big data strategies for both structured and unstructured data. When measuring climate impact, we can consider weather data as unstructured and continuously changing, and climate as longer-term structured data. Weather affects building temperature, but humans cannot control it. A new model is needed to solve complex problems like sustainability, which considers multiple aspects of a building's system of systems.

SYSTEMS DESIGN AND THE QUEST TO TAME COMPLEXITY

THE PROBLEM WITH SYSTEM-OF-SYSTEMS PROBLEMS

When problems arise in a system of systems, manually finding the cause can be like searching for a specific needle in a needle factory without inventory tracking. To solve a complex problem, organize the approach using frameworks and deconstruct into smaller sub-problems or steps. Analysis first needs to determine whether something is a root cause or a symptom of a problem elsewhere through a trial-and-error process. Fault detection and diagnosis are not straightforward in integrated systems. Even if the problem is corrected, changes to one system may affect others due to interdependence. Remember the lesson of our robotic cat ERWIN—actions have consequences, potentially even from observation.

THE ECOSYSTEM OF APPLIED SYSTEMS DESIGN

Systems design combines a design-led approach with a systems-thinking mindset to address this complexity. Rather than looking at individual systems (HVAC system) or individual use cases (thermostat settings), systems design looks holistically at all the systems, processes, and personas that affect and are affected by the problem space. Figure 5.2 illustrates the concept through shapes arranged in several logical constructs.

This perspective aids in the identification of problem causes, and improvement and innovation opportunities become more evident than before. For an office building biometric entry control system,

the problem space is better understood once the analyst understands tenant privacy concerns, HR data status, sensors, building
layout, and entry points. These systems—human, HR, infrastructure, and architecture—combine to influence a biometric entry control system, which is one of many systems in an intelligent building.

Figure 5.2. **Applied Systems Thinking**
Source: Infosys Knowledge Institute

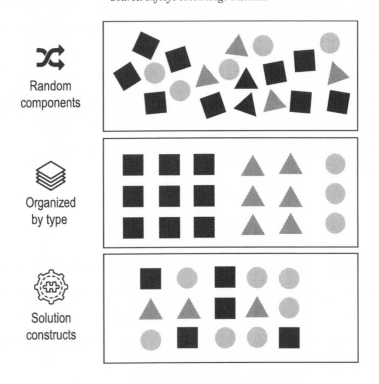

Applied systems design considers interfaces, architecture, and
data points based on problem type and context. It arranges these
attributes into an ecosystem organized into eight categories, as
shown in Table 5.1.

Table 5.1. **Attribute Ecosystem for Applied Systems Design**
Source: Infosys Knowledge Institute

Attribute	Description
⚙ Functionality	System ability to do the work for which it is intended
🛡 Reliability	Probability that a system performs correctly during a specific duration
🔍 Extensibility	Ability to extend a system and effort level to implement the extensions
✂ Connectivity	Structured relationships between spatially or temporally distinct entities
🔒 Privacy	Relationship between legal policy and the collection and dissemination of data and technology
🔒 Security	Inclusion of all facets of accessing physical and digital assets
✋ Usability	Quality of effectiveness, efficiency, and overall satisfaction of user experience when interacting with products or systems
✖ Flexibility	Ability of system processes to manage existing and potential product variety

Systems design creates systems that adapt to real-world solutions and assist engineers in solving complex problems. They sort through calculations, reason, and show whether a solution is feasible. From a reasoning perspective, they ask whether society will accept a solution. Is the business case viable, and is it a solution that functions in the expected operating environment? As buildings became complex and intelligent, applied systems design emerged to develop and operate building systems effectively.

TAMING SYSTEMS FOR THE BUILT WORLD

The world is complex. Our wicked problems are complex. Buildings have gotten complex too. Buildings have moved from systems to a system of systems, and a new approach is needed to solve these problems and take full advantage of opportunities. Applied systems design is the answer, and using this proven discipline in buildings is the practical way to implement smart spaces. Below is an applied systems design framework that synchronizes the physical and digital components in an agile manner that validates technical feasibility, user desirability, and business viability (see Figure 5.3).

Figure 5.3. **Applied Systems Design Framework**

Source: Infosys Knowledge Institute

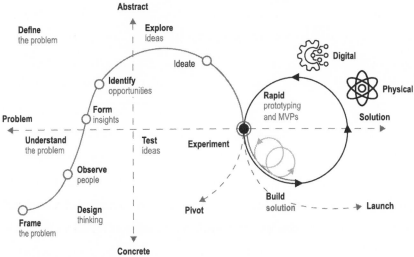

This framework blends Agile and Lean into a single framework. It uses design thinking with rapid technology proofs of concept to identify how a complex system functions. It allows for different speeds for digital and physical components in product design and implementation. For example, over six months, it may be possible to deliver four software sprints and one physical product design cycle for a new air ventilation system leveraging IoT and cloud data services. During COVID, we designed, piloted, and installed this type of solution for over twenty buildings covering twenty million square feet.

Given this complexity, smart spaces use systems design to define a problem, test ideas, and validate solutions through rapid proto-typing. Opportunity identification experiments allow decisions to either move forward with the solution or pivot to a new tact before expending expensive time and resources. All stakeholders and activities follow a single system-wide approach. Creating a robust experience map requires interviews with the building stakeholders. Facility managers, owners, tenants, and visitors provide rich insight into not only how a system currently works, but more importantly, how it *doesn't* work and steers away from pursuing ideas without merit.

When building project professionals assume they already know the issues and skip the discovery step, they lose the clarity, insight, and alignment this map creates. This understanding gap increases the difficulty of diagnosing problems and identifying innovation areas.

A large real estate management company used smart spaces to reimagine their properties. The initiative launch coincided with the COVID-19 pandemic, and the leaders quickly identified a safe workplace as the priority for their tenants. The team mapped the impacted people, processes, and technologies, focusing on three representative groups. The first group was functional leads: legal, marketing, HR, building engineering, and design. The second was a combination of cloud platforms and third-party service vendors, whose services included bathroom cleaning, people counting, and oxygen-density monitoring. Finally, facility managers, property managers, and tenants represented the customer perspective.

Their mapping exercise increased understanding of potential changes, and it also quantified expected value. The analysis determined which features and capabilities could be effective and were financially viable. One use case was the ability to track bathroom cleaning by floor. Through vendor interviews, the team learned they needed CAD drawings of floor plans that the platform could interpret. Otherwise, it could not correctly display floor maps. A tenant may need to know that a bathroom is safe, but the property managers are responsible for scheduling and tracking the cleaners.

While systems design defines architecture, functionality, and data, smart spaces must also consider how this system of systems is interconnected and the relationship of inputs and outputs. The applied systems framework understands elements and how they relate and impact each other.

PRACTICAL CALCULUS FOR PRACTICAL SUSTAINABILITY

"Practical" anything is appealing because it is, well, practical. The idea of practical calculus comes from Oliver Heaviside and James Maxwell's theorems on electric dynamics.[7,8] The difficulty of converting theoretical science to working products challenges inventors who build tech businesses based on complex science. An air-ventilation system may use sensors that recognize atmospheric particles at a micron level, but the inventor lacks a scientist's understanding of how it all works. Science is the basis for why and how things work, and practical calculus makes scientifically valuable ideas more universally available and valuable to makers. This accurate simplification will democratize the development of intelligent spaces.

Heaviside was a mathematician who simplified Maxwell's complex equations into practical, usable calculus that enabled thousands of inventors. Heaviside's peers never acknowledged him in his time, yet we would not have technologies like cloud computing and wireless without Heaviside's work in the 1890s. It is both appropriate and ironic that the upper layer of the earth's atmosphere is named after Heaviside because he theorized that the earth's magnetic core and the reflective barrier that encases our planet enabled radio wave transmissions.[9]

Just as Heaviside simplified code concepts, practitioners and subject matter experts today utilize so-called low-code and no-code software to develop applications. People who never thought they could program can now create new tools. So too can policymakers set climate goals and investors determine ESG credit risks. They all contribute by applying Practical Sustainability grounded by complex science. Property managers and supply chain leaders can spend more time on high-touch activities to control their destiny or pursue options through partnerships and outside firms.

EXPONENTIAL CONVERGENCE

CONNECTIVITY

Even in the modern era, complex buildings and spaces still contain siloed "dumb" systems. Proprietary systems have constrained buildings from collaboration, yet buildings are complex and often part of a collaborative system beyond the building. As spaces are digitized to make them intelligent, architecture has moved from full-stack, proprietary solutions to open source and standards. Smart spaces arise from diverse-point solutions connected to and integrated with applications, data, and IoT devices. Information technology codified connectivity as a new source of value, and IT systems will revolutionize what buildings deliver individually and as ecosystems across campuses, companies, and cities.

IT systems drive the digital economy. They sense input, initiate response, and shape the responses that drive business and citizen outcomes. Connectivity extends reach and creates the network effect. Across the places where we conduct business and socialize, information technology services have expanded beyond the traditional realm of IT specialists to a much broader society of digital natives, powered by the proliferation of smartphones and the app economy. Smart spaces will exponentially amplify this phenomenon and further democratize the digital economy.

CLOUD UBIQUITY AND RESILIENCE

Imagine a disaster scenario such as a flood that prevented teams from working together in-person at an office, and that at the same time, they experienced a cloud computing failure. Remote workers would be unable to collaborate and deliveries would break down. Already stressed emergency services would experience surges with fewer tools to manage them. Buildings that relied heavily on the cloud would face disruption of their required functions and services.

Companies must build resilience into their cloud structure by testing it in continuous and even chaotic ways to avoid cloud failure. Resilience represents a higher standard for computing systems than typical operating conditions. Companies should progressively test their systems to migrate to cloud services for stability, availability, reliability, and, overall, resilience. Smart spaces have the advantage of a mature, affordable cloud IT backbone to address the many aspects of sustainability. Leaders should start with the expectation that something will go wrong, and cloud-enabled infrastructure systems need to be structured and tested to respond.[10] As illustrated in Figure 5.4, resilience is the ultimate stage for cloud maturity.

Figure 5.4. **Cloud System Maturity Model**
Source: Infosys Knowledge Institute

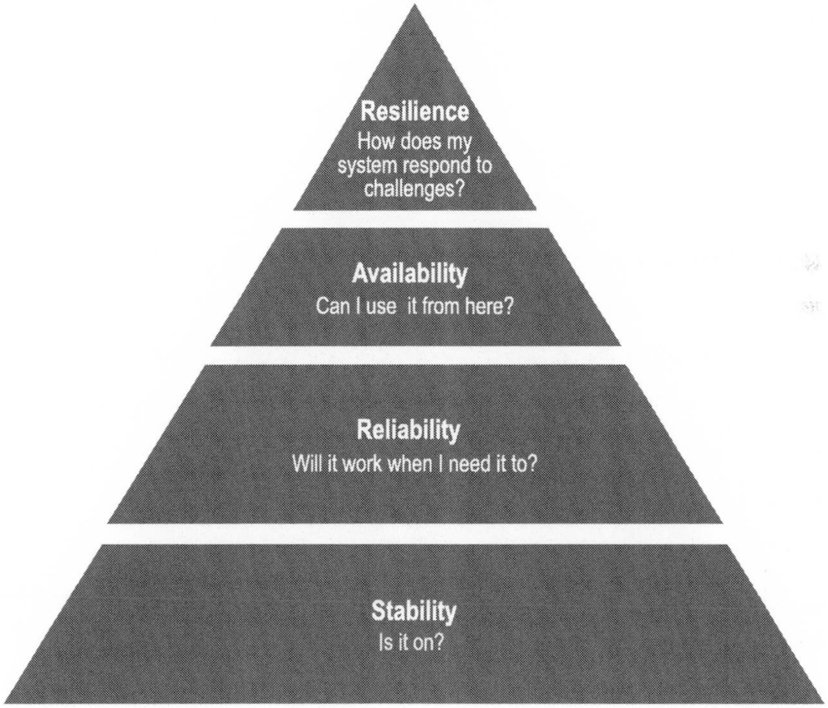

Resilience
How does my system respond to challenges?

Availability
Can I use it from here?

Reliability
Will it work when I need it to?

Stability
Is it on?

IOT: LIFE ON THE EDGE

Microsoft CEO, Satya Nadella, predicts the world will have fifty billion connected devices by 2030, fundamentally changing business thinking and data usage.[11] Forrester projected edge computing market growth of 50% in 2020.[12]

To deliver sustainable services and products, companies should tie their sustainability agenda to their digital transformation. IoT and edge computing make this practical, automating data capture, modernizing applications, and innovating at the edge, the area expected to generate growth.

Sustainability mandates require businesses to understand the edge, making decisions, conducting transactions, performing work, and capturing data. A growing number of companies see the vital role played by the flood of new data gathered and managed at the edge. This information drives efficiency and provides real-time ESG analysis that allows companies to make smarter decisions and create new business models.

Research by Gartner, an advisory firm, showed that two-thirds of organizations intend to use 5G networks to bolster their edge-computing capabilities. Gartner predicts that enterprises will fully deploy edge-computing infrastructures between 2025 and 2030 to support digital transformation and sustainability goals.[13]

CONVERGENCE

Technological convergence refers to the tendency for unrelated technologies to intertwine as they develop. As technologies converge, they spawn new products and services.[14] While current exponential technologies rule the headlines, technological convergence is not a recent phenomenon. The internet converged with print media, radio, video, and computers to create new products and services. Each was a separate entity before the internet. Now radio is online and movies are on demand. The same convergence has happened with cloud, connectivity, and IoT. They have converged, and when applied to the built world, they enable smart spaces and drive sustainability.

The increasing affordability of computing power, low-cost IoT devices, and widespread 5G connectivity has further enabled these capabilities. Building an IT infrastructure was expensive to set up before cloud-computing power and low-cost IoT hardware and sensors. Now anyone with a smartphone, credit card, and email can leverage cloud storage.

Smart spaces are entities with assets that range from people to IoT sensors and to physical assets like HVAC, lighting, and water systems. There is a dizzying array of source data that IoT sensors now collect: lighting, air quality, occupancy, weather, and many other sources. IoT devices support use cases spanning climate, greenhouse gas emissions, energy transmission, material usage, security, wellness, and wayfinding. The cloud enables building owners and occupants to use sensor data accessed through an IoT platform. Sensors capture massive amounts of data that require storage and quick access. Real estate operators or manufacturers require sensor data to make rapid decisions and access that data whenever needed. The combination of IoT and cloud technology enables this access. As this occurs, enterprises evolve from connected to observing to aware, or sentient. Research from *The Live Enterprise: Create a Continuously*

Evolving and Learning Organization showed that technology convergence provides the combination of awareness and response capability needed to succeed in a disruptive market.[15] These same sentient principles provide building and sustainability leaders the tools to improve performance and resilience.

ROOT CAUSE AND RECOMMENDATION ENGINES

The predictive power of artificial intelligence acting on sensor data streamlines the time and effort to determine the root cause of building problems. When the system can find faults and respond across systems, it becomes prescriptive. Analysts use systems design mapping to understand the relationships within a building ecosystem. This structured approach enables a better, more interdependent system that improves visibility and responsiveness.

While building engineers traditionally had measurement indicators—like pump RPM—technicians manually checked them at intervals paced by staff capacity and budget. Daily or even less frequent measurements were standard operating procedures to monitor status. Smart sensors instead take measurements at much shorter intervals and feed data into an intelligent building management system. Volatility and impact on overall system performance now drive these intervals. Even if the system takes readings several times per second, data can be parsed and sent only when needed to monitor leading performance indicators. In addition to simple time-series data such as temperature, more complex data such as vibration monitoring paints a predictive picture that anticipates faults. The system learns these best practice corrective actions for faults like pump cavitation based on historical records of defects detected and their applied resolutions. Should a pump need to be taken offline for more intensive fixes, the predictive system recommends an optimal time to minimize adverse effects on the overall system. It can even pre-order the necessary parts and schedule a repair team to complete the resolution process.

KRTI 4.0 is an example of an intelligent prescriptive system.[16] Poyry, an international consulting and engineering firm specializing in energy and industrial sectors, developed KRTI 4.0 along with Nokia and Infosys after noticing that industrial enterprises had to analyze performance data manually before performing corrective action. The platform reduces system maintenance costs and expensive operation shutdowns by improving reliability, enhancing employee safety, and complying with environmental requirements. KRTI 4.0 accomplishes these business objectives by enabling predictive maintenance, pervasive connectivity, and knowledge sharing. The system acquires real-time information from field assets and uses advanced analytics to determine current asset health. It integrates with reliability models and correlates asset health parameters to analyze and provide insight into risk exposure. The risk exposure is then aggregated from plan to enterprise level, enabling decision-makers to plan and take necessary action on inventory and operations. See Figure 5.5 for a summary view of KRTI 4.0 architecture.

Buildings are complex systems, much more than the structure visible to tenants and visitors. The system of systems mindset allows leaders to deconstruct the complexity into manageable components yet retain the critical, holistic perspective to understand the interdependent challenges and opportunities to address sustainability that intelligent buildings and infrastructure provide.

Figure 5.5. **KRTI 4.0 Technical Architecture**
Source: Infosys Knowledge Institute, Pöyry

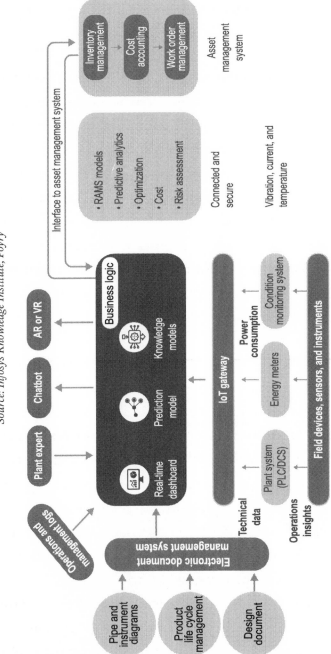

SMART SPACE OPERATING MODEL

INTERSECTION AND SYNCHRONIZATION

Smart spaces in offices and residences lag technology adoption in industrial-connected factories. A positive consequence of this delay is that technology has become more ubiquitous and mature, increasing potential benefits and decreasing implementation risk. For example, the electrical monitoring of older assets has always been a challenge. However, new low-cost industrial applications made the leap to smart devices, like electrical current transformers with logic that provides utility meter quality at a fraction of the cost.

The smart spaces operating model organizes this array of technology options into three layers to show the complexity of the systems involved and how they relate. Figure 5.6 illustrates the smart spaces operating model.

The first layer is Digital Foundation, and it's a *system of things* comprised of technology, sensors, and equipment. We call it foundational because the entire operating model depends on the technology to accurately gather and report data for the other two layers to function. The second layer is Digital Mesh, and it's a *system of insights* using AI and ML to facilitate historical, real-time, and predictive analytics for such functions as energy management, assets, and service management. The third layer is Decision-Making, and it's a *system of actions* to facilitate business productivity, process application, and employee well-being.

For the intelligent spaces operating model, Phil Christensen, VP Digital Systems at Bentley Systems, told us, "The nature of this work and its problems require much more cross-discipline collaboration.

Figure 5.6. Smart Spaces Operating Model

Source: Infosys Knowledge Institute

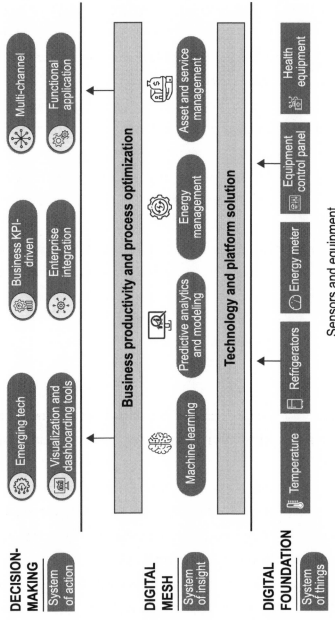

The system of systems view is effective to tame these wicked problems."[17] System of systems challenges exceed the capabilities of point solutions and need solving through a consortium partner ecosystem model. The more complex a system, the larger the network is required to service it to succeed.

Many smart solution providers exist for point solutions like digital signage, access control, and smart parking. The challenge for these companies is to integrate their solutions into building operating systems. Before a technology provider can implement their solution, systems integrators must bring together building systems and a secure cloud to store readily accessed data. As a result, no single company can claim they deliver the full spectrum of industry expertise, IT, cloud, IoT, and data science on their own. To achieve the full potential of smart spaces, organizations require an ecosystem of highly skilled partners.

BMS AS AN OPERATING SYSTEM

Campuses typically have buildings of varying ages, each with their own building management system (BMS) and infrastructure. Even if these dated systems are too expensive to replace, a new lightweight BMS platform allows them to modernize with software, increasing transparency and adding new functionality. As Marc Andreesen, noted entrepreneur and Silicon Valley venture capitalist, rightly stated, "Software is eating the world."[18] This iconic quote translates to software replacing physical goods and digitizing work itself through automation. This phenomenon is undoubtedly occurring in the built world, and BMS is how building owners and operators use it to their full advantage.

A multinational semiconductor giant had offices and factory buildings across the globe, with building management systems from different vendors, of varying age, and often unsecured. As an Infosys client, they developed a standard enterprise building management system across these campuses, from which multiple sites were monitored and controlled with a consolidated dashboard. Multiple partners contributed to the new solution, which increased visibility across facilities, enhanced security, eased user management, and reduced redundancy. Given the complexity involved, each partner's complementary set of skills increased the potential for success and reduced risk. The value of partnership is a common theme the authors have seen across smart space initiatives.

MORE IS MORE

The integration of rich data into our physical spaces has increased productivity and redefined space asset valuation. More productive spaces create greater personalized experiences, guard our safety and well-being, and command a premium fee in the market. Reed's Law, which calculates the value of a complex system made up of many participants, provides insight into the importance of smart space organizational network size (see Figure 5.7).

David Reed of MIT published Reed's Law in 1999 to explain the effect and utility of large networks, particularly social networks.[19] It states that the value of a network scales exponentially with the size of the network based on the number of possible pair connections by participants.[20] Reed's practical calculus formula to measure network value is:

Figure 5.7. **Reed's Law**
Source: David P. Reed

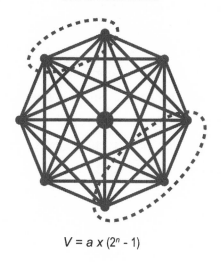

$$V = a \times (2^n - 1)$$

$V = a \times (2n - 1)$, *where*

V *is value of a network (dimensionless)*

a *is Reed's coefficient (dimensionless)*

n *is number of network nodes (dimensionless)*

The proliferation of smartphones is an excellent example of how this works. Smartphones are significantly more expensive than their voice-only counterparts, so why the explosion of smartphone adoption? With smartphones, consumers get an mp3 player, high-quality camera, GPS, and health monitoring, which validates the premium price, all of which attracts a more significant number of users (N), which exponentially increases the value of the smartphone network. This is why network service providers discount phones to attract and retain subscribers. It's also why an entire ecosystem of companies has thrived by providing apps on mobile communications networks. Smartphone technology redefined how mobile phones were valued, because they added perceived value and attracted lots of network participants.

The same concept applies to smart spaces, as they increase building value by adding more valuable services, as perceived by property managers, occupants, and visitors. Smart spaces networks consist of building structures and systems, users, and many endpoint devices.

Smart space networks multiply the value function within Reed's Law. They go beyond the "N," which initially represented the number of people that populate and utilize a network socially. The new exponential reality that updates Reed's Law is that digital influencers like endpoint devices, cloud computing, and AI magnify the number and impact of digital agents, making decisions and driving outcomes. Smart spaces have the potential to deliver significantly higher value through these additional non-human network participants, and also increase sustainability and enrich human experience.

Creating intelligent and sustainable spaces happens either through retrofitting older buildings for efficiency or through new construction designed to be smart spaces. A study published by the Rocky Mountain Institute (RMI) shows that a deep energy retrofit of a standard 500,000 gross square foot, twelve-story office building costs $25–$150 per square foot.[21] This analysis indicates that retrofitting could increase a building's value by $2 to $3 for each $1 spent. The calculation measures gross capital cost and avoided cost, and then nets the two amounts. The figure below illustrates the value concept using the example of the Empire State Building retrofit, in the form of a waterfall chart.

Figure 5.8. **Empire State Building Retrofit Marginal Capital Cost**
Source: Rocky Mountain Institute

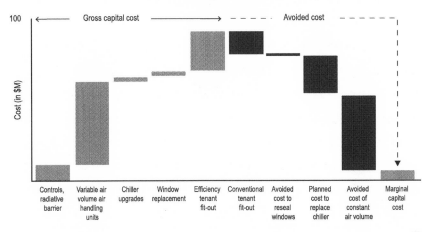

New high-performance green buildings can increase building asset value up to 7% and reduce operating cost by 8% in the first year.[22] The average cost for LEED-certified construction is $440 per square foot, compared with $436 for non-LEED, less than 1% difference, which makes a strong case to build green when building new.[23] While investors may challenge retrofit proposals to justify increased short-term costs, the ultimate ROI is substantial, and a simple payback period can be in the range of two to three years[24] for both new and retrofitted buildings.

Dean Hopkins, COO of commercial real estate leader Oxford Properties, believes that buildings with intelligent technologies will continue to command a premium. Much like a smartphone, people will pay more to get additional technology and experience from their buildings. Smart spaces will benefit the corporate ESG agenda with potential 36% reduction of GHG emissions, reduced-water consumption (30% for indoor and 50% for outdoor), and over 50% reduction in waste consumption. In addition, smart spaces can reduce annual electricity costs by up to 50%.[25]

ADAPTION THROUGH ANALYTICS

Data and analytics enable smart spaces. Understanding selected metrics while keeping the strategic view in mind enables companies to generate immediate value from analytics and still adapt as needs evolve.

Smart spaces rely upon many sensors that generate massive data volumes, ranging from energy usage, air quality, emissions, room temperatures, water consumption, occupancy, and ingress and egress. Facility operators harness these data points to view historical trends, uncover hidden insights, and produce actionable recommendations. As advanced analytics and charts proliferate, the traditional dashboard approach quickly becomes overwhelming, as humans simply cannot track the sheer amount of output from all these disparate systems.

To deliver value to smart space tenants, managers must move beyond descriptive analytics to command centers, digital twins, and automation tools to increase visibility. They must evolve capabilities beyond reviewing historical trends and monitoring current performance to perform predictive analytics, suggesting what will happen. These forward-looking insights provide early warning for breakdowns and malfunctions, or even temporary changes, like needing to compensate building comfort controls during an event that draws an influx of visitors. Ultimately, a system of systems provides the foundation for prescriptive analytics that brings smart spaces to life and delivers more value to the managers who lead them.

RECAP

- Applied systems design provides a robust framework to synchronize complex digital and physical systems into a feasible and viable execution map.

- The system of systems approach increases potential financial and sustainability benefits with significant ROI and payback in two to three years, whether new or retrofitted green building construction.

- The larger and more complex a system, the more extensive the network is required to service the system. This application of Reed's Law increases the value of a building by including endpoint devices in the network, thereby adding more services and value to property managers, occupants, and guests.

- Leaders must start with the expectation that something will eventually go wrong, and cloud-enabled infrastructure systems need to be structured and tested to respond. Companies should progressively test their systems to migrate to cloud services for stability, availability, reliability, and resilience.

- To deliver sustainable services and products, companies should tie their sustainability agenda to their digital transformation. IoT and edge computing make this practical by automating data capture, modernizing applications, and innovating at the edge, the area expected to generate significant growth.

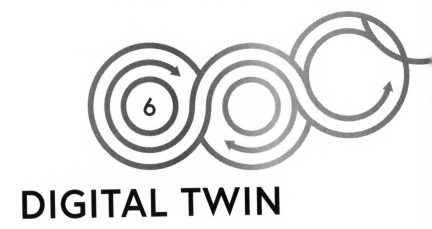

DIGITAL TWIN

CONTEXTUAL AND SPATIAL DATA RELATIONSHIPS

GALLOPING GERTIE, MILLENNIUM WOBBLE

When completed in July 1940, the Tacoma Narrows Bridge was the third-longest suspension bridge on Earth, linking to Tacoma, Washington. The financing had been a problem, leading to a radically innovative design: a slender steel ribbon stretched across Puget Sound. Construction workers called the bridge Galloping Gertie due to the way it swayed even in moderate winds. Four months after opening, forty-mile-per-hour winds caused a catastrophic failure, and the bridge collapsed into the waters below.[1]

The Tacoma Narrows bridge became famous as a precautionary tale in engineering history. It collapsed due to aeroelastic flutter, the twisting of one part of the bridge reinforcing another twist further along.[2]

Sixty years later, in London, the Millennium Bridge opened in June 2000. A 320-meter-long suspension bridge linking both sides of the River Thames, designers hailed its steel-glass elegance "an absolute statement of our capabilities at the beginning of the 21st century." Very soon, however, the bridge made an unexpected statement—it started to wobble, slowly at first, then alarmingly from side to side. Pedestrians looked like they were walking on ice. As a result, this $40 million "pure expression of engineering structure" was closed almost as soon as it opened.[3]

The problem with the Millennium Bridge was synchronous lateral excitation—2,000 people walking in unison caused the bridge to sway, forcing people's footsteps to go with the sway, causing the bridge to sway even more.[4]

Structures are big and complex, and it's crucial to model and simulate what's going on below the surface. It took two years before the Millennium Bridge reopened—an entire decade for a replacement across the Tacoma Narrows. Engineers digitally modeled the Millennium Bridge to find and fix the problem—silicon was as crucial to the structure's fate as concrete and steel.

A digital twin provided the Millennium Bridge historical modeling, real-time status, and future-cast simulation. Digital twins were the literal bridge to success, analyzing historical data, real-time operations, and simulating future performance.

DIGITAL TWINS

Practical Sustainability is a physical and digital journey, and at the core is the digital twin. The digital twin collects wide-ranging data from smart spaces, manufacturing, maintenance, operations, and operating environments. It then uses this data to create a unique model of each asset, system, or process, focusing on a critical behavior, such as life, efficiency, or flexibility.

Analytics are applied to these models to detect anomalies in the system. The twin then determines the actions that optimize priority metrics and generates forecasts for planning. These modeling and analytical techniques allow the enterprise to rapidly create, tune, or modify parameter settings.

The digital twin uses analytics to deliver specific sustainability outcomes using environmental and operational data. This consistent data flow enables the digital twin model to continually adapt to changes in the environment or operations and deliver optimal results.

Figure 6.1. **Digital Twin Ecosystem**
Source: Infosys Knowledge Institute

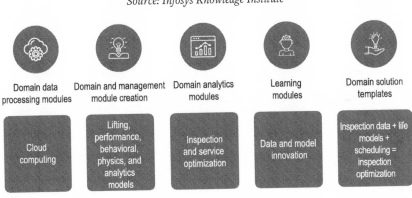

The digital twin becomes a living model of the physical asset or system, discovering productivity improvements and even new revenue opportunities. Working assets, systems, and processes unlock value and achieve productivity benefits. These twins can also rapidly scale for quick deployment for other applications.

OCEANS OF DATA

Buildings and supply chains contain massive amounts of data related to activities, building systems, and the surrounding environment. Even the building design and construction stages create valuable data. There are also static data trapped in manuals, visitor logs, and maintenance histories, but it is often disconnected and overlooked. Like the ocean and its surface or stars in the universe, only a tiny portion of this vast data is visible and accessible to those who need it. Figure 6.2 depicts the types of data found in buildings.

Figure 6.2. **The Data Contained in Buildings**

Source: Infosys Knowledge Institute

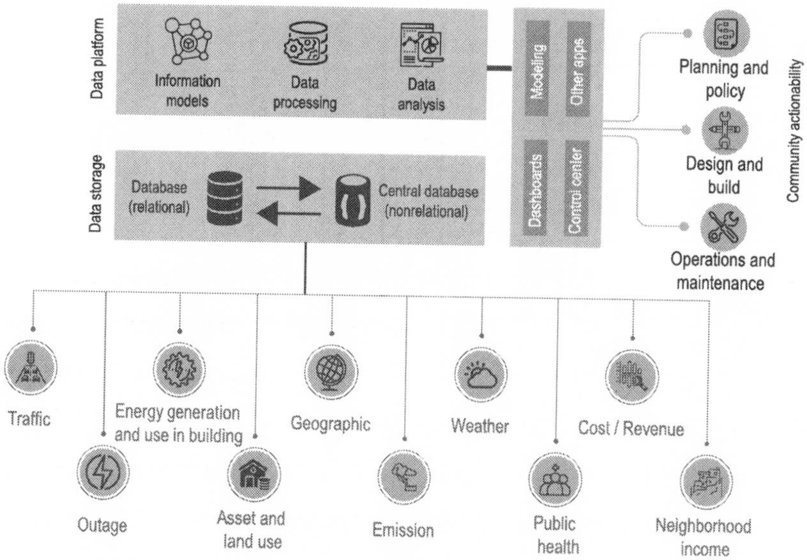

We established in the previous chapter that many disparate systems constitute the buildings and supply chains in the Practical Sustainability model. These systems influence each other, even when apparently segregated into silos. Consider lighting and HVAC systems, which are not directly connected but certainly interact. While one lighting fixture may not have much thermal impact, entire lighting systems produce significant amounts of heat, which HVAC systems must work to offset. A facilities team cannot see how these two systems interact if their data is managed and stored separately.

NO FLOW-THROUGH

Data flow in the built world has not kept pace with other industries, and the construction process provides a relevant example. When building construction completes, a junior construction employee enters data into an asset register, and mountains of building paperwork and manuals eventually make their way to the facility manager's desk. The manager might get this data on a USB drive, but they typically place this trove of data in a drawer and essentially forget about it. They do not leverage the information created from the building design and construction stages.

This visibility gap is where the digital twin concept demonstrates its value. Josh Ridley, CEO of leading digital twin software firm, Willow, says that the builders created 86,000 static data points throughout the construction of an 80,000-square-foot facility in Sydney, Australia.[5] However, no one knew if the data passed through each construction stage aggregated into a single data store. Further, facility managers did not use these data points in operations or planning. These leaders created a mountain of data during construction but derived little value from it. This gap represents a largely untapped source of value for buildings.

Construction managers and contractors need to understand the significance of the data they create and proactively manage data during building construction. This data includes structural designs, drawings, network diagrams, and asset manuals. Poor data management is a significant source of delay in construction during building handover, and this delay impedes operational readiness.

Building and asset data generated during construction is key to managing the much longer building operations phase. For example, a facility manager can quickly check a piping drawing and valve location while reacting to water leakage and plan for corrective action instead of searching archives to find and access the data. Building managers can also determine the liability of a leakage fix if warranty data and user manuals are readily available, saving significant time and repair costs to repair the leak.

Sustainable building planning is an integrative design process where building designers and stakeholders engage early on building designs and the desired attributes of each subsystem design.[6] For example, if the building incorporates efficient artificial lighting, the designer optimizes the air conditioning system design based on a good lighting system design. Likewise, each building subsystem designer benefits from the design performed by others to ensure that the overall design is solid. Correctly sized equipment and systems increase building efficiency and reduce initial capital expenditure.

Building operations data is crucial to sustaining performance, as they have a long life, typically fifty to one hundred years. While buildings often do well in their first three to seven years of operations, as a building ages, its performance starts to deteriorate. This increases per capita energy use, maintenance costs, user complaints, and deterioration in indoor environmental quality. In manufacturing, supply chain modeling and performance are critical factors for a facility to evolve and remain productive. Transitioning from a linear flow to a circular loop evolves how data is used to support decarbonization and product life-cycle requirements. Data management enables operators to control these metrics and optimize throughout a building's lifetime.

HIGH VALUE, SPATIAL RELATIONSHIPS

Building Information Modeling (BIM) systems increasingly manage building data, capturing many data elements related to building design and construction.[7] BIM continues to update with data during the operations stage of the building life cycle, as well as during redesigns and upgrades.

Contextual data influences decisions on building design and upgrade projects. These decisions include geographical alignment, available infrastructure (rail, roads, traffic), environmental factors (orientation to sun, weather), and demographic information. For example, rainfall information and the presence of a floodplain alter the choice of building material and the design for basement ramps. Geographical information systems capture this contextual building information. Combining BIM and GIS systems unlocks opportunities for sustainability design and engagement with civic agencies and service providers for disaster preparedness.

The combination of building data and context is valuable to facility operators who retrieve and reuse this information when undertaking retrofits and modernization projects. Combining operations data with building data and geospatial information enables a wide range of use cases, such as elevator maintenance condition monitoring. Asset data locates a fault, while the system compares equipment operations data to planned performance criteria to determine root cause and then develops a corrective action.

SINGLE PANE OF GLASS

VISIBILITY AND THE SINGLE VIEW

Building systems and asset data are allies in the quest to manage buildings efficiently. Data visibility and latency issues result in inefficient decisions, increased operations cost, reduced asset life, and inconsistent maintenance. Digital twins bring to life data scattered across multiple systems and improve operations performance.

Digital twins create visibility into the multiple building systems provided by original equipment manufacturers (OEMs), like HVAC, fire, lighting, and elevator control systems. Building automation systems automated these applications, but building managers accessed each one individually. The need to centrally control and operate a building as a single system of multiple subsystems led to the adoption of Building Management Systems (BMS), which integrate data from all systems into a single platform. BMS became the single source of truth for all building operational data. It enables a dashboard to view all the systems in real-time in a single view, giving rise to the term "single pane of glass." BMS is instrumental in increasing the visibility of building operations data.[8]

The next stage of BMS evolution is to do more with this vast amount of data generated by buildings. A typical building can push over 80,000 data points through subsystems operating all aspects of a building.[9] While analytics generate decision insights, predictive models need simulation support to assess the effectiveness of these models.

Digital twins are more than a digital replica of a physical environment or asset. Digital twins enable users to manipulate 2D and 3D models to optimize system-operational scenarios. They allow people to observe, model, and interact with the systems that make up built environments. Digital twins provide a single-pane-of-glass perspective—an integrated view to the multiple connected systems in a building.

Figure 6.3. **Single Pane of Glass**
Source: Infosys Knowledge Institute

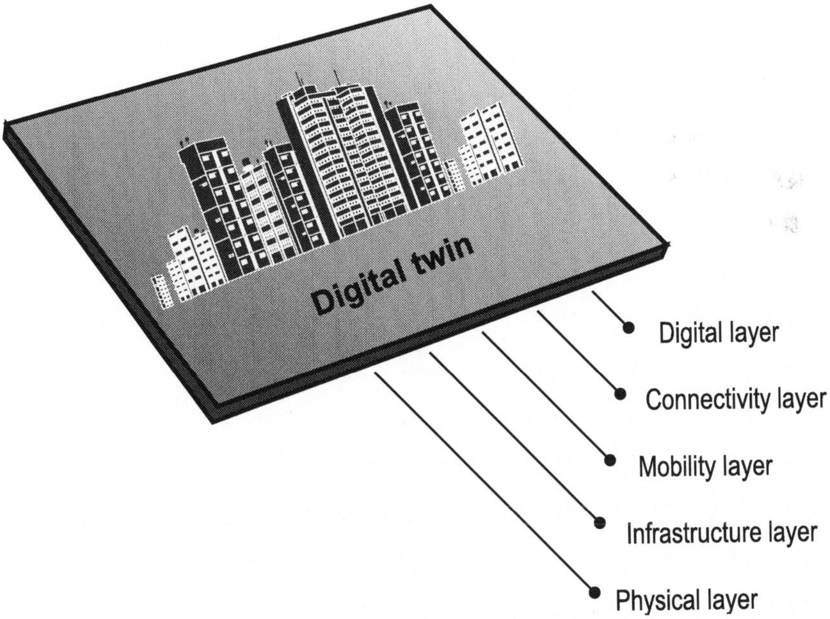

- Digital layer
- Connectivity layer
- Mobility layer
- Infrastructure layer
- Physical layer

HOUSTON, WE'VE HAD A PROBLEM: CENTRAL COMMAND CENTERS

Digital twins enable the smart space ecosystem. They blend buildings and their systems into a unified view aided by sensors streaming data. A command center model manages this unified view and delivers a 24/7 mission control capability for building systems operations and analytics.

Figure 6.4. **Digital Twin Command Center**
Source: Infosys Knowledge Institute

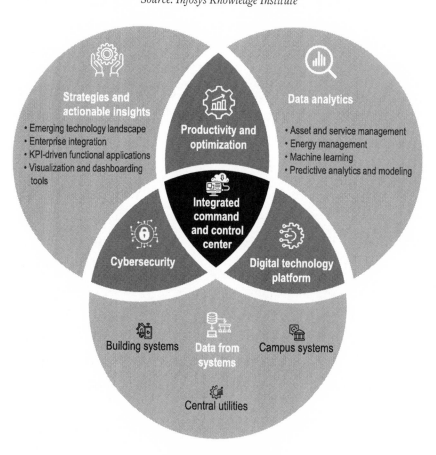

The command center is to buildings what Mission Control is to NASA. NASA's Mission Control helps flight controllers on Earth manage space missions from launch to mission completion. Without Mission Control, the famous Apollo 13 mission would have failed and lives would have been lost.[10] A building command center, enabled through a digital twin, helps facilities teams manage, analyze, and act on building problems—whether COVID-19, equipment failure on a factory line, or natural disruptions like flooding.

Our previous chapter discussed our robotic cat ERWIN, a real-world example of the command center with a digital twin. Infosys has a facilities command center in Bangalore, India, where the team remotely manages "ERWIN's box" through a digital twin (they also manage fifty million square feet of smart spaces across Infosys campuses). Multiple dashboards track many parameters, including temperature, gas level, humidity, and occupancy rates, based on data streamed from ERWIN and its box. The system uses artificial intelligence to ensure ERWIN's box operates properly and checks for anomalies. Operators observe what happens across multiple criteria and create simulations.

Digital command centers bring each aspect of building operation into full view for facility managers. In principle, a single glass pane can visualize anything that a human or machine can connect. Command centers monitor, track, and report data for utilities (energy, water, air quality), occupancy, space utilization, physical security, access control, and asset-operating conditions.

THE HUMAN RELATIONSHIP TO SPACE

The traditional tenant-landlord relationship has followed the same path with little variation:

1. The tenant signs a lease.
2. The tenant occupies the building.
3. The landlord maintains the building, keeps it clean, and makes sure it properly operates.
4. The landlord reengages the tenant to sign up again once the term ends.

While the norm, this approach is far from perfect. Scott Rechler, CEO of RXR Realty, a commercial real estate firm, explained that tenants are often unhappy and do not re-sign when they realize they did not optimize their space or amenities or were disappointed with their experience. Tenant attrition is among the highest costs to the real estate industry. One year of vacancy can cost a real estate company three years of rent when the loss of rent is added to the cost to find a new tenant, says Rechler.[11] Reducing attrition is a significant cash flow opportunity for owners.

Digital twins redefine relationships between tenants and landlords, and they reveal how tenants utilize space and amenities and provide feedback loops to enhance experience and productivity.

The future of tenant-landlord relationships will be data-driven.[12] Imagine if the landlord provides tenants with data about how they currently use their space six months into a lease with recommendations to utilize their lease better. Landlords will analyze the data generated from connected buildings to enhance tenant experience frequently, deliver operational savings, and provide flexibility in facility-usage patterns.

Tenants of the future may take up office spaces on a project-by-project basis. Landlords will ensure that building operations design, optimize, and adjust office space to project needs, rather than merely providing space for a given duration. Digital twins will be the primary tool to design office space solutions and simulate project outcomes.

VISIBILITY AND REGULATIONS

The COVID pandemic more than reinforced the need for safe, healthy workspaces.[13] Leased offices of the future will enable ready integration with wearables, occupant biometric data, and integration with tenant healthcare and wellness programs. Workers will do all this while complying with local privacy regulations. Buildings will capture more data than ever and use it to ensure that people experience a safe and healthy work environment. Digital twins will become indispensable to visualize and analyze this data to conduct simulations for managing occupant health risks.

With more people moving to remote or hybrid work and using office spaces as collaboration areas, landlords will participate in monitoring, time management, motivation, and engagement activities, as tenants may not be able to staff these capabilities. Tenants will expect landlords to provide services like social and networking events to help them improve employee engagement.

THE DIGITAL SUPPLY CHAIN

DIGITIZATION OF THE INDUSTRIAL MARKETPLACE

Digital twins have pioneered IoT-based industrial monitoring and diagnostics. This platform has established new standards and accurately forecasts physical and digital asset sustainability.

Digital technology proliferation and rapid adoption are increasing global alignment, participation, and accountability in the race to carbon neutrality. This technology is not just efficient; it shapes social and economic landscapes as it analyzes the past, monitors the present, and predicts the future.[14]

The continuous collection of data about each component in the value chain powers circular commerce. The circular model reduces waste, maximizes reuse or recycling, and delivers a more sustainable life cycle. Companies match end-user consumptive behaviors to production modeling through data analytics using AI and machine learning. Digital twins operate as a platform, not just isolated analyses, to rapidly identify, adapt, and implement new capabilities and services.

Digital twins function in manufacturing, maintenance, and operations, and they model assets, systems, and processes. While they do improve efficiency and flexibility, digital twins also incorporate sustainability parameters and circular supply chain performance metrics. They provide historical, real-time, and predictive forecasting to audit and plan activities for the long term. Digital twins uncover anomalies in the system of systems that comprise the value chain. Environmental and operational data are the fuel to automate quick adaptations. The sentient digital twin quietly and ruthlessly captures the data quantitatively for reports and audits. Accurate models aid the rules-based grind to squeeze additional performance using traditional analytics. These models set up transformational improvements through insights derived from complex patterns and uncovering operational arbitrage opportunities.[15]

Circular supply chains use digital twins to reduce inefficiencies on the path to achieving zero waste in operations and facilities. Digital twins minimize energy use and greenhouse gas emissions through continuous monitoring and production-line tuning. Control centers and labs use digital twins to develop low-carbon tech and test products. Since the twin is a digital doppelganger of the physical asset or system, it extends to physical, real-world analytics to identify demand patterns and future product configurations. This turbocharged simulation accelerates transition and deployment at scale while minimizing impact to business operations.

PREDICTION, SELF-LEARNING, AND OPTIMIZATION

Industrial digital twins measure and predict likely outcomes at the asset level. Enterprise-scale digital twins simulate complex systems interactions, performing probability scenarios, and recommend key performance indicators.

These simulations leverage data sources for emissions, weather, performance, and operations. This data enriches scenario modeling across operations, supply chain, and logistics. For example, power-generation customers use digital twins to plan energy management and deliver committed electrical power output through options, such as renewable energy sources or minimal fuel consumption models.

Railways use digital twins to illustrate the comparative advantage of locomotives to transport options like trucks by computing weight, train car configuration, topography, and route environmental conditions. In this example, digital twins simulate calculated components like fuel economy and operational trade-offs to optimize fuel use, safety, and scheduling. This vivid simulation creates a more compelling story of lower fuel cost and emissions, punctuated by 300 miles per single gallon of diesel fuel, providing evidence of transitional value to markets and regulators eager to close the door on fossil fuels.[16]

DIGITAL TWINS ARE DIGITAL BRAINS

Picture a factory powered by a solar farm deployed in a nearby field, with its array of gleaming panels producing electricity for years. One day the control system for a newly installed solar panel senses a random sensor input that is unrecognizable.

This input triggers the offending sensor to communicate with older well-functioning panels and learn if they experienced this irregular input pattern before and if there were any associated events. It receives information from these "mentor" panels that indicate they experienced this as part of an unusual weather condition and that actions may be necessary to optimize the performance of the potentially faulty panel. The digital twin advises the new panel to determine the impact on its components and configuration. In this scenario, digital twins are in frequent communication and constantly learn from each other, generating factory power and transforming industrial services through their ability to diagnose issues and forecast the future.

We live in a world of machines that communicate with each other, think through problems, and make decisions autonomously. By 2030, there will be fifty billion connected machines, and digital twins will be the Iron Man suit that powers each industrial asset on the global journey to carbon neutrality.[17]

RESPONSIBLE DESIGN

3D PRODUCT AND PACKAGING VISUALIZATION

Digital product life cycle management is an integral part of our sustainable future, and design decisions lock in a large percentage of product cost early in the life cycle. Less obvious, yet just as important, is the packaging that surrounds, protects, and brands the product inside. The 3D product and packaging visualization reduces the carbon footprint by eliminating physical models and relies upon digital twins for rich modeling and simulation.[18] Cloud-based visualization platforms enable 3D assets to flow from product asset to virtual store or even fixture setting. With 3D technologies, e-commerce platforms showcase the product in multiple sellable forms in a complete virtual experience on web, AR, and VR at scale. Use cases range from internal design activities to customers selling in a highly immersive experience that is low carbon and low waste.

The digital twin makes possible 3D product and packaging visualization and review, visual merchandising, and an immersive digital showroom. It is an effective alternative to traditional packaging and merchandising development, since it does not create physical packaging during conceptual design and marketing. No physical store is required to showcase the product to consumers. It can also be integrated into circular supply chain workflows, creating a sustainable practice across design, sourcing, creation, merchandising, and sell stages. These tools make a real difference. A leading consumer goods company deployed an XR visualization platform (developed by Infosys), and they reduced time to market by 30%, reduced 80% costs in logistics and transportation, and decreased physical sample setup by 60%. Other manufacturers have used this platform and similar ones to improve safety management, guide workers through complex assembly instructions, and superimpose maintenance manuals over automobiles for repair.[19]

CONSUMER PACKAGING BUYBACK IS A WIN-WIN

According to the US EPA, containers and packaging used to wrap or protect consumer goods generated 82 million tons of waste in 2018.[20] These containers and packaging shipped, stored, and protected products, yet they provide little direct value to consumers.

Physical packaging should be designed for circularity, not for our landfills or, even worse, our oceans. Big ideas require big goals, and more enterprise leaders aspire to achieve 100% packaging reuse or recycling. Consumer packaging buyback is an emerging example of responsible design concepts.[21] This model requires leaders to develop reverse logistics programs and integrate them with their sales network to improve packaging reuse or recycling returns. They then create a secondary value stream for the network, like carbon credits linked to container return. Beyond sustainability, the consumer packaging buyback model improves connection with consumers

Figure 6.5. **Consumer Packaging Buyback Model**

Source: Infosys Knowledge Institute

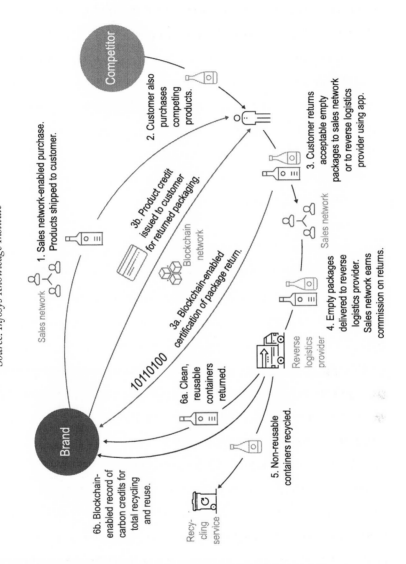

who increasingly value brands that provide this convenient service. Figure 6.5 illustrates this closed loop, regenerative system.

Create programs where the distributor of goods can accept returns and issue reward credits to customers who participate in the program. Reward the sales network with additional earnings for handling the reverse logistics. Expand the program for customers by accepting returns of reusable or recyclable packaging of competitor products. Benefits could include:

- Reduces waste
- Reduces carbon footprint from packaging
- Builds the sustainability brand
- Generates credits for consumers for future product purchases
- Creates additional revenue streams for sales network
- Gains carbon credits from excess returned packaging
- Potentially shifts future purchases from other brands to yours

A reverse logistics program with responsible packaging reclamation is a fresh idea in business model evolution, as it reduces the packaging carbon footprint and provides new sales and marketing benefits in crowded, mature markets.

DIGITAL TWINS ARE OUR REALITY

Growth of the digital twin is inevitable since the data we can now harvest will continue to increase dramatically, and the digital twin uses data to create incremental sources of value. We will become 100% dependent on systems that can visualize historical, real-time, and future simulations. We will trust and depend on our computing, sensor, and connectivity technologies to help us make choices to realize desired outcomes, such as sustainability. It is a natural conclusion that digital twins will play a dominant and vital role in how we view the world and ourselves in all aspects of our work and lives. As we view our world through this lens, this becomes our new reality.

HISTORIC MODELING, REAL-TIME STATUS, AND FUTURECAST SIMULATION

IT TAKES A VILLAGE: THE MANY ROLES OF A DIGITAL TWIN

Architects cannot solve data or systems design issues without technologists. Technologists cannot solve building design or construction issues without architects. Cross-discipline collaboration is needed to solve wicked problems in the built world. Digital twins are the ultimate expression of this cross-discipline collaboration. They involve the convergence of distinctive disciplines, data, and multidisciplinary algorithms for intelligent automation. Phil Christensen, senior vice president of Digital Cities at Bentley Systems, says the "crossing the chasm" moment has already happened for digital twins.[22]

Cross-discipline collaboration starts at the beginning of digital twin solution development. Ideation sessions leverage insights and experiences from product owners, designers, developers, and architects. While the product owner is responsible for the vision and goals, the team's collective power is the driving force that designs solution features and functionality.

Armed with ideas, the project team develops solution features. A feature is a service that fulfills end-user needs with a well-described benefit, hypothesis, and acceptance criteria and briefly describes the context. Dashboards, voice-based support, and chatbots are examples of features that enrich digital twin-based solutions.

Architects use these descriptions to develop features or user stories and sketch their physical manifestation. The feature's expected impact determines its priority in the development backlog, the initial view to achieve the overall vision.

BUILDING INFORMATION MODELS

Change is constant throughout a building's lifespan. Some changes, like corrosion, are small and take a long time to become visible. Other changes are significant and move fast, like a water line burst. Facilities operators can track these changes if they instrument a building to collect data, similar to how health devices track the human body as a data-generating system of systems.

As humans, our vital statistics fluctuate across our bodily systems, and wearable devices can track this data with little or no manual intervention. Wearables track heartbeats, distance, workouts, sleep, and multiple other bodily characteristics. They help people optimize their bodies and protect them, nudge them to take a walk, and even recommend improving sleep. Digital twins are similar but on a much larger, more complex scale.

Digital twins complement Building Information Models (BIMs). Where BIMs rely on creative data representations of a building, digital twins use accurate real-time building virtualizations. Digital twins are informed in real-time by intelligent devices and sensors connected at the edge that collect data from building assets.

The digital twin captures changes that occur in the physical building. If building occupancy rises, a digital twin can identify if HVAC output needs to increase. If social distancing orders are in place, digital twins can track compliance.

A digital twin learns and predicts future actions based on the data it consumes and the tasks it performs. For example, an HVAC twin continues to learn the needs for cooling and ventilation based on occupancy patterns combined with ambient data, building operating conditions, and maintenance schedules. The digital twin lowers operating costs by optimizing the energy mix and providing accurate forecasts of cooling and ventilation needs.

Change is constant, and facilities teams cannot afford to determine manually what systems need attention. Digital twins provide facilities teams a unified view of their building landscape to respond to problems and address issues before they become serious.

HINDSIGHT IS 20/20: HISTORICAL ANALYSIS

Buildings are a treasure trove of data and include BIM, OEM specifications, building design, operating conditions, sensor data, and equipment setup. Data lakes store large amounts of structured, semi-structured, and unstructured data in raw form. Information is tagged and converted into structured data only when needed for use by the digital twin. Examples include occupant traffic, video streaming, ambient condition, and sensor data like GIS information. The data warehouse typically stores more structured data, which is ready for analysis. Examples include equipment specifications, operating ranges, and equipment performance rating.

Historical data provides data mining opportunities to evaluate current operating conditions and predict building systems behavior by learning from past patterns. The digital twin analyzes structured and unstructured data sets to predict equipment failure by observing performance data or optimizing energy demand by monitoring occupancy trends, as examples. Without occupancy data, energy is wasted by only regulating temperature through setpoints. However, active manipulation of set points is cumbersome in large buildings with many rooms and open areas like lobbies. To overcome this constraint, facility managers use intelligent automation to determine heating or cooling needs and plan energy load efficiently.

Facility managers analyze historical data from operating conditions, OEM specifications, and control settings to predict equipment performance and failure patterns well in advance. This advanced awareness reduces the need for excess inventory by timing equipment shutdown with minimal impact on operations. Predictive analytics on equipment performance improve asset availability, eliminate breakdowns, improve asset efficiency, and prolong useful asset life.[23]

Facilities operators can also use predictive analytics to adjust alerts management. Typically, OEMs provide threshold settings for operating performance and failure points to set up alerts. Through equipment performance observation, facility managers optimize alerts by adjusting deviations between the min-max range or the alert criticality classification. This performance tuning can significantly reduce operations costs for building operators.

The digital twin not only enables analytics but also aids decision-making through predictive modeling and simulation. Machine learning capabilities can help a twin simulate the impact of decisions, and minimize or even avoid costs, like parts replacement.[24]

FUTURECASTING: ARE WE IN A SIMULATION?

The so-called simulation hypothesis traces its origin back to antiquity and remains relevant today. The basic premise is that all reality is artificial—either in the mind or through technology. This idea is so pervasive that it is the basis for many science-fiction movies and series. While interesting to contemplate, simulation is even more compelling because it already exists in several forms. Simulation modeling creates content for safety tests, scientific exploration, and, yes, movies like *The Matrix*, which may be the poster child for sci-fi digital twin simulation on a global scale. Digital twins create real-world processes in a controlled digital environment. Simulation modeling is also prevalent in futurecasting, the definitive what-if scenario analysis, a practice used in many industries to strategically plan for an organization's future.

Figure 6.6 illustrates how a building chiller plant uses a digital twin for predictive maintenance at the Infosys Mysore campus.

In built environments, facility managers and property owners are limited in their ability to futurecast because they lack the means to simulate. The physicality of buildings constrains options for building owners and forces them to gamble on new building solutions, says Dean Hopkins, COO of Oxford Properties, a property management firm. "Many asset managers try new building solutions with no way to visualize or determine if they work."[25] Facility managers waste significant time and money on trial and error. To use an old analogy, they are trying to change the tires on a moving car.

Figure 6.6. **Digital Twin Simulation for Predictive Analytics**
Source: Infosys Knowledge Institute

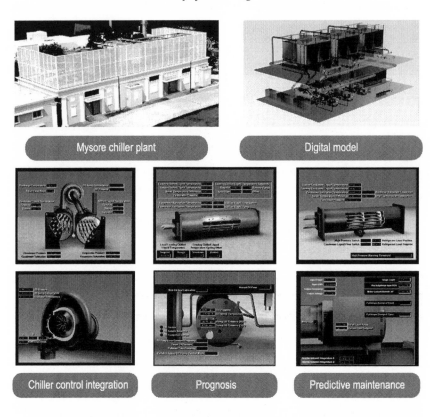

Digital twins offer the best option to develop and test new solutions because they accelerate development cycles and maximize the impact of R&D budgets.[26] They foster innovation through experimentation with new ideas in the digital model without spending large amounts of money and time developing physical prototypes or conducting expensive pilots. With increased emphasis on personalizing building occupant experiences, solutions need multiple variations that become impossible to test using conventional techniques. A digital twin offers the most effective and cost-efficient method to test solutions in practice.

With more aspects of personal and business life going digital, information security is paramount. Digital twins provide a collaborative platform for users to test security and safety compliance, and to simulate business-critical situations for a more quantitative approach to new building system design and operation.

Digital twins allow facilities leaders to test new scenarios and solutions in a safe, digital environment that mirrors the physical. Digital twins are highly accurate replicas of physical buildings, so what happens in the digital world will accurately reflect the physical and vice versa. Simulations provide the ability to optimize energy performance and anticipate failures without intervention in the physical world.

For example, when deploying an adaptive lighting system in a building, the solution needs to be optimized based on occupancy patterns, space usage types, exposure to ambient light, user preferences, and energy consumption. A digital twin affords a nonintrusive and cost-effective method to simulate the solution in action and test effectiveness of the design and control sensors. The simulation also reveals how sensors, connectivity infrastructure, and other architecture considerations significantly impact costs and long-term solution effectiveness.

RECAP

- We live in a world of machines that communicate with each other, think through problems, and make decisions autonomously. By 2030, there will be fifty billion connected machines, and digital twins will be the Iron Man suit that powers each industrial asset on the global journey to carbon neutrality.

- Digital technology proliferation and rapid adoption are increasing global alignment, participation, and accountability in the race to carbon neutrality. This technology is not just efficient; it shapes social and economic landscapes as it analyzes the past, monitors the present, and predicts the future.

- The digital twin collects wide-ranging data from smart spaces, manufacturing, maintenance, operations, and operating environments. It then uses this data to create a unique model of each asset, system, or process, focusing on critical behaviors, such as life, efficiency, or flexibility.

- Change is constant, and facilities teams cannot afford to determine what systems need attention manually. Digital twins provide facilities teams a unified view of their building landscape to respond to problems and address issues before they become serious.

- Preparedness is critical to engage ESG investors and deal with regulatory requirements reporting, as CDP disclosures have grown significantly and are likely to continue to increase going forward.

SMART SPACES

THE CASE FOR SMART SPACES

HINGE OF FATE

Winston Churchill said, "We shape our buildings; thereafter, they shape us."[1] In shaping us, they shape history too. When we read his words and revere their impact, few appreciate the exact location where Churchill mobilized the English language and made it fight. The wartime 'hinge of fate' occurred in a small room in a gothic palace, the British Parliament's House of Commons in the Palace of Westminster, stretching along the River Thames in London. Its very design influenced its effectiveness. Unlike most parliaments, members sit facing each other. When standing to speak, there's nowhere to hide—it's visceral and gladiatorial—your foes a phalanx in front of you, supporters a wave of noise behind, careers built or broken on a single speech. Prime minister Tony Blair called it "the arena that sets the heart beating a little faster."[2]

Even the building flourishes and details up the ante. The Commons' green leather benches are cramped with only 427 spaces for 646 members, reinforcing the design objectives of collaboration and discourse. Red lines on the floor, two sword lengths apart, separate opposing sides (giving us the phrase "toe the line").[3] These design flourishes emphasize and influence how its occupants interact.

"We shape our buildings; thereafter, they shape us." This shape is heavily influenced by technology in the digital age, from sensors to automated climate control. However, the real opportunity is to weave the physical and digital together, using intelligent building design for rich experiences, operational efficiency, and financial returns.

BUILDINGS MUST DO MORE

Taken together, the events of the past decade have accelerated the need for buildings to do more. They need to again become symbols of the era, of progress. While the stream of innovations has included plumbing, electricity, telephones, and the internet, now buildings need to reflect and enhance the human experience.

The concept of a building has changed. Instead of concrete, commanding and efficient buildings are green, inviting, and sustainable. This change includes both the physical building concept and the mental concept perceived by the market and society. The pandemic illustrated that the notion of spaces is changing. Spaces have become digital, remote, physical, and in-person. The workspace may be remote, at home, in a coffee shop, or even in transit. The world is in perpetual motion, and people want their space to keep up.

We expect supply chains and spaces to do more than ever and to answer questions never asked before, like, "Do you need an office building?" and "What is the new purpose of the spaces we inhabit?" COVID-19 accelerated an existing trend. Work is now an experience, not just a location. For many, the location is also a conscious choice.[4] For buildings to fulfill their promise and guarantee their future, their managers must step up to the expectations of modern society.

Emerging technologies can make the so-called built world better by merging infrastructure initiatives with the call to action on sustainability—how do we convert buildings that produce such a high percentage of global carbon emissions into sustainable ecosystems?[5]

BRAVE NEW BUILDING

Issues related to sustainability, human experience, and Practical Sustainability are not new. However, the pandemic highlighted the gap between what buildings offer now, what technology makes possible, and what people desire. Josh Ridley, CEO of leading digital twin software firm, Willow, says the COVID-19 pandemic brought a "bit of the Wild West, the gold rush" to the built world.[6] Companies saw the opportunity and did their best to seize the moment. Building managers increased investments because they had to—occupant safety became the mandatory use case. Existing building tech firms ramped their marketing, and new entrants pivoted quickly to offer building solutions. The built world has historically struggled to keep up with the pace of technology. Beyond keeping up, smart spaces are at an inflection point where they can drive significant benefits to building stakeholders and the planet overall.

Former Microsoft Smart Places innovation executive, Rimes Mortimer, says, "Our clients' major concern is how to future proof a building project, but this is a real challenge. The least static thing going into buildings is technology because it's changing so fast."[7]

Technologies like compute, edge devices, and cloud continue to race down cost and maturity curves, and providers have opened their protocols to enable easier connection and integration. Building owners historically were slow to change but, even before the pandemic, they understood the imperative to adopt Practical Sustainability—the missing link was guidance on how to do it.

MAKING SPACE MATTER

Traditional approaches to the built world were developed for a world that no longer exists. The list of changes is lengthy: heightened occupant expectations, stringent environmental requirements, converging exponential technologies, and broader societal obligations. Where buildings once focused solely on efficiency, construction cost, and operating expense, they now must evolve with the times, providing occupant experience and complying with ESG requirements while still generating acceptable returns. After the pandemic collapse, commercial real estate's renaissance hinged on envisioning and communicating an essential role to the market.

The framework below describes the major components of smart spaces, which interweave physical infrastructure and digital technology to empower collaboration, fuel sustainability, increased operational efficiency, and transformed occupant experiences.

Figure 7.1. **Smart Spaces Overview**
Source: Infosys Knowledge Institute

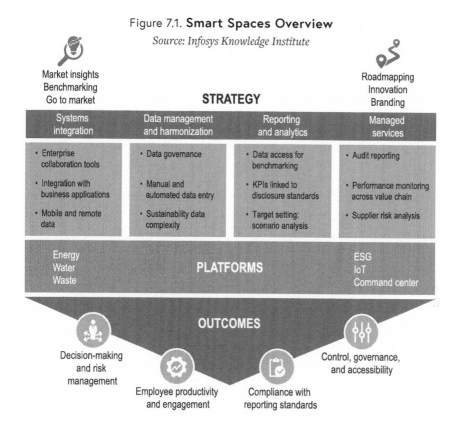

Market insights
Benchmarking
Go to market

STRATEGY

Roadmapping
Innovation
Branding

Systems integration	Data management and harmonization	Reporting and analytics	Managed services
• Enterprise collaboration tools	• Data governance	• Data access for benchmarking	• Audit reporting
• Integration with business applications	• Manual and automated data entry	• KPIs linked to disclosure standards	• Performance monitoring across value chain
• Mobile and remote data	• Sustainability data complexity	• Target setting: scenario analysis	• Supplier risk analysis

Energy
Water
Waste

PLATFORMS

ESG
IoT
Command center

OUTCOMES

Decision-making
and risk
management

Employee productivity
and engagement

Compliance with
reporting standards

Control, governance,
and accessibility

The smart spaces framework guides a building's strategic purpose, technology platforms, and desired outcomes. Despite sharing common goals for asset productivity, user experience, and sustainability, buildings vary significantly across industries and value chains. Consider the difference between buildings used for pharmaceutical discovery, manufacturing, and a hospital. All three are part of the healthcare value chain, yet each has its dynamic and unique needs for space utilization.

In the built world, the approach to doing business has changed little in three decades. As Willow CEO Josh Ridley shares, "People tend to build new spaces that follow their traditional ways, which has been to get a physical asset, finance that asset, and generate sufficient cash flows. They task an architect or engineer to design a new building. The problem is that there is now a new source of value called digital, and these professionals do not have the experience to design buildings with this new layer."[8]

Technology-enabled strategies will drive necessary change in the digital layer to meet environmental and social metrics for today's world.[9] Architects cannot solve data or systems design issues without technologists. Yet, technologists cannot solve building design or construction issues without architects. Cross-discipline collaboration is needed to solve wicked problems.[10] A practical, digital roadmap for physical buildings provides the foundation and typically starts with initiatives that leverage IoT technologies. The following chapter on implementation covers the journey to smart spaces and Practical Sustainability.

ENTERPRISE OFFICES AND CAMPUSES

DESIGN FOR SERVICE AND EXPERIENCE

Traditional building design has been architecture-led, with architects leading planning, layout, appearance, and material to construct a building in compliance with regulations and client expectations. Customer-centric design and innovation are now required to enable buildings to remain relevant in a continually evolving, digital-influenced environment. Creative use of space to rapidly cocreate new products and capabilities offers a unique opportunity to combine innovation, customer experience, and emerging technologies. This return on space investment also indicates the capability to keep pace with changing market needs.

For example, building architecture may incorporate natural lighting to reduce dependence on electrical lighting, create a visually driven productive environment and reduce total building energy cost.[11] Smart technology minimum ventilation rates control fresh air intake, which effectively reduces the carbon footprint.[12]

Smart space design helps buildings become extensions of the communities they serve. Typical design elements include recycled materials in construction and furnishings, low emission (plastic-free) design, and municipal infrastructure and transportation integration. This enlightened design approach minimizes environmental impact, increases transportation options, addresses community resilience to natural risks, and creates a more sustainable community.

Building services are the systems that make buildings comfortable, functional, efficient, and safe. Traditionally, building services focused on designing and operating mechanical, electrical, and plumbing systems. They have been connected and controlled through proprietary technologies, typically provided by original equipment manufacturers (OEMs) and managed through significant manual effort. IoT has enabled new data sources (air quality, ambient lighting, and occupancy) combined with traditional measurements to elevate the human experience, delivering new building services like indoor environment quality and wellness indices (health monitoring). New York City real-estate innovator RXR Realty created a platform to integrate multi-sensor data from building management systems to measure building wellness. The market viewed this index as a positive step during COVID to ensure compliance with health protocols and an overall emphasis on occupant safety.[13]

The digital leap has driven building design to improve occupant interactions and deliver new experiences. These interactions increase security, create go-no-go zones for visitor safety, and video analytics for incident monitoring and reporting. Solutions improve productivity through bot-supported check-ins, integrated parking solutions, and space reservations. Moving up Maslow's hierarchy of needs, experiences like personalized signage, low-wait intelligent elevator banks, and intelligent vending make the occupants feel special and provide a personalized touch.

BEST BUILDINGS ATTRACT THE BEST TALENT

Companies everywhere are engaged in a battle for talent. While hiring enough workers—period—is challenge for many firms, having sufficient workers fluent in digital skills is a strategic edge for any organization to succeed in the post-pandemic era. This talent pool works flexibly, is progressive, and expects the built world to reflect these values. Millennials and now Generation Z workers want assurance that their employers embrace sustainability goals and reflect this in the products and services they sell,[14] plus the buildings where they work. Organizations need to design dynamic spaces that are human-centered, feel authentic to the brand, and allow room for growth and new technologies as they arrive.

In the post-COVID era, Gartner predicts that in 2022 more than half of the US (53%) and UK (52%) workforce will be hybrid, only working part-time from the office. Globally, 31% of all workers will be remote.[15] Working spaces must rapidly evolve to address the needs of this hybrid workforce and deliver on their needs to collaborate and work flexibly. With employees accustomed to working in their home environment, offices may include features that look like an extension of homes: lounges, fireplaces, and cafés.

The hybrid workforce wants to collaborate, which is their compelling reason to come to the office.[16] Working spaces must support this need through open spaces, flexible meeting rooms, and integrated communications.

THE CAMPUS AS ECOSYSTEM

The corporate campus has evolved into a large, subsidized space, traditionally on city peripheries, and emphasizes learning and innovation along with collaboration through proximity. Not surprisingly, technology companies were the early adopters of this form of office space.

A campus is a cluster of buildings designed and located within a bounded area with a sense of purpose, occupied by one or more organizations, and connected through the spaces in between. Modern campus planning no longer maximizes building placement in an aesthetic surrounding but is increasingly an urban planning project. Campuses are vibrant collections of people and infrastructure, where occupants are present 24/7, and services need to accommodate multiple types of interactions between occupants and the built space.

The around-the-clock presence of people requires campus designers to include elements of recreation, commerce, and social interactions, in addition to considerations for health, efficiency, security, and sustainability. Smart in-campus navigation, parking visibility, intelligent transportation, retail integration, and food services must integrate for a seamless campus experience. In-campus transportation must integrate with public transport schedules to provide convenient transport options for people to commute. Similarly, resource consumption like water and energy must align with city infrastructure without straining resource availability for city residents.

Figure 7.2. **Infosys Mysore Campus**
Source: Infosys Knowledge Institute

Infosys has a corporate educational campus in Mysore, India, housing over 12,000 trainees who live, learn, and work in its lush 340 acres (See Figure 7.2). Entertainment, sports, food, retail, and transportation services perform seamlessly with the learning and working environment. Cashless transactions, mobile access, and integrated physical security function across all the services offered at the campus. Externally, the campus is also well-integrated with local city administration by sharing transport schedules, weather information, and waste management. The Mysore campus has evolved from a symbol of excellence as a corporate learning center to a role model for sustainability and experience design.

IT'S ALL ABOUT THE DATA

Through their many sensors, connected buildings churn out a lot of data, estimated in 2020 to be 37.2 zettabytes (a zettabyte = a thousand exabytes = a billion terabytes = 1 trillion gigabytes—a massive amount). There is approximately thirty times more data created by buildings at the time of writing than there was just ten years ago and almost a 30% increase from 2019 to 2020.[17] Measurement parameters span temperature, humidity, energy, light, air quality, and occupant movement. These data points traditionally resided in siloed systems, but IoT technologies, cloud adoption, and edge processing allow these data points to integrate like never before.

While data has long been heralded as the new oil, organizations struggled to develop meaningful use cases until the emergence of smart spaces. Efficiency and cost savings are the obvious immediate opportunities, driven as much by integration as the application of existing analytics. Another promising area is regulatory reporting, which streamlines building certification audits, and eases compliance with sustainability goals and other statutory requirements. Looking ahead, building data can also improve decisions on peak-load management, equipment downtime, and equipment-failure predictions.

COMMERCIAL REAL ESTATE

The pressure on commercial real estate has been building for years, facing challenge after challenge. First, the large superstores ravaged small businesses in America, who were, in turn, themselves gutted by online marketplaces, such as Amazon. Due to COVID and the consequences of a permanent work-from-home culture by an estimated 25% of the workforce,[18] corporate real estate had to pause. Residential housing became less available, and costs increased as the population shifted due to the cost of living and opportunities.[19] These scenarios have two things in common:

1. Sustainability will become the most significant challenge and last for generations.
2. Buildings can transform and become better using available smart space technology, fair governance, and clearly communicated regulation.

Sustainability in commercial real estate is no longer just doing the right thing. Sustainability has moved beyond cost reduction to become a driver of revenue and brand strategy.[20] Stadiums, arenas, multi-tenant housing, retail spaces, and entertainment centers increased focus on sustainability to mitigate the cyclic nature of rentals and property valuations, which reeled due to the pandemic's impact.

THE IMPACT OF URBANIZATION

Analysts estimate that by 2050, over two-thirds of the world's population will live in urban areas.[21] Rapidly rising demand for housing and inflexible housing stock drive unaffordability, leading to housing shortages and an aging housing infrastructure that is expensive to maintain. Housing contributes roughly 20% of GHG emissions of any city, and consequently, cities are under scrutiny to upgrade their infrastructure.[22] Urban areas have a diverse mix of poverty and wealth, which influences jobs, well-being, education, and housing. Generally, people residing in the inner city lead a poorer quality of life. These gaps impact who has access to sustainable housing and the benefits it creates. For sustainable initiatives to succeed, they must deliver at scale and serve the entire social and economic spectrum of the urban population.

Multi-tenant real estate provides much of the urban housing in cities. These organizations require significant investment to ensure their property portfolio stays current with sustainability standards. These changes, like energy-efficient appliances and water waste reduction, are capital intensive and increase the cost of already expensive housing. While affluent and environmentally conscious individuals may be ready to pay extra for greener living, the entire population needs housing, and much of the urban housing stock is resource intensive.

Real estate developers must look for innovative solutions to accelerate modernization. Smart sensors optimize the performance of energy-intensive appliances like elevators, boilers, and HVAC systems. AI and machine-learning algorithms optimize power consumption to match the availability of greener (and possibly less expensive) power from the grid or rooftop solar power generation. These measures may increase initial costs but yield recurring benefits in lower operating costs, utility bills, and repair costs.

The residential housing industry has been slower to adopt sustainable practices.[23] They have not yet felt the pressure of green initiatives, but the momentum is growing, like building codes and tax credits for green energy and water-consumption efficiency. New work-from-home practices should be counted as part of a company's ESG footprint, requiring data capture and reporting shared with employers. Banks are exploring credit availability to favor green residential projects, and government green infrastructure programs include housing. This financial support will encourage lean construction techniques, recyclable and local materials, and integration with local communities. If persistent, these actions will create a virtuous circle of positive impact on new job creation, incremental homeownership, and green mortgage lending.

SUSTAINABILITY = FLEXIBILITY FOR RETAIL

The pandemic wreaked havoc on the retail industry, with store closures, corporate bankruptcy, restrictive operating hours, employee furloughs, and an accelerated shift to e-commerce. In the post-COVID era, retail spaces must continually adjust to changes in buyer behavior and the fortunes of big retailers. Most large US retailers closed stores (Gap and Macy's) or filed for bankruptcy (J Crew and Neiman Marcus), and retail mall space faced continual pressure to maintain traffic and sales. There is also a shift towards strip malls and neighborhood shopping points to get closer to the customer, a trend accentuated by the success of Footlocker and similar brands.[24] On the other hand, Amazon and large retailers like Walmart have experienced resounding e-commerce-fueled growth. Consumers have embraced their low prices and extensive product selection, avoiding travel to a physical store and stocking up while staying locked down in their residence.

This increased dependence on e-commerce, contactless payments, and curbside pickups may alter some retail spaces. However, most retailers must wait for the physical return of consumers as local authorities rescind COVID restrictions. For real estate owners, their spaces must exude health, safety, and human experience. Shopping centers and the high street need to position themselves as beacons of energy efficiency and the sustainable lifestyle instead of appearing as transactional temples of consumerism. To stay relevant, stores need to adopt sustainable practices aggressively, including locally sourced materials for store interiors, natural lighting, and environments promoting health and well-being. More practices include energy-efficient signage, LED lighting, solar power, paperless operations, and even reuse of air-conditioner condenser water to water plants. These measures not only enhance a sustainable brand reputation but also reduce operating costs.

THE YEAR-ROUND VENUE

Stadiums and arenas are typically significant city structures created with the help of taxpayer money like grants and tax holidays. Most stadiums and arenas are used a few days a month and excessively demand local resources. Their energy needs and GHG emissions spike exponentially on event days and, in most cases, the energy they consume comes from grids fed by non-renewable power sources. On event days, stadiums also generate enormous amounts of trash, which mostly goes into landfills, not to mention the tremendous strain on the host city's water management system.

The sports industry, its leagues, and franchises are adopting practices to increase the sustainability of these facilities. Digitalization is driving the smart stadium market as visiting fans expect a more intuitive experience, and stadium owners seek new ways to increase the return on their investment. A study by Mordor Intelligence reports global smart stadium market value of $7 billion in 2020 and annual growth of nearly 22% to reach $18 billion by 2025.[25]

Fans expect a richer experience with better seating, pervasive wireless coverage, and interactive media, which is also expensive to provide. Venues must become platforms and progressively add capabilities that improve sustainability, enhance safety, security, simplify operations, and embrace technology to maximize fan experience. These upgrades and retrofits are expensive undertakings, and the investments cannot be justified for infrequent property use.

These capabilities are feasible only with a consistent revenue flow from facility operations. The pandemic had a catastrophic impact on scheduling and revenue from sports and other live events. As the live event market returns, venue leaders have an opportunity to refine their vision and approach to fill seats and drive revenue.

Stadiums must adapt to support multiple events throughout the year, including concerts, political gatherings, trade shows—likewise for housing and office complexes, hotels, and other entertainment centers. Successful venues will integrate into the surrounding community to drive their economic development and overall well-being. Stadiums and arenas will optimize environmental practices, support local businesses, and generate revenue through increased energy-efficient appliances, incorporate natural lighting, and reduce water waste engagement.

INTEGRATED WORKFORCE MANAGEMENT

A hybrid workforce requires a new model to bring people and space together in a meaningful way. Intelligent office buildings serve workers' needs while providing facility managers with vital information. They deliver the employee "wow" experience that creates a compelling reason to come to an office. Figure 7.3 shows an example of an intelligent office building in action with several amenities to serve workers and visitors.

A workforce command center synchronizes people and business operations across multiple floors and even multiple properties. New York City's RXR Realty developed and deployed their workforce command center, which they refer to as a building insights platform. This platform considers every aspect of building performance, workplace, and tenant experience. A team of customer specialists developed this phygital solution that merged the physical built environment with digital technologies and tools to optimize work-space operations and enhance employee experience.

Figure 7.3. **Commercial Real Estate Smart Space**
Source: RXR

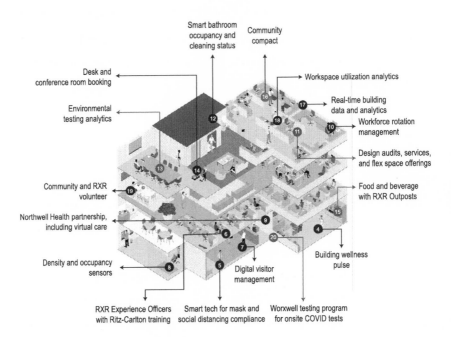

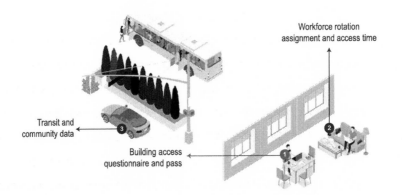

This suite of tenant solutions includes onsite COVID testing and tracing and supports many work amenities across twenty million square feet of prime real estate.[26] The RXR platform solution is deployed in twenty-six office buildings in New York City and enabled nearly 1,000 businesses and 70,000 employees to return to work as the COVID pandemic receded.[27] The integrated workforce command center manages over 900,000 data points across these properties, collecting data on occupancy, safety, and central utilities.

SMART FACTORIES

INDUSTRY 4.0

The industrial sector's share of US GDP was 11% in 2019,[28] yet it contributed 23% of total carbon emissions, according to the Environmental Protection Agency (EPA).[29]

The US Energy Information Administration (EIA) forecasts carbon dioxide emission by industry sector with multiple scenarios that pivot around crude oil price. Transportation and electric power were the two leading emissions contributors in 2021.[30] However, according to EIA projections, if oil prices are high, the industrial sector will overtake electric power as early as 2030.[31] Factories are at the nexus of buildings, supply chains, and voracious energy-consuming equipment. Given the ominous projections, factories carry additional responsibility to reduce emissions, and smart spaces are essential. This sustainable set of tools includes efficient energy usage, renewable energy, and alternate fuels, plus carbon capture, storage, and material recycling. These steps begin with measuring current levels and then a closed-loop model for ongoing improvement with Industry 4.0 as the foundation. The broad tenets of Industry 4.0 are:

- Interoperability for connected assets to communicate with each other.
- Technical assistance for rational decision-making with supporting analytics.
- Information transparency to simulate systems proactively.
- Decentralized autonomous decisions based on preset rules.

Infosys published a six-stage maturity model for Industry 4.0 in collaboration with Germany's RWTH Aachen University and Acatech consortium.[32] The report provides the roadmap to advanced manufacturing and is required reading for anyone in manufacturing in the twenty-first century. Beyond a better way to serve customers and reduce costs, Industry 4.0 is also the path to sustainable manufacturing.

The four rules above generally correspond with Stages 2 through 5, with Stage 1 as baseline computerization, and Stage 6 as an autonomous version of the previous stages (think Skynet in the *Terminator* movies). For more information about this maturity index, please refer to the white paper.[33] The maturity model is an approach to identify status and develop a roadmap to attain targets in Industry 4.0 adoption.

Figure 7.4. **Industry 4.0 Model**
Source: Acatech, Infosys Knowledge Institute

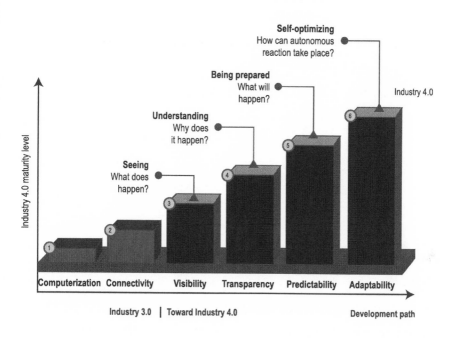

CONNECTING ASSETS, SYSTEMS, AND PEOPLE

The first tenet of Industry 4.0 is interoperability, where assets, systems, processes, and people talk to each other. Connectivity makes the factory closed loop with a continuous feed of critical parameters to aid rational and timely decisions. Interoperability is essential for diverse communication protocols and operating systems used in machinery to talk to each other. Table 7.1 shows the themes in each functional area, approaches to adopt technology, plus practical recommendations.

Table 7.1. **Smart Factories Drive Sustainability**

Source: Acatech, Infosys Knowledge Institute

Smart factory functional areas	Emission control and reduction themes	Approaches and technologies	Recommendations
Production	Minimal energy consumption, machine idle time, and consumable usage	Connected assets and internet of things to measure vital parameters	Sensor installation on plant assets for continuous metrics
Supply chain	Optimized logistics chains for minimal distance and maximum truckload	Location monitoring of shipments, with tags for track and trace	Plan for deep visibility into the supplier ecosystem
Quality	High first-pass yield in manufacturing to avoid waste, rework, and scrap	Poka-yoke (mistake proof) manufacturing, with sensor-aided inspection	Digitization of traditional poka-yoke methodologies
Maintenance	Proactive measures to ensure minimal asset downtime and repair time	Proactive, with machine learning to train systems with historical data and predictive maintenance	Identification of failure modes for bottleneck assets
Environment, health, and safety	Minimal water usage, ergonomic workplaces, and employee monitoring while respecting privacy	Measurement of critical resources and wearables for human health monitoring	Expand beyond profits to include environmental, social, and governance (ESG)

THE i4.0 INDEX

Industry 4.0 is a complex combination of advanced manufacturing technology and related systems. However, at its core, it's all about efficiency, making good decisions, and reducing risk. Infosys developed an index to measure this efficiency as a proxy for factory maturity using the principles described above. The i4.0 index measures four dimensions: resources, information systems, organization structure, and people and culture.

The critical **resources** in a manufacturing plant are the personnel, machinery, and equipment used for manufacture, tools, materials, products, and the information network systems used to communicate. **Information systems** integrate diverse systems to aggregate critical data, process them, and deliver valuable insights from user data for in-context consumption. **Organizational structure** explores the internal organization, employee relationships, and the ability to collaborate with external networks. The **people and culture** aspect addresses a willingness to change, an appetite for continuous learning, and information technology as a decision-making tool.

In addition to these four dimensions, the i4.0 index measures asset efficiency in four functional areas: engineering, supply chain, services, and operations (maintenance, performance, information, and energy). This efficiency becomes practical through use cases, and Table 7.2 shows a snapshot of common use cases where Industry 4.0 helps humans make faster decisions with increased accuracy.

Table 7.2. **i4.0 Index: It's All About Efficiency**
Source: Acatech, Infosys Knowledge Institute

Use cases	Actors	Metrics	Benefits
Measure critical product parameters	Shop floor manager, quality manager	Physical dimensions and defect rate	Scrap and rework avoidance and on-time order fulfillment
Monitor usage of electricity and consumables	Facilities manager	Monthly usage of electricity and consumables	Reduction in resource usage and cost saving
Measure critical equipment parameters	Maintenance manager	Mean time between failures and mean time to repair	Reduction in machine downtime and repair time
Track shipment status and location	Supply chain manager	Percentage of on-time arrival and income stock quantity	Compliance with audit requirements and decreased inventory
Monitor workforce parameters	Shop floor, human resources	Human considerations and compliance with regulations and geographic boundaries	Improvement in safety metrics and regulatory standards

ANALYTICS IN THE FACTORY

Peter Drucker's famous statement "you can't manage what you can't measure" applies to smart factories too. Industry 4.0 improves the measurement of critical operational parameters, but measurement alone is not sufficient. Analytics is the next step to managing data volume, velocity, and variety, analyzing this data, and identifying actions. There are three broad types of analytics:

- **Descriptive:** Historical data and trends study a system and enable an improvement plan. Example: trend charts of critical parameters like electricity usage, levels 3 and 4 in the Industry 4.0 maturity index, and the visibility to understand what is happening.

- **Predictive:** Historical data extrapolates and predicts future values of critical parameters. Relationships between multiple parameters are established statistically and analyzed. Example: equipment vibration patterns used to predict failure cause (say, blunt-cutting surface). Level 5 in maturity index.

- **Prescriptive:** Historical data in conjunction with real-time data to understand why something is happening. Suggests a course of action, even without human intervention. Level 6, highest in the maturity index. In the vibration example above, once fault attribution to a blunt-cutting surface occurs, part rotation speed can be reduced gradually, and an alert issued to replace the tool.

The strategic goal of Industry 4.0 is to increase asset efficiency, and this directly generates sustainability benefits. Smart factories are vital to Practical Sustainability: intelligent buildings that use less energy, intelligent equipment that wastes less material, and embedded analytics that optimize scheduling.

SMART CITIES

THE CHANGING LANDSCAPE

City governments vary but have similar leadership and responsibilities. They have a public face (mayor), operations leader (city manager), front line (city worker), partner (private service provider), and citizen.

Even in the best times, cities constantly struggle to provide comprehensive, quality public services with seemingly insufficient budgets. This pressure requires creativity from city leaders, and from sharing resources like public safety to squeezing the most value from their technology investments.

Local government has traditionally viewed technology investment as an expensive luxury. However, this attitude is changing as technology prices fall and digital native citizens demand more tech solutions from their government. For example, web-based self-service chatbots provide the public answers to many questions, and other tech automates requests and approval workflows, improving citizen experience.

There is no truly smart city yet, although some are smarter than others. London regularly graces smart city lists for its Office of Technology that coordinates multiple smart city projects.[34] Singapore also ranks high on smart city lists for its extensive use of IoT with its Smart Nation program, where one use case is to detect people smoking in designated nonsmoking areas.[35] There are many smart city pilots, and lessons have already emerged.

The authors interviewed Alice Charles, Head of Cities and Real Estate at the World Economic Forum (WEF), for her views on urban sustainability. According to Charles and WEF research, the path to Net Zero Carbon Cities has four components: ultra-efficient, connected buildings; smart energy infrastructure; clean electrification; and high urban density.[36] Further, Charles highlighted that the role of the private sector is changing from "selling widgets and gadgets to cities" to "promoting an outcome-driven model."

Smart cities promise to apply technology to improve urban citizen quality of life. They will also help in achieving ESG targets and reducing per capita energy and resource consumption. Integrated with a command center, they can deliver insights through predictive capabilities and optimize across many buildings and other infrastructure assets.

PUBLIC-PRIVATE PARTNERSHIPS

Partnerships between local governments and the private sector have traditionally been transactional, prioritizing price and overlooking broader metrics such as environmental impact. Fortunately, this is changing, thanks to the efforts of pioneers like Gordon Feller, former Cisco executive and founder of Meeting of Minds, an urban innovation and sustainability organization. Mr. Feller has increased public-private partnership interest and smart city funding for many local governments.[37]

Kansas City partnered with Sprint to create free public Wi-Fi across fifty city blocks and their streetcar transport service. The service was free to Kansas City taxpayers because Sprint was allowed to use 50% of the network for its purposes. The streetcar platform also benefited from interactive kiosks installed by Cisco, self-funded through advertising.[38]

Mastercard stepped into the smart city arena through City Possible, an initiative it launched to help cities advance inclusive and sustainable development. Thanks to urban inclusion and sustainability, City Possible expanded beyond individual cities to form a network. Maddie Callis, Director at City Possible, puts it this way: "When we shifted to form a network and identify common challenges across communities, we found a lot that can be shared. As a network, we gained more attraction, and the network became invested in the successes and the outcomes." City Possible has nurtured a network of cities and partner companies spanning every continent on Earth.[39]

While still evolving, these examples show the potential of smart city public-private partnerships when they address a worthy problem of common interest.

EXPERIMENTATION AND CITIZEN ENGAGEMENT

San Mateo County Labs (SMC Labs) offers a regional perspective on public-public partnerships, covering the twenty diverse cities in the San Francisco Bay area. SMC Labs director, Ulysses Vinson, found that connectivity was the key to making government services more efficient and a means to improve citizen quality of life—with access as the foundation for everything else.[40]

SMC Labs improved connectivity by installing one hundred public Wi-Fi hotspots, then created a smart city sandbox to experiment, rapidly sharing knowledge across the county. Since San Mateo County includes Silicon Valley, SMC Labs has ready access to leading tech firms to test solutions. For example, SMC labs tested sensors from several local firms to pilot an air quality sensor program.

Civic leaders traditionally engaged the public through surveys, town halls, and the oft-maligned yet still enduring complaints department. Integrated communications have revolutionized citizen engagement by reducing the effort and expense to connect with leaders and organize with like-minded citizens. Twitter may be the most well-known channel, but even a city website chat function can provide effective communication.

Chief Innovation Officer for the City of Sacramento, Louis Stewart, engaged the public through demonstrations of new technology capabilities. Beyond routes around city hall, he took technology into the community, so citizens experienced it firsthand. When autonomous cars go to elementary schools in underserved areas, kids see that autonomous vehicles are actual and not just on TV.

Citizen engagement is essential to mitigate inequality and social exclusion, which have emerged as unwelcome by-products of urbanization.[41]

UNIVERSITY AS CATALYST

Universities are central to smart city programs through their fundamental R&D and innovation agendas, yet they have only played a limited role until recently. A notable exception is Arizona State

University (ASU), which partnered with Phoenix government bodies to build and sustain a smart region initiative.[42]

Diana Bowman, ASU's Co-Director for the Center for Smart Cities and Regions, was one of the core architects who established The Connective, a highly successful local public-private-academic tech consortium.[43] For Bowman, this approach to building and sustaining a smart city or vision offers advantages over previous models: "Elected officials reduce political risk by partnering with a university, the private sector, and a local not-for-profit, and leveraging assets across partners. Using the university as the testbed, solutions are tested, evaluated and only after deemed fit for purpose, taken back to the mayor as a potential solution."[44] These partnership opportunities also allow students to work with public and private sectors to create real-world solutions and open access to new funding opportunities for cities and regions. While the model developed by ASU and its partners in the Greater Phoenix region is considered the first of its kind, several cities and regions worldwide are considering similar governance structures for their smart city initiatives.

Since the World War II postwar period, Pittsburgh, like many other cities, was burdened with sizable transportation and economic challenges as populations and industrial bases fluctuated. During the latter part of the twentieth century, local, state, and federal governments put in motion several initiatives to remake and revitalize downtowns and surrounding suburbs, resulting in the construction of buildings and roads. These revitalization efforts created a modern highway system and access to and from the downtown business district, but they also created an access disconnect for many low-income neighborhoods.

In 2006, Carnegie Mellon University teamed with the City of Pittsburgh to create the Metro 21 program, a living lab to develop smart city solutions.[45] One program won the US Department of Transportation's (USDOT) smart city challenge by focusing on the relationship between transportation and energy.[46] Working together, they developed an open platform and functional governance structure to improve the safety, equity, and efficiency of the city's transportation system and its correlation with energy and communications systems. They created a series of Smart Spine corridors that connect with critical city areas and services. The Smart Spine produces data that will improve mobility for all city residents. The platform is open source, allowing the City of Pittsburgh and its partners to offer and share a national standard for a municipal service delivery platform, which increases industry and innovation.[47]

How we build, use, and operate our buildings, infrastructure, and cities has always influenced our happiness and longevity. As we have progressed building new nations and economies, cities are the engines of progress, innovation, wealth, and poverty. Currently, 55% of the world's population lives in urban areas, which is forecasted to increase to 68% by 2050.[48] The EPA estimates that the average American spends 87% of their life inside buildings,[49] and the authors have already cited the significant level of emissions from buildings.

Using technology, we can make our buildings and cities intelligent, decarbonize our environment through policy-shaped targets, and nurture fairness through an equitable society. These are vital, impactful opportunities that are within our reach using known and near-future technologies.

RECAP

- Traditional approaches to the built world were developed for a world that no longer exists. Where buildings once focused solely on efficiency, construction cost, and operating expense, they now must evolve with the times, providing occupant experience and complying with ESG requirements while still generating acceptable returns.

- Smart spaces are the largest connected network of smart sensors and human interactions in a secure, sustainable system of systems that amplifies our ability to be productive and thrive.

- Buildings are a critical path to achieve global sustainability goals. Regional tech consortiums reduce risk and leverage assets through partnership between local government, the private sector, and universities. Universities serve as an effective experimentation lab, where solutions are tested, evaluated, and deployed only after deemed fit for purpose.

- Spending on buildings is second only to costs invested in the workforce. They are related because investment in smart spaces benefits the individuals working in those buildings.

- Banks are exploring credit availability to favor green projects. This financial support will encourage lean construction techniques, recyclable and local materials, and integration with local communities. If persistent, these actions will create a virtuous circle of positive impact on new job creation, incremental homeownership, and green lending.

IMPLEMENTATION

MINDSET SHIFT

WHERE THREE ROADS MEET

R ome became the first smart city in 312 BC, when water began
to flow on the Aqua Appia, Rome's first aqueduct transporting
water to the city.[1] This was around the same time that Rome's
architects designed the initial stages of the Appian Way, the first
superhighway that revolutionized transportation.[2]

Necessity was the mother of the Aqua Appia and Appian Way.
Before the Aqua Appia, Romans relied on local water sources that
could not support large populations or future growth. The aqueduct
moved water to the city, supplying public baths, toilets, fountains,
and even private homes.[3] The Aqua Appia also supported commerce,
like mining, milling, and agriculture.[4] It enabled Rome to scale and
overcome the constraints of water scarcity.

The primary purpose of the Appian Way was to transport troops and supplies to outer regions and across the empire.[5] Extensions to the Appian Way transported Roman settlers to expand the Roman empire. Roman roads covered most of Italy—372 great roads totaling 250,000 miles connected 113 provinces and cemented Rome's status as a superpower.[6] In this time and place, all roads literally did lead to Rome.

Through war and peace, feast and famine, civic leaders have innovated over the centuries to modernize cities around the needs of their citizens, especially those with authority or status. This civic innovation has driven societal progress and served as a primary channel to build utilities for basic needs as well as infrastructure for communications, travel, education, and culture.

As for culture, a "trivium" was where three Roman roads met, a good place for the public to communicate and authorities to announce the latest news. This communications channel gave us a word derived from the plural of trivium. In Rome, *trivia* was anything but trivial.[7]

CARBON NEUTRAL AND EMPLOYEE POSITIVE

In 2008–09 the world experienced the Great Recession, yet from that crisis arose growth and opportunity. To keep pace with business growth and plans, Infosys co-founder N. R. Narayana Murthy knew Infosys needed many more employees, along with a massive increase in real estate footprint. This talent initiative also provided Infosys with the opportunity to pursue sustainability aggressively by decoupling business growth from resource consumption. In 2008 Infosys committed to becoming carbon neutral by 2020, which the market viewed then as bold and progressive.[8] At the time of writing, only a quarter of Fortune 500 companies have committed to carbon neutrality by 2030,[9] a full ten years after Infosys achieved its target.

The Infosys carbon neutrality team identified smart buildings as the initial focus area for this Appian Way to sustainability. Infosys had forty-three-plus million square feet of campus area, with twenty-eight-plus million square feet of office buildings across sixteen campuses under continuous monitoring. Across this enormous real estate footprint, the company delivered a 50% per capita reduction in energy consumption over ten years ending in 2020. That decade brought a revolution in mobility, low-cost internet, and cloud-based solutions. The rise of IoT significantly influenced Infosys facility implementation and management efforts, as IoT and connected solutions captured building data and improved operations efficiency.

The increase in mobility drove new ways for end-users and building managers to interact with their buildings and harmonize with nature. These technological breakthroughs were instrumental for buildings to be appreciated as flexible, interactive environments to make occupants more secure, comfortable, and productive. Figure 8.1 illustrates the Infosys sustainability strategy as an example pathway to achieve carbon neutrality and set strategy.

Like the Infosys sustainability journey, a journey should begin with quantitative objectives to reduce resource consumption and environmental burden, and should consider human experience as a core component within the model. Professionals spend a third of their lives working in buildings, yet the traditional facility management approach delivered an unproductive, mostly negative occupant experience. Infosys leadership sought a duality of carbon neutrality *and* richer human experiences throughout their real estate portfolio.

Figure 8.1. **Infosys Sustainability Strategy**
Source: Infosys Knowledge Institute

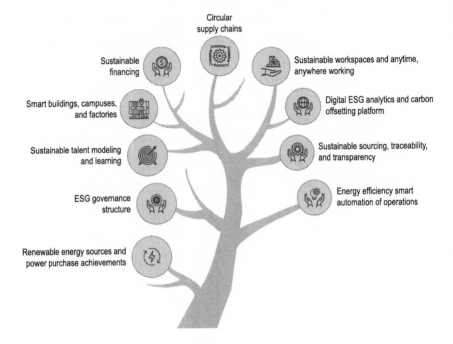

Infosys achieved carbon neutrality in 2020, and the United Nations officially recognized our climate program and smart-building approach. The ideas discussed in this book were launched, implemented, and for the most part, successfully adopted for Infosys buildings, with several painful lessons along with rewarding successes. This chapter shares an approach to implementing smart spaces shaped by our own experience, along with advice from practitioners and leading technology experts that make smart spaces possible today and essential tomorrow. Each step in the smart space journey should be a conscious decision informed by sustainability, human experience, and financial goals.

JOURNEY TO PRACTICAL SUSTAINABILITY

In writing this book, the authors have had the opportunity to speak with many industry experts, clients, academic authorities, and government institutions, all seeking a sustainable future. We are also fortunate to be part of a major global technology firm that is net carbon neutral and specializes in digital transformation and smart space solutions at scale. We recognize both the significant challenge for all of us and the urgency to execute with results. Organizations need to set aggressive targets yet deliver micro-actions every day across operations and supply chains. Actions consistently applied to built environments will achieve practical results and cumulatively a sizable impact. The rest of this chapter explains how to make this a reality.

These categories progressively come to life through a six-stage journey. See Figure 8.2 for the journey to Practical Sustainability.

Figure 8.2. **Journey to Practical Sustainability**
Source: Infosys Knowledge Institute

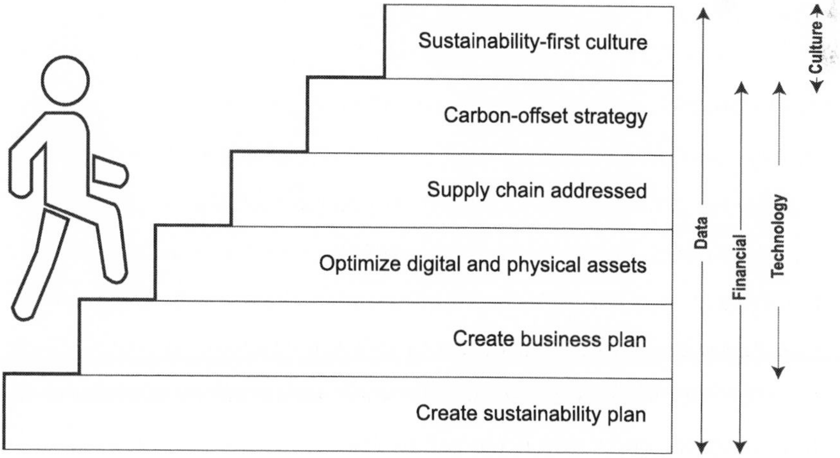

STAGE 1: SUSTAINABILITY PLAN

The first stage is a sustainability plan, which involves selecting metrics, data, and science-based targets. Enterprises determine how to collect data for monitoring, compliance, and operational purposes. This stage establishes the intergenerational well-being of each asset, along with their trade-offs and interactions, so that operations become systematic and sustainable.

STAGE 2: BUSINESS PLAN

The next stage is the business plan and how it will complement the sustainability plan—it's not an either-or alternative. Traditional growth areas still apply: market penetration, product development, market expansion, and diversification. The twist is that sustainability criteria influence each area, considering the related levers of carbon footprint, regulatory requirements, market perception, and policy-driven investments.

STAGE 3: DIGITAL AND PHYSICAL ASSETS

Digital and physical assets must support the sustainability plan alongside service delivery in the operating model. Physical assets are easier to understand than digital. While digital agendas have been prevalent for a few years, the sustainability overlap is less mature and less understood. Integrate physical-asset carbon-emissions reduction with the enterprise digital agenda, and track through the ERP system of record. This integrated view will improve reporting and

strengthen the corporate scorecard for triple bottom-line accountability. Start with buildings and rolling stock for asset-based views,
and then include technology assets in smart spaces.

STAGE 4: SUPPLY CHAIN ADDRESSED

Address supply chains and decide how far to drill down into the firm's
ESG footprint. This stage builds upon the asset base and incorporates
assets into a circular value delivery system. This system could be the
traditional conversion of raw materials into finished products at the
point of sale. Value delivery may also be defined as service-intensive
work delivered through a combination of office-based and remote
work. Beyond conventional financial return on assets, buildings and
supply chains require robust measurement for Scope 1, 2, and 3 emissions and eventually carbon offsets as a formal part of strategy.

STAGE 5: OFFSETS STRATEGY

The carbon offset strategy is an essential component of financial
institution portfolios, alongside investments, carbon trading, green
bond issuance, and corporate social responsibility. Corporate Social
Responsibility (CSR) is an essential component to meet the social
impact of ESG, though sometimes it's cynically equated with greenwashing or corporate virtue signaling. Resources and reporting are the links between CSR and operating performance with
recruitment, skills (re)development, and retention each a potential
driver of financial returns. Community outreach goes beyond the
veneer of corporate branding to nurture meaningful local and global

relationships that increase resilience, grow loyalty in good times, and overcome future adverse events.

STAGE 6: SUSTAINABILITY-FIRST CULTURE

Sustainability becomes a behavioral trait for all employees and guides strategy and everyday activities. In practical terms, leadership progressively increases the influence of sustainability on decision-making and governance. Sustainability as a cultural norm converts vague noble purpose and regulatory compliance into a North Star and compass. Changing organizational culture to establish sustainability is not easy. However, in a world of fractured and evolving interests, a sustainability-first culture is a unifying force.[10]

CONTINUOUS IMPROVEMENT

Companies need to frequently review their asset portfolio to understand access to new energy options, technology tools, and regulatory requirements. This intelligence enables better decisions on existing and future buildings and assets. Smart spaces become central to operational and financial objectives as they aid complex retrofits and new builds. In similar fashion, invest in circularity for supply chains to reduce waste and increase reuse. Retool with equipment that requires less energy to operate. Increase the use of renewable energy sources and reduce the use of fossil fuels. Hydrogen and biomass can also reduce CO_2 emissions. Use carbon capture and carbon storage technologies,[11] and monitor operations through digital twins and AI-enabled command centers.

DELIVERING VALUE IN FIVE DIMENSIONS

Unfortunately, smart space initiatives do not generate immediate financial return on investment. They may take three years or longer to achieve a 30% reduction in energy costs.[12] However, spaces deliver value in multiple dimensions as they become more intelligent by learning insights and tuning building operations, as they capture more data over time.

Figure 8.3. **The Five Dimensions of Smart Space Value**
Source: Infosys Knowledge Institute

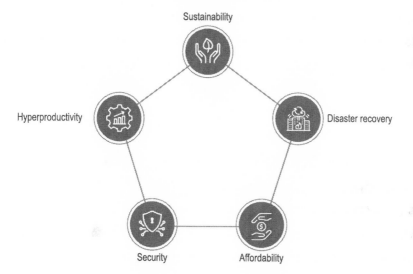

- **Security.** Physical security makes spaces, buildings, and campuses safe as well as intelligent. Digitization in the management of physical security is a growing trend for smart spaces. Beyond personal safety and asset protection, physical security digitization improves operational efficiency and reliability.

- **Affordability.** Safe and resilient, buildings become affordable as smart spaces optimize operating costs. With 50% of building energy and water resources wasted,[13] organizations have massive opportunities to improve resource efficiency. Infosys recycles over 90% of its water through advanced technologies like smart metering to monitor water usage and automation.

- **Sustainability.** Conventional buildings generate significant carbon emissions in construction and operations, and smart spaces reduce them directly.[14] In its sustainability journey, Infosys used intelligent buildings to address energy consumption. Since 2008, we have reduced per-capita-energy consumption by 55%, and we source 40% of energy needs through renewables.

- **Hyper-productivity.** Smart spaces enable people to do more in the ways they wish to do them. They create environments that promote wellness, safety, connectivity, efficiency, and enabling technology.[15] The classic example is a meeting room automatically adapting to the profiles of its occupants and their productivity needs, and then customizing the experience through room reservations, temperature, connectivity, and collaboration tools.

- **Disaster Recovery.** Smart spaces adapt to dynamic threats and are more resilient than traditional spaces. This resilience develops because smart spaces consume and analyze data to better respond and recover from adverse events. For example, intelligent buildings equipped with sensors and wayfinding apps can direct ingress and egress patterns during emergencies. Digital twins and command centers use AI-driven diagnostics to automatically deploy over-the-air fixes to malfunctioning components or dispatch field service workers who "speak" with the building to diagnose and efficiently implement repairs.

Leaders should set ambitious ESG goals to build a sustainable digital ecosystem. Documenting concerns in a system of record quantifies the issue and the potential business value of its resolution. Scorecards tame this complexity as the most crucial ESG issues are defined, prioritized, and addressed. The example shown in Figure 8.4 is a scorecard used to report ESG status and progress.

Figure 8.4. **ESG Scorecard**
Source: Infosys Knowledge Institute

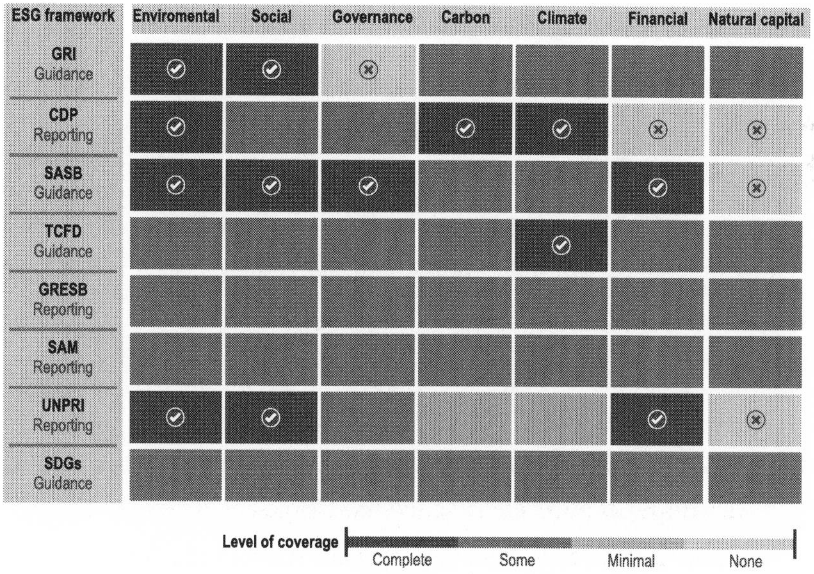

ESG framework	Enviromental	Social	Governance	Carbon	Climate	Financial	Natural capital
GRI Guidance	✓	✓	✗				
CDP Reporting	✓			✓	✓	✗	✗
SASB Guidance	✓	✓	✓			✓	✗
TCFD Guidance					✓		
GRESB Reporting							
SAM Reporting							
UNPRI Reporting	✓	✓				✓	✗
SDGs Guidance							

Level of coverage				
	Complete	Some	Minimal	None

For ESG reporting to be valuable, create a realistic and comprehensive view of operations. Each of the five value areas above requires observation and quick response, guided by strong governance. Without decisive action, even the best scorecards become exercises in data collection instead of agents of change.

ARCHITECTURE

SMART SPACE *ARETE*

Ancient Greeks used the term *arete* to describe excellence in all forms.[16] *Arete* (pronounced "uh-rate") applied to the excellence of a home, the excellence of a horse, and the excellence of people.[17] The earliest appearance of the term was the notion of people living up to their full potential—the fulfillment of purpose or function. A person's training spanned the best physical, mental, and spiritual elements with the individual considered incomplete if they lacked in any of these three elements.[18] As with the ancient Greeks, so it is with today's smart spaces.

A smart space's construction, technology, and experience represent *arete*'s physical, mental, and spiritual elements in a unified manner. This potent mix of disciplines moves buildings toward *arete*—excellence.

Smart space designers consider the symbiotic relationship between construction, technology, and user experience. Physical space is just a lifeless and underutilized structure unless the technology is carefully applied to enhance the occupant experience. When the physical environment incorporates technologies that enable personalized experience, performance in the building improves, driving productivity and collaboration. Siemens, a leading industrial firm, asserts that lighting, temperature, and CO_2 monitoring affect the health and wellness of the occupant.[19]

Figure 8.5. **Arete in Smart Spaces**
Source: Infosys Knowledge Institute

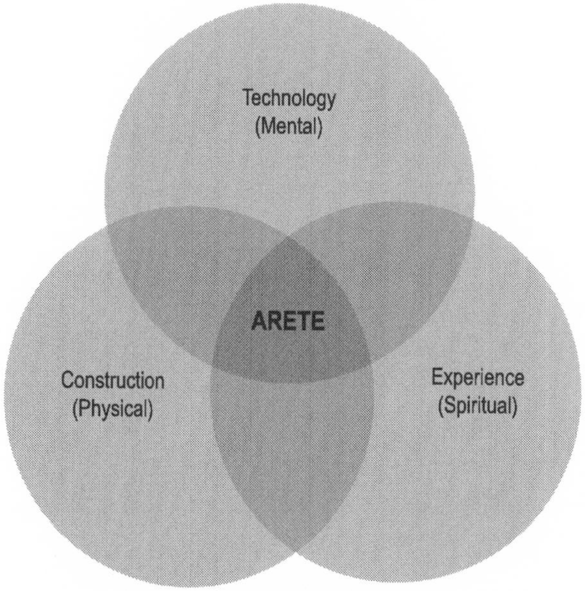

GUIDING PRINCIPLES

Smart spaces reimagine existing physical infrastructure through digital technology. They aspire to empower collaboration, achieve higher operational efficiency, and enrich the human experience. Twelve foundational principles guide smart space architecture and design.[20] These guidelines are listed in Table 8.1.

Table 8.1. **Smart Spaces Guiding Principles**

Source: Infosys Knowledge Institute, University of New Hampshire

Construction	
Enduring	Sustainable in the planning, design, and construction process
Efficient	Efficient regarding energy, maintenance, waste, water, materials, and cost
Secure	Secure for user needs, health, security, safety, accessibility, and comfort
Adaptable	Adapt to changes in user preferences, use, and contexts to serve future generations
Meaningful	Meaningful and engaging for user and the community
Technology	
Secure	Secure and protect each entry point from potential attacks through cybersecurity
Intuitive	Anticipate user and building needs and learn from data to make decisions
Accessible	Accessible and interoperable across needs of entire organization
Experience	
Inclusive	Inclusive personal experience for all occupants, visitors, clients, or facilities teams
Personalized	Personalized user experience
Frictionless	Friction and barriers removed for user
Productive	Productive for user to excel in tasks and activities

Taken together, these principles of construction, technology, and experience create secure, productive, healthy, and inclusive environments for users. Smart spaces make buildings extensions of ourselves, much like smartphones and our computing devices, but at a level where we coexist with each other and the technology. Properly designed, it becomes an immersive experience that amplifies our abilities, and at the same time, helps us live and function more sustainably.

ARCHITECTURAL FRAMEWORK

Smart spaces architecture is the organizing construct that translates technology to the functionality and user interfaces that bring use cases to life. The solution requires proper integration, or the data will not be accurate or useful. The logical architecture stack has a foundational layer of infrastructure, a middle layer of smart space operating system, and a top layer of experience and use cases. Each layer builds upon the one below. Figure 8.6 shows an example of smart space architecture.

Infrastructure is the foundation of an intelligent building. This technology includes network, connectivity, and physical building systems like HVAC, water, and lighting. Whether the building is a brownfield or greenfield potential smart space, these foundational systems are present with even historic buildings like the Palace of Versailles offering free Wi-Fi. When a building's physical foundation is faulty, the building will experience problems, such as plumbing issues and structural cracks. Without robust technology infrastructure, data and integration problems will spread to other areas.

The smart space operating system builds upon the infrastructure and represents a building's skeletal structure and muscles—how things get done. This middle layer consists of IoT platforms, digital twins, data storage, and automation, enabling smart spaces to think and connect. The operating system layer links the data among field equipment, sensors, and applications, and it supports the ERP backbone of essential IT services. Like a brain and nervous system, it senses inputs, distills insights from building operations, and enables occupant experiences like smart power, light, and thermal comfort.

Figure 8.6. **Practical Sustainability Architecture Framework**

Source: Infosys Knowledge Institute

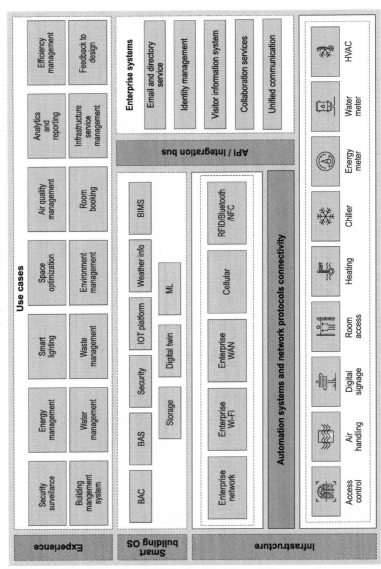

The final layer of smart space architecture is experience. It consists of building operations management and occupant experiences like space personalization. Systems collect and rationalize data from the operating system and infrastructure layers, then analyze to optimize user experience and automate building operations. The aesthetics of a well-designed traditional building already provide more than just a visual experience. Examples like the Vatican, Taj Mahal, and Great Pyramid come to mind as delivering functional utility and even evoking spiritual experiences.

Smart space experience goes further still and employs high-volume sense and quick response to evolve the user experience based on continuing input and feedback. It combines multiple touchpoints into a customized workspace based on stored user preferences, like the experience of a luxury car that auto-adjusts to the driver's ergonomic needs.

SECURITY PRINCIPLES

Security by design is the approach for platform services to embed security at the design stage.[21] Developers can then consider security guidelines and practices and ensure compliance during the entire engineering process. Sensors and video can surreptitiously collect and report data that is also personal in nature. Leaders must establish, communicate, and enforce clear policy guidelines to maintain occupant trust while also delivering the safest environment possible. Applications often provide user opt-in controls through permission settings. Complete security solutions should include policy and governance components to address regulatory, corporate, and individual requirements.

Security by design occurs through the following concepts:

- **Identity as foundation.** An identity service to authenticate users through multimodal authentication and authorize actions across a centralized or federated model. Identity services should cover all key stakeholders—employees, customers, partners—and provide the flexibility to operate anytime and anywhere across the enterprise ecosystem.

- **Zero-trust architecture.** Traditional perimeter-based security will not be enough for companies now operating across hybrid cloud and edge and forming their enterprise ecosystems. There is a need to trust no one and instead apply security controls and checks across all architectural layers and interactions that occur system-to-system, system-to-user, and user-to-user.[22]

- **Multi-cloud and data security.** Most enterprises operate across the hybrid (public-private) cloud and edge cloud,[23] and they also manage widespread data across these hybrid and edge clouds. Monitoring and securing data, containers, AI services, and applications across multi-cloud environments is a critical success factor. Autonomous techniques maximize the impact of emerging methods like security as code, policy as code, and monitoring as code.

QUANTIFIABLE SCIENCE-BASED TARGETS

THE SCIENCE-BASED TARGETS INITIATIVE

Companies recognize the importance of climate change and their role to reduce (GHG) emissions to minimize global temperature rise compared to pre-industrial temperatures.[24] This is based on the 2015 "Paris Agreement Under the United Nations Framework Convention on Climate Change," commonly known as the Paris Agreement.[25] ESG investors have demonstrated they perceive companies setting these targets as more innovative, socially responsible, and profitable.[26]

The Science Based Targets initiative (SBTi) is a leading example of science-based climate initiatives. SBTi collaborates among CDP, the United Nations Global Compact, World Resources Institute (WRI), and the Worldwide Fund for Nature (WWF). SBTi defines, promotes, independently assesses, and validates targets, and they advise companies how to reduce GHG emissions to non-harmful levels.[27]

Companies submit proposed science-based targets to SBTi for approval. The targets are consistent with the levels required to meet the goals of the Paris Agreement and are aligned with reductions needed to keep warming to well below 2.0°C threshold trajectories.[28] Companies set targets covering GHG emissions from all three scopes to achieve carbon neutrality goals and increase resilience in the transition to the low-carbon economy.

SBTi supports companies in the following ways:[29]

- Call-to-action campaign for companies to demonstrate their leadership on climate action by publicly committing to set science-based targets.

- Showcases companies that have set science-based targets through case studies, events, and media to highlight the benefits of doing so.

- Defines and promotes best practices in setting science-based targets with the support of a technical advisory group and a scientific advisory group.

- Offers resources, workshops, and guidance to reduce barriers to adoption.

Companies that commit to science-based targets face less regulatory risk and enjoy higher consumer confidence because their GHG emissions reductions are verifiable.[30] Smart spaces accurately capture efforts to reduce carbon, so combined with science-based target setting, they are a comprehensive approach that any business can pursue. SBTi provides industry and regional carbon budgets and shows thousands of companies committed to set targets, allowing peer review.

THE BENEFITS OF TARGET SETTING

Science-based targets deliver a verifiable, independent means to reduce GHG emissions backed by science. The Practical Sustainability strategies and methods shared in this book make setting science-based targets more attainable, even for small companies and those without large budgets.

Setting ambitious targets can transform businesses through leadership and employees who become invested in sustainability-based innovation. Ironically, businesses are more likely to achieve bold goals than modest ones.[31] This innovation approach can also introduce new services and products and attract long-term loyal customers, employees, and even investors. Sustainable financing practices, such as internal carbon pricing, may improve financial performance measures. Carbon taxes can indirectly stimulate the research and development required to achieve ambitious targets.[32] They can also potentially generate iterative cycles of investment capital that support the triple bottom line.

Company preparedness is critical for future regulatory reporting. As an example, Carbon Disclosure Project (CDP) disclosures have grown from an investor asset base of $64 trillion in 2010[33] to $96 trillion in 2019[34] and will likely continue to increase. While CDP disclosures are currently voluntary, they are an indication of the regulatory requirements that companies may soon face as governments mandate reporting across sustainability components, namely environmental, social, and governance. Enterprises can develop and refine ESG reporting capabilities on their own timeline by starting now. A first step for CDP disclosure is to set a carbon budget, experiment with several methods, and identify ambitious targets. Develop decarbonization strategies that promote short-term reductions and minimize cumulative emissions.

PATHWAY TO DECARBONIZATION

Targets recognized by SBTi can be calculated based on multiple science-based targets with options for measurements and ambition level. Science-based targets should meet all primary criteria, including the

GHG Protocol Corporate Standard, Scope 2 Guidance, and Corporate Value Chain (Scope 3) Accounting and Reporting Standard.[35]

Within the five-step process to set science-based targets, the second step—develop a target—utilizes three target-setting methods: carbon budget, emissions scenario, and allocation approach. Method selection varies based on duration and targets. Figure 8.7 describes the three elements of a science-based target method.[36]

Companies can quantifiably reduce their global GHG emissions, which tends to generate positive branding and the potential for financial benefits from ESG investors and consumers of their products and services. Smart spaces are a practical means to achieve science-based targets and a fundamental component of sustainability practices.

Infosys is a real-world example of how Practical Sustainability achieves the benefits outlined above. Over the last decade (culminating with carbon neutrality in 2020), Infosys has consistently demonstrated leadership in the climate action area:

- It reduced the per-capita energy footprint by more than half from 2008 when Infosys began its climate-action journey and increased its usage of clean and renewable energy sources.

- Infosys community-based carbon offsets delivered beneficial climate action and, by helping 102,000 families, created a significant positive impact beyond its corporate boundaries.

- Infosys set a carbon-neutral target that seemed unattainable a decade ago (2010). However, the company has achieved this audacious target through innovation and policy changes

Figure 8.7. **Developing Science-Based Targets**
Source: Science Based Targets Initiative

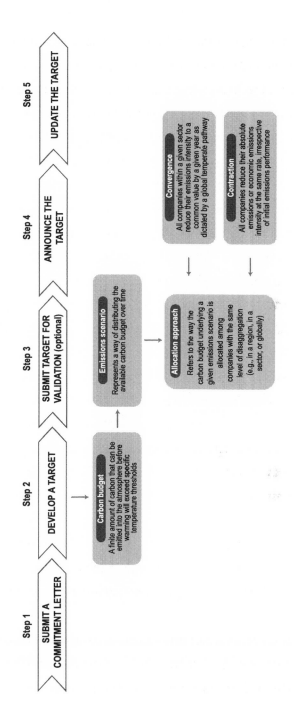

and became carbon neutral in 2020, thirty years ahead of the timeline set by the Paris Agreement.

The Infosys sustainability philosophy seeks that their business, their clients' business, suppliers, and its influenced ecosystem are all sustainable. The approach is sustainability at the enterprise level, with execution enabled with visibility through quantitative data-enabled smart environments, assets, cloud, and connectivity.

Digital transformation delivers Practical Sustainability by setting targets such as SBTis, and then validating them through quantifiable data. Consider the massive amount of data related to occupant activities, building systems, and the building's relationship to its environment. Digital twin methodologies build a living digital model of the physical asset and use this data to uncover a broad range of productivity-related savings and even revenue opportunities. Operations and supply chains also benefit from this modeling, which improves asset life-cycle management and efficiencies.

ASSESSMENT

FACILITY LIFE CYCLE ASSESSMENT

Sustainable development needs methods and tools to measure the environmental impact of human and technology activities. These impacts include emissions and resource consumption. Environmentally conscious buildings, whether for workspace or manufacturing, are created by understanding the environmental impact of their entire service life. Life cycle assessment (LCA) is a tool to understand a building's sustainability over its life cycle.[37] To determine the total environmental impact of a structure and its functional activities over decades of use, consider all stages, from preconstruction until post-demolition.

LCA quantifies the environmental impact of each stage in the infrastructure life cycle. LCA considers all the steps from raw material to manufactured product, plus materials extraction, energy consumption, transportation, use, recycling, and end of life.[38] The methodology quantifies how a product or process affects climate change, nonrenewable resources, and the environment. LCA's strength lies in the fact that it considers what happens before and after the final product is used by customers and measures effects over a long period.

The assessment analysis should include a full cradle-to-grave life cycle review. The LCA team collects a large amount of emission data: emissions from energy production, waste produced, and raw materials. These emissions are captured in different formats since the emissions from harvesting raw materials are different from those that produce electricity. Convert emissions data into actionable metrics, each addressing a specific impact category, like energy consumption.

ENVIRONMENTAL COST INDICATORS

Impact categories are not the only means to measure environmental impacts. In many cases, it makes sense to translate them into a single aggregated metric that enables comparison to other data. Environmental Cost Indicator (ECI) is a popular metric for this comparison. Generally, most products do not create emissions at a production facility but along a supply chain, which an LCA can measure.

Scores need to be weighted and merged to create a single, comparable number like the ECI. Environmental impacts are weighted based on the shadow price method. The shadow price is the highest cost level acceptable for governments per emission control unit,[39] known as prevention costs. Since government price setting determines these costs, leaders need to assess the risk of future price fluctuations and incorporate change protocols and arbitration clauses before committing to long-term programs.

Environmental data comes from multiple sources, and environmental impact measures vary greatly. Different impact categories measure data, and as a result, these numbers can be hard to compare. Figure 8.8 depicts the required steps from input through characterization and weighting.

Figure 8.8. **Environmental Cost Indicator**
Source: Ecochain

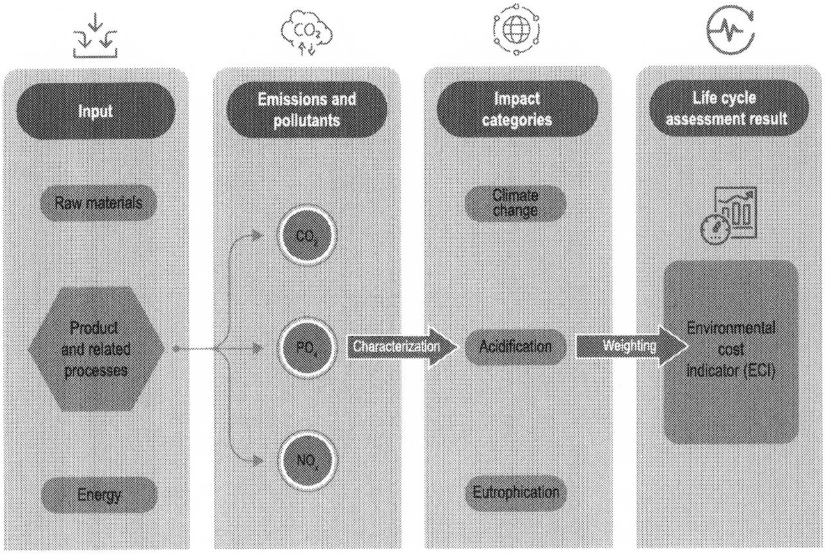

The Environmental Cost Indicator simplifies and unites differ-ent environmental data points into one monetary number. That one indicator compares the financial number across industries to bench-mark a sustainability program.[40]

BUILDING MATURITY ASSESSMENT

Building operations and design assessments require frameworks and tools to build systems across disciplines and assign importance to technical performance and stakeholder requirements.

While life cycle assessment (LCA) is a tool used to understand a building's overall sustainability over its entire life cycle,[41] Building Maturity Assessment (BMA) evaluates building systems design spe-cifically to reduce their life cycle cost and environmental impact. The BMA also assesses readiness for digital transformation. The tool evaluates trade-offs among alternative solutions to optimize building performance. As an example: environmental goals are diverse, complex, and interconnected, while local, regional, and global objectives also often conflict. Reducing impacts on one prob-lem (e.g., air pollution) may increase implications for another (e.g., solid waste generation).

The assessment starts with problem definition, and the flow pro-gresses through data collection and analysis, incorporating weight-ing for value and normalization. After scoring and ranking, leaders develop a roadmap and determine sustainability readiness. See Figure 8.9 for building maturity assessment flow.

The Building Maturity Assessment Framework (BMAF) addresses many building aspects organized into nine categories: Technology,

Figure 8.9. **Building Maturity Assessment Flow**
Source: Infosys Knowledge Institute

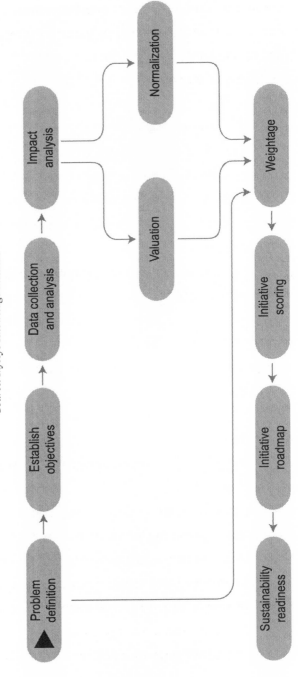

People (Resources), Space (Real estate management), Sustainability (Environment), Data, Assets (Building Infrastructure), Process and Operations, Policies and Standards, and Security.

The framework evaluates and assesses buildings based on the life cycle and comparative risk. Each step in the BMA process is needed to conduct the evaluation. The assessment follows a standard flow but is tailored to a specific building or campus, as its decision parameters are weighted based on the stakeholders involved. The BMA provides a comprehensive set of indicators to assess building sustainability preparedness. The framework assesses building data maturity relative to a standardized framework covering policies, governance, data management, building type, and stakeholder engagement.

The BMA framework is a helpful tool during the entire sustainability journey. Company leadership should conduct an evaluation regularly, helping building leaders increase their understanding of data and institutionalize good practices. This periodic assessment also supports innovation, collaboration, co-creation, and research in the building industry.

The Building Maturity Assessment Framework measures building performance and sustainability readiness. It is based on the building ecosystem and considers the dynamic interrelationships of buildings to their occupants and the larger environment. The framework is organized similar to the periodic table of elements and is tailored to buildings. Companies can use the framework, shown in Figure 8.10, as a single source of truth for assessments, blueprints, and required modifications to create a smart space.

Here is how the BMA framework works:

Figure 8.10. **Building Maturity Assessment Framework**

Source: Infosys Knowledge Institute

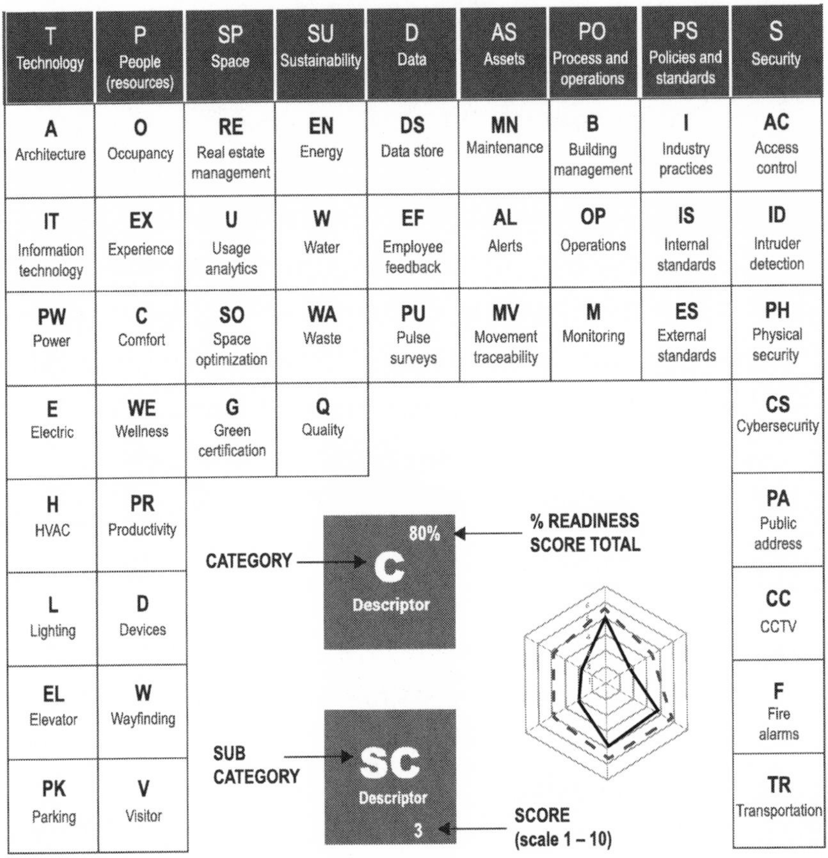

T Technology	P People (resources)	SP Space	SU Sustainability	D Data	AS Assets	PO Process and operations	PS Policies and standards	S Security
A Architecture	O Occupancy	RE Real estate management	EN Energy	DS Data store	MN Maintenance	B Building management	I Industry practices	AC Access control
IT Information technology	EX Experience	U Usage analytics	W Water	EF Employee feedback	AL Alerts	OP Operations	IS Internal standards	ID Intruder detection
PW Power	C Comfort	SO Space optimization	WA Waste	PU Pulse surveys	MV Movement traceability	M Monitoring	ES External standards	PH Physical security
E Electric	WE Wellness	G Green certification	Q Quality					CS Cybersecurity
H HVAC	PR Productivity							PA Public address
L Lighting	D Devices							CC CCTV
EL Elevator	W Wayfinding							F Fire alarms
PK Parking	V Visitor							TR Transportation

CATEGORY → **C** Descriptor — 80% % READINESS SCORE TOTAL

SUB CATEGORY → **SC** Descriptor — 3 SCORE (scale 1 – 10)

1. The top row is organized by nine key master categories:

    a. Technology

    b. People

    c. Space

    d. Sustainability

    e. Data

      f.   Assets

      g. Process and Operations

      h. Policies and Standards

      i.   Security

2. Each master category has an associated set of subcategories that are the building blocks or elements that make up the master category. For example, the sixth master category on the chart is Assets (**AS**), and it has three subcategories. Each subcategory generates a capability maturity score on a scale from 1 to 10 (10 being maximum).

      a. Maintenance (**MN**)

      b. Alerts (**AL**)

      c. Movement Traceability (**MV**)

3. For illustrative purposes, say the three Assets subcategories sum to a score of fifteen (of thirty possible). In this case, the Assets % Readiness would be 50%, suggesting potential for improvement.

4. Review all the top row master categories to generate a complete view of BMAF Readiness and develop a plan to address gaps in performance objectives.

Our experience shows several practical means to gather the data used to generate the sustainability Readiness score. It could be through a manual assessment like a series of questions in a survey or a physical onsite inspection entered in a spreadsheet.

Technology is a better way to enter data, whether building a new structure or if an existing structure is being retrofitted to become green. Technology enables and drives a sustainability culture through smart spaces.

Tech is the most accurate way to collect and verify data, since it's automated and less susceptible to human error. For example, maintenance personnel should use IoT devices and eliminate the human risk to collect, understand, and translate data. Once the data is collected, it can be extracted, visualized, and analyzed with AI and ML. IoT is the most efficient means to collect data related to sustainability. When combined with the cloud, it can be used in more ways, increases insight, and creates the potential for more value.

TAKING ACTION

MICRO-CHANGE MANAGEMENT

People are resistant to new ways of thinking and working because it challenges their reality—a reality reinforced through repetition, training, and shared experience. When confronted with change, people resist for several reasons. The most common reasons are the risk involved with change, the effort required to change, and the desire to remain comfortable.

Resistance to change leads to less-perceived value realized and more significant failure in smart space projects. Spyros Sakellariadis is familiar with this resistance from his work with a remote-monitoring system for a company in Asia. The company spent a year implementing the new system, yet it failed to deliver the original promised value. Their leaders reached out to Spyros and his team to audit and understand what caused the system to fail initially.

During the audit interviews, the facilities team who was supposed to use the new system said they did not use it. The team had switched the entire system to manual override because that was the method they used in the previous system. Throughout the audit, it became clear that the team did not think the new system could replace their twenty years of experience. While true, the objective was never to replace the workers. The new, remote monitoring system enabled workers to do a better job: carbon and silicon, human and technology, working in unison.[42]

From our multi-year (sometimes painful) transformation at Infosys and working with dozens of clients, *lasting change at scale* is the hardest yet most valuable and rewarding aspect of leadership. The insight from our research is that lasting change occurs from a series of small, irreversible changes whose compound effect delivers an exponential result. This concept is called micro-change management, covered in detail in *The Live Enterprise: Create a Continuously Evolving and Learning Organization*.[43]

These changes accompany the now-standard agile approach, with a nudge instead of a hammer to get users to adopt the new change. This incremental approach moves the communications and change-management function from infrequent, large, splashy campaigns to a regular cadence of barely perceptible modifications to behavior—a new screen button here, an alternate process step there, with little user angst. The additional benefit of this incremental approach is that changes flow directly from the agile teams, which incorporate learning and course correction during sprints. The other benefit is that this approach delivers value more quickly, and demonstrated success is the crucial tonic to drive adoption even for the most reluctant user.

This "micro is the new mega" model is tailor-made for smart spaces and sustainability initiatives, which are rapidly evolving as IoT, cloud, and AI continue to spawn new use cases and sources of value. Further, there is a societal sense of urgency on all things environmental, especially carbon-emissions reduction and micro-change management as it nurtures adoption from concept to scale.

Micro-change management plays a significant role in smart spaces initiatives, from small incremental projects to large transformational programs. We recommend a change management track that focuses on people for human resources and culture change perspectives. Define action plans that incorporate the intelligent solution implemented as a new service in the building. Elements of this parallel track and its action plan include:

1. Create an employee experience live lab:
   a. Test technology at an early stage and in a safe environment.
   b. Test partner skills and teamwork in an early stage.
   c. Bring scenarios alive, test journeys, and detect adjustments in a live setting.
   d. Initiate collaboration among digital experts, facility services, and building operations.

2. Promote communication and adoption:

   a. Create enthusiasm across the organization through the lab as a show-and-tell environment for program sponsors and colleagues.

   b. Use the ADKAR change model (Awareness, Desire, Knowledge, Ability, and Reinforcement) to help individuals understand, change, and adopt new behaviors.[44]

Figure 8.11. **ADKAR Change Management Framework**
Source: Jeffrey M. Hiatt, ADKAR

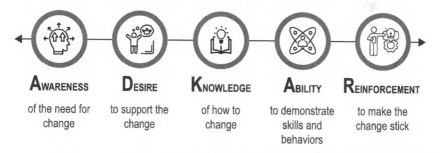

AWARENESS	**D**ESIRE	**K**NOWLEDGE	**A**BILITY	**R**EINFORCEMENT
of the need for change	to support the change	of how to change	to demonstrate skills and behaviors	to make the change stick

ERP and large-tech programs traditionally favored a single significant event—the "big bang" approach. Smart spaces programs lend themselves to an incremental method of micro-actions that deliver continuous small changes, addressing a portion of the new solution and experience at a time. This strategy means that change constantly adjusts to user needs and for their benefit. It is important to empathize with users and understand that individuals are at different readiness levels at different points across project timelines. A user-centric approach and personalized experience remove the friction that commonly occurs with new technology. This user-centricity maintains interest and retains the wow factor, starting with building entry or dashboard view and proceeding with further aspects of the new experience. Aim to evoke a feeling of understanding and enrichment—avoid uncertainty and distress.

INCLUSION IN ACTION

As companies promote inclusion, they first need to respect all relevant local and national laws. Any company introducing measures to promote equality needs to be aware of the diversity of language, culture, and family circumstances in their workforce. Managers and supervisory staff should understand the different types of discrimination and their effect on employees. A prominent example is ensuring equal pay for equal work. Women constitute a growing proportion of the workforce, but studies have shown that women earn less than their male counterparts. Also, employees with disabilities have needs to meet, where reasonable, to have the same opportunities as their peers.

Companies can take specific actions to address discrimination and eliminate it within the workplace. Some examples follow.

In the Workplace[45]

Institute company policies and procedures that make qualifications, skill, and experience the basis for recruitment, placement, training, and advancement, with inclusivity, diversity, and accessibility at all levels. Assign senior responsibility for equal employment issues, issue clear company-wide policies and procedures, and deliver frequent mandatory training through self-guided learning platforms. Use these platforms to guide equal employment practices and link advancement to desired performance. Determine on a case-by-case basis whether a distinction (like a four-year degree) is an inherent job requirement, and avoid requirements that systematically disadvantage certain groups. Keep updated records on recruitment, training, and promotions and provide a transparent view of opportunities for employees and their progression within the organization. Where discrimination is identified, develop grievance procedures to address complaints, handle appeals, and provide recourse for employees without retaliation to the whistleblower who recognized and reported the grievance.

Be aware of formal structures and informal cultural issues that can prevent employees from raising concerns and grievances. Reasonably adjust the physical environment to ensure health and safety for employees, customers, and other visitors with disabilities. Establish programs that promote access to skills development training and promote greater workplace awareness.

In the Community of Operation[46]

Encourage and support efforts to build a climate of tolerance and equal access to opportunities for occupational development, such as adult education programs, health, and childcare services. In foreign operations, accommodate cultural traditions and work with representatives of workers and governmental authorities to ensure equal access to employment by women and minorities.

Enterprise CSR programs as offset mechanisms can be powerful extensions of an organization's diversity and inclusion goals.

They promote local sustainability and economic development in underserviced communities, becoming an extension of its business handprint. Create foundations and funding that target specific communities in need, with clear goals and timelines, and enable company staff to participate in service programs of personal interest.

ENTERPRISE

Practical Sustainability thrives on a foundation of green buildings and circular commerce loops, inherently resource-efficient, safe, and healthy. Exponential technology solutions are incorporated to augment or replace existing technology and build intelligent systems. Each smart system starts with an assessment and progresses to design, requirements development, implementation, operations, and maintenance. Physical asset upgrades need to incorporate low-carbon or zero-carbon components. Areas of a physical environment that don't require a human presence to function, such as a robotic assembly line, may not require lighting and environmental comfort controls. Digital components should use efficient coding and reside on cloud platforms that are tuned to have the lowest possible GHG emissions. Edge technologies should integrate with the enterprise ERP system of record, with the data collected readily measurable for ESG audit requirements. The best way to achieve this is to make the sustainability agenda part of the digital transformation journey.

Smart spaces are not exclusive to new, greenfield buildings. Much of the built world needs to be updated and retrofitted. This is not an easy task, given these buildings were not originally designed with future technologies in mind. Experts forecasted the global non-residential green buildings market to grow from $69 billion in 2020 to $79 billion in 2021 (15% growth).[47]

Most conventional buildings were designed for aesthetics, maximizing occupancy, and structural safety. So much more is possible now, from efficiency to experience and sustainability. An assessment is often the starting point for creating energy-efficient buildings and enhancing occupant well-being, while caring for the building—and the environment—using modern technology.

An assessment scope typically includes building-management systems, asset health and connectivity, and data quality. To support current operations, retrofits must also align with IT policies on cloud infrastructure, cybersecurity risk, and partner roles. These inputs, combined with future state capabilities and experiences, determine the complexity of the building transformation needed.

INDIVIDUAL ACTION—MAKE A DIFFERENCE

For smart spaces to be effective, take action at the individual, grassroots level to complement what leaders do on a more formal corporate scale. Individual action is empowering, energizing, and provides direct feedback that a single person can indeed make a difference. That also generates a positive ripple effect for enterprise and societal action.

Smart spaces are not successful due to appearance, usability, and feasibility alone. They must also be relevant to the people who occupy them. Proofs of concept (PoCs) are an effective method to create successful solutions. They are structured to demonstrate quick, partially formed solutions that attempt to be technically feasible, emotionally desirable, and financially viable. Our research has shown that a high volume of PoCs is ineffective (except to show executives that people are busy). Over time, success comes from short-cycle, iterative PoCs that demonstrate value, embodying the micro-change management approach described in *The Live Enterprise* (Kavanaugh and Tarafdar, 2021).[48] Short-cycle PoCs allow organizations to experiment, refine, evolve, and rapidly iterate to improved solutions. This short interval cycle also limits the time and investment in solutions that are not feasible, desirable, or viable.

Individuals play a significant role in making their own smart space and can take steps to make their space smarter, regardless of their level and position in a company. We advocate a local approach and offer the following ideas to consider.

- **Environment.** At the individual level, you can directly impact the use of materials. Eliminate plastics, remove waste bins from work areas, conserve water and power, adopt dark mode on digital devices, and print less. Make conscious choices to use responsibly sourced consumable products. Arrange to work from home for one to two days per week on rotational workforce scheduling, reducing transportation and the daily energy, water, and waste systems' footprint required in the workspace. Use meeting technologies to replace business travel when possible. Form carpools with coworkers or use mass transit for your daily commute.

- **Social.** Proactively get involved in inclusive teams, both on work projects and in CSR initiatives. Learn about other cultures by having lunch or coffee with people who are not typically part of your social circle. Form teams to execute on a leader's ESG goals. Volunteer to own CSR initiatives. Dive into learning about ESG and find sustainability mentors or become a mentor yourself. Perform at least one sustainability activity every day, either at home or in the workplace. Keep track of these activities in the same way you would track your diet or physical activity programs.

- **Governance.** Start your day with a "Fifteen-Minute Sustainability Stand Up" with team members to identify what you will do that day to impact the sustainability agenda positively. Create a digital scorecard to track progress and gamify through healthy competition among colleagues and teams. Communicate and meet with leadership regularly to communicate progress, share challenges, and align on upcoming activities. Be a leader, a voice to hear, and an example to follow.

And have fun. Approach sustainability as your gift of grateful service, an opportunity to make a difference, and part of the social contract for whatever benefits this world has sent your way. Practical Sustainability embraces insights and innovation, not just austerity and avoidance. Sustainability will fulfill its ultimate goals when people lean into it, and that will happen from purposeful joy, not dour duty.

Individuals, businesses, governments, and even countries seeking carbon neutrality can be overwhelmed with the task before them.

This section presents a set of practical steps to start your journey, measure your progress, and report your results. This model offers a framework that you can apply to your specific path regardless of maturity level. As the ancient Chinese proverb says, "A journey of a thousand miles begins with a single [sustainable] step."[49]

RECAP

- Companies that commit to science-based targets face less regulatory risk and enjoy higher consumer confidence because their greenhouse gas-emissions reductions are verifiable. Smart spaces accurately capture efforts to reduce carbon, so combined with science-based target setting, they are a comprehensive approach that all businesses can leverage.

- Establish a strategy to achieve carbon neutrality in an aggressive timeline. Use Practical Sustainability frameworks and the six-stage journey to organize, implement, measure progress, and adjust for continuous improvement.

- Create smart spaces to make a significant impact and deliver results on your sustainability agenda. Reimagine existing physical infrastructure with digital technology, following themes of sustainability, hyper-productivity, security, affordability, and disaster recovery. Scorecards are an effective means to track and score initiatives.

- Leaders should set ambitious ESG goals to build a sustainable digital ecosystem. Documenting concerns in a system of record quantifies the issue and the potential business value. Scorecards tame complexity as ESG issues are defined, prioritized, and addressed.

- Create a sustainability-first culture using an incremental approach of proofs-of-concept and micro-actions that deliver continuous small changes. Constantly refine change to user needs and for their benefit.

- Lead by example and take individual action to be part of the solution. With an attitude of grateful service, identify doable daily activities, such as eliminating plastics, or stepping outside your set routines and established circles of interaction. Embrace diversity and new cultures. Become a voice to hear and an example to follow.

METAMORPHOSIS

THE CRITICAL CROSSROADS

In January 2021, the Davos Agenda identified a world at the "critical crossroads" in need to collaborate for the common good, across stakeholders, and across geographies. What the United Nations has described as the Decade of Action is now bookended with COVID-19 at one end and seventeen UN Sustainable Development Goals (SDGs) at the other. Global pandemic drove us off course for sustainable development and UN SDG delivery. At the same time, the pace of digitization and innovation was breathtaking, fueled as much by urgency and courage as underlying exponential technology. While the stories of ingenuity and resilience were widespread, in the words of the UN General Secretary António Guterres, the pandemic also "exposed and exacerbated existing inequalities and injustices."[1]

The authors wrote this book to share the Practical Sustainability role of circular commerce and smart spaces on society and our well-being. The primary focus was on buildings as they offer a positive path forward, and they play an integral role in work and personal life. They exert significant influence on decarbonization initiatives through their emission contribution in construction and operations. Buildings hold the promise to get the United Nations SDGs back on course and to lead the way with real progress on decarbonization. This book highlights the valuable role intelligent buildings play in sustainability, but the clock is ticking. In 2021, the UN Financing for Sustainable Development Report highlighted that business closures and fragile supply chains cost 114 million jobs, plunged 120 million people back into extreme poverty, and left 132 million undernourished.[2] To achieve all seventeen SDG goals by 2030, let alone reach Net Zero, what Klaus Schwab called the "AC," or after-COVID era has increased the need and urgency to act.[3]

This pandemic also highlighted that disasters affect us all, regardless of borders or economic level. As the world recovers post-COVID, experts expect CO_2 emissions to rebound by 1.5 billion tons—the second-largest increase since records began.[4] We spend 90% of our time in buildings and, with more than half the global population already living in cities,[5] urban living already accounts for 70% of CO2 emissions.[6] With expected population growth and two-thirds of all people to live in cities by 2050,[7] unless we laser-focus on smart spaces, circular commerce, and improved human experience, we will fail to recover better, together—to paraphrase the UN's António Guterres.[8]

Buildings are fundamental to modern life yet often fall short of their sustainable promise. As Liu Zhenmin, Head of the UN

Department of Economic and Social Affairs, explained, "To rebuild better, both the public and private sectors must invest in human capital, social protection, and sustainable infrastructure and technology."[9] We stand at a crossroads—technology offering tremendous possibility for planet and profit, yet also daunting complexity and uncertain societal implications.

While certainly an inflection point, the pandemic accelerated the underlying megatrends already in motion—revealing a $2.5 trillion market for smart buildings and cities,[10] and the merging of intelligent buildings and infrastructure into an intelligent local network. The following five megatrends have elevated sustainability to the forefront: environment, digital technologies, energy transmission, social, and financial.

A sustainable world requires more than government policies; it also demands exponential change in the built environment. Practical Sustainability is about more than saving the planet. It's also about the next business boom—the need to merge the physical and digital, using intelligent building design for rich experiences, operational efficiency, and financial return. With $16 trillion of existing commercial real estate needing to become intelligent and sustainable,[11] traditional approaches no longer apply. Our generation's moonshot requires new models of thinking on an enterprise, national, and global scale.

An excellent reference to learn more about Practical Sustainability is the 2021 report, "Decarbonize, Democratize, and Digitalize India's Built Environment: A Transformative 2050 Vision for Wellness and Resilience," written by Reshma Singh of the Lawrence Berkeley National Laboratory and Monto Mani of Indian Institute of Science, Bangalore, India, and Swapnil Joshi of Infosys.[12]

The Infosys sustainability journey and our collaboration with industry experts, academia, and global think tanks offer clues for others on the path. The vision was rigorously practical, and we focused on quick wins for long victories, achieving carbon neutrality in 2020, a full three decades ahead of the Paris Agreement timeline. We designed to evolve and to cascade sustainability throughout our enterprise. The triple bottom line return on investment was tangible and significant:

- Forty-four percent of our total energy needs met through renewables.
- Forty-three percent reduction in carbon emissions since 2008.
- Fifty-five percent reduction in per-capita energy usage, equivalent to $225 million in energy savings.
- Reduced water consumption by 60%.
- Twelve million square feet of corporate real estate certified as the highest-rated green buildings.
- The elimination of single-use plastics and 100% recycling of plastic waste.

We share these results as inspirational examples of what is possible, and leaders can apply these concepts to their context and situation. In the words of the UN motto, "This is your world." Across the world, organizations are eager to accelerate the next stage in their evolution. What's missing is the underlying framework and fresh approach. Practical Sustainability provides a model built on five essential elements:

- **Regenerative future:** Buildings and commerce play a critical role in advancing environmental metrics, while supporting regulatory requirements. The path ahead shifts from extraction to sustainability, and then from sustainability to regeneration.

- **Circular commerce:** Circular commerce is the enlightened combination of data, physical goods, and finance to conduct business in innovative ways that also respect the environment. Enterprises can—and must—move from recycling to reuse, using technology to minimize consumption and waste while optimizing experience.

- **Human experience:** The human experience is a fundamental requirement for physical spaces and the flow of goods. It is human-centered, elevating people to the creative work only they can do by automating repetitive, low-skilled actions and using sensing technology to improve human factors. Privacy and security are vital in the ethics of intelligent buildings and supply chains.

- **System of systems:** Systems design is a practical discipline that transcends individual systems used to manage buildings and supply chains. It helps us observe to improve, employ technology to understand, and contextualize the world through data-driven insights.

- **Digital twins:** Digital twins create a single pane-of-glass view to replicate the physical world into living digital models. They help us learn from history, optimize today, and simulate a better tomorrow.

In June 1940, when Britain stood alone, Winston Churchill stood in the House of Commons and warned, "If we fail, then the whole world...including all that we have known and cared for, will sink into the abyss of a new Dark Age made more sinister, and perhaps more protracted, by the lights of perverted science."[13] In the post-COVID era, we face a choice: do we recover better together through the promise of regenerative, human-centric smart tech, or sink into the abyss of a new dark age exacerbated by unsustainable profit, destructive policies, and excessive consumption?

SMALL STEPS AND GIANT LEAPS

For inspiration, perhaps we should look up, 250 miles above our heads.

In July 2011, the space shuttle *Atlantis* made its final flight—the closing chapter in the shuttle's three-decade story of tears and triumph. The mission destination was the next stage of our human journey, the International Space Station (ISS),[14] perhaps the ultimate smart space. The ISS circles the planet every ninety minutes, traveling five miles every second, a privileged witness to sixteen sunrises and sunsets every day.[15] The ISS has two bathrooms, one gym, and six sleeping quarters, all watched by fifty onboard computers and eight miles of cabling.[16] Almost 250 people from nineteen countries have made ISS their home, the perfect example of a regenerative smart space that is literally in space, dedicated to improving the human experience.

The *Star Trek* mantra "to boldly go" has inspired us before. The month after DARPA's first contact in October 1969, NASA made their second shot at the moon. Thirty-six seconds after lift-off, lightning struck the Apollo 12 spacecraft, the flight facing jeopardy. A NASA technician, John Aaron, stayed calm and saved the mission,[17] his colleagues later calling him "a steely-eyed missile man" (the movie *The Martian* later paid tribute to him).[18] The following year, Aaron was central to bringing Apollo 13 home too.[19] If, as they say in Bhutan, "we borrow from our children," we must flip the script on sustainability from negative to positive, giving our children a positive vision of the future to innovate and achieve, not simply scare them through dystopian and doomsday scenarios. In the race to sustainability, we need our steely-eyed missile men and women to guide us home—or perhaps, to guide us to our next home.

Practical Sustainability offers a positive, science-based mindset that delivers on the triple bottom line of people, planet, and prosperity. It provides a blueprint for individuals, governments, and society to evolve with purpose while addressing the structural problems and opportunities that will define the future of business and, ultimately, life itself.

We share this planet with nine million species of plants and animals.[20] Our choice is exponential change or exponential consequences. Like the people of Amazonia, we can innovate to regenerate our world. Like Darwin and Hooker on Ascension Island, we can architect an exponential Eden. Like the Zabbaleen of Cairo, we can create a circular economy, regardless of how humble our circumstances are. We must work together to meet the challenge, to rediscover both modern miracles and a golden age—on this blue planet or another.

To succeed, we must break the journey down into small steps of rigorous Practical Sustainability. It is only through small steps that we will make the giant leap, and someday one small step for an individual may once more be a giant leap for humanity—and a sustainable reality.

ACKNOWLEDGMENTS

○

TO INFOSYS

We thank the following people at Infosys for their encouragement and support:

Nandan Nilekani, for his leadership and guidance in leading the Infosys sustainability journey.

The Infosys ESG Operations Council—Salil Parekh, UB Pravin Rao, Nilanjan Roy, Deepak Padaki, Sumit Virmani, Krish Shankar, Inderpreet Sawhney, and Manikantha AGS for their strategic guidance.

Ravi Kumar S, Mohit Joshi, Ashiss Kumar Dash, Shaji Mathew, and Prasad Joshi, for their sponsorship and support.

The Infosys Green Initiatives team—Bose Koorliyil Varghese, Mathsy Kutty, Chetan Raghupathi, Guruprakash Sastry, Mangesh Narayan Lokhande, Manoj Bhaskar Hegde, Murali Ramalingam, Nand Verma, Nilandri Prasad Mishra, Prasad Gowande, Sandeep Rachapalli, S Jayachandran, and Vijayalakshmi S.

The Sustainability Governance and Reporting team—Aruna Newton and Tanuja Manohara.

The Infosys Diversity and Inclusion team—Nisha Atey, Suja Warriar, Pooja Umesh, and Harsh Kalra.

The Infosys Sustainability team—Irenie Poitras, Sharada Prasad, Peter Tevonian, Krishan Kant Agarwal, Scott Confer, Swapnil Madhukar Joshi, Todd Roazen, Punit Hemant Desai, Vikas Makkar, Nagaraju Kacham, Jaisal Singh, Bisesh Kumar Mahato, Ashutosh Tiwari, Heather Howton, Madeline O'Dwyer, Oliver Lorey, Madhav Apte, Alexandre Akchatel, and Angela King.

The Reform EcoWatch team—Lax Gopisetty, Raj Srinivasan, Rithika Hannah Messiahdas, Debanjan Desarkar, Sankar Konduru, Sanjay Ladha, and Vinoth Subramanian.

The Smart Spaces team—Vikas Gupta, Semra Barutchu, Abhishek Goyal, Ravi Kumar G. V. V. Kamlesh Kumar Anuragi, Krishnananda Shenoy, Saurav Kanti Chandra, Kedar Barve, Praveen Bhat, Sriram Panchapakesan, and Arunkumar Ranganathan.

The SDC team—Raja Rajeshwari Chandrasekhara, Jean-Francois Guillou, Promod Singhvi, Christopher Okamoto, Kurt Schafer, Joel Hill, Ben Larsson, Anoop Mohan, Dana Boatwright, Douglas Wills, Julia Shao, Ian Kowza, Ljubica Popovic, Madeleine Roberts, Harish Reddy, Jessica Bicknase, Kenneth Kaplan, Kumaragurubaran Lakshmipathy, Priya Sharma, Prakhar Kiyawat, Shweta Nayak, Vinod Kizhakke, Tad Bowen, Anoop Mohan, Samy Eswaran, Shreya Nim, Onkarnath Pandey, Rajesh T, Manoj Neelakanthan, and Raj Janardan.

The Marketing team—Vijay Varadarajan Srinivasa, Tania Thanda, Harini Babu, Navin Rammohan, and Bharat Malhotra.

The Analyst Relations team—Sandeep Mahindroo, Suyog Purushottam Shetty, and Jayaram Ponnada.

TO OUR EXTERNAL CONTRIBUTORS

Alice Charles, Ankush Patel, Bert Von Hoof, Bob Bennett, Chris Hoemeke, Dean Hopkins, Eyal Feder, Gordon Feller, Jeff Martin, John Elkington, John Porter, Jonquil Hackenberg, Joshua Ridley, Louis Stewart, Maddie Callis, Mark Boyd, Monto Mani, Nitesh Bansal, Phil Christiansen, Reshma Singh, Rimes Mortimer, Rushi Rama, Russ Argusa, Scott Rechler, Spyros Sakellariadis, Ted Maulucci, Tom Davis, Jamie Metzl, Max Jarrett, Matthew Peterson, Tony Shakib, and Ulysses Vinson—for their generous time to share ideas, learnings, and experiences.

Special note of thanks to Arizona State University—Amy Scoville-Weaver, Diana M. Bowman, Lev Gonick, Michael Crow, and Patricia Solís—for their insights and science.

COREY GLICKMAN

The idea of authoring a book linking sustainability to smart spaces, commerce, and the human element transformed from an ambition to a reality thanks to the culture and support we received throughout Infosys and the many industry peers we are privileged to interact with regularly. I would like to thank Infosys for enabling me to lead the company's Sustainability & Design Practice and the interactions with the many clients and partners who recognize the critical role in all our hands. At the time of our publishing this book, Infosys has now been carbon neutral for two years, which is thirty years ahead of the Paris Agreement. This accomplishment provided the confidence that we could present and share our ideas as being practical and actionable.

Writing *Practical Sustainability* would not have been possible without the mentorship and collaboration of my co-author Jeff Kavanaugh, Director of the Infosys Knowledge Institute, and his invaluable team, most notably Kerry Taylor, Dylan Cosper, and Nikki Seifert. I would also like to acknowledge the many industry and academic thought leaders inside and outside of Infosys. They generously contributed their time and ideas to the authors and, ultimately, the readers of this book. Also, particular thanks for the true spirit of collaboration to Dr. Michael Crow and Arizona State University, Gordon Feller, and John Elkington. Thank you to the good people at Scribe Media for making the publishing of this book a smooth process.

Lastly, and most importantly, I thank my wife, Denni, and my children, Lex and Jane, for their boundless ideas, support, and encouragement.

JEFF KAVANAUGH

Practical Sustainability is a story we needed to tell, yet like sustainability itself, a book is only possible with the help of many generous contributors. I thank the many people across Infosys mentioned in our nearby Infosys acknowledgment. I also thank the many business leaders and subject matter experts whose work we cite in the book, especially those who shared their experiences with me through the

Infosys Knowledge Institute, as a client, in the classroom, or over a good glass of whiskey.

This book would not have happened without my co-author and friend, Corey Glickman, who has been a fantastic collaborator, supporter, prodder, devil's advocate, subject matter expert, and voice of reason.

Also, I would like to extend my heartfelt thanks to our publishing manager, Becca Kadison, the chief Scribe himself, Zach Obront, and the rest of the team at Scribe Media. They have supported me over several years on this and previous projects and enabled my ideas to find a home in print and on the digital page.

Thanks to Infosys for allowing me to guide and grow the Infosys Knowledge Institute, which provided support for research and interviews for the book. Thanks to the Knowledge Institute team, especially Kerry Taylor and Dylan Cosper, who poured their head and their heart into this project. Thanks to Nikki Seifert and Jeff Mosier for their support as well.

Last, I thank my wife, Melanie, and daughters, Katherine and Terri Lynn, and my dog Oscar, the most literary and supportive Yorkie you will ever find.

NOTES

CHAPTER 1

1   Nikolas Kozloff, *No Rain in the Amazon: How South America's Climate Change Affects the Entire Planet* (New York: St. Martin's Publishing Group, 2010), 53.

2   Carl F. Jordan, "Amazon Rain Forests: Although Similar in Structure to Forests in Other Regions, Amazon Rain Forests Function Very Differently, with Important Implications for Forest Management," *American Scientist* 70, no. 4, 1982, pp. 394–401, www.jstor.org/stable/27851547?seq=1#page_scan_tab_contents.

3   Jonas Gregorio de Souza, Denise Pahl Schaan, Mark Robinson et al., "Pre-Columbian Earth-Builders Settled Along the Entire Southern Rim of the Amazon," *Nature Communications* 9, no. 1125, March 27, 2018, www.nature.com/articles/s41467-018-03510-7.

4   Monica Prestes, "Black Earth: The Amazon's Sustainable Farming Legacy," Diálogo Chino, May 16, 2019, https://dialogochino.net/en/agriculture/26853-black-earth-the-amazons-sustainable-farming-legacy/.

5   Ibid.

6   Ibid.

7   Clare Fieseler, "Mysterious Island Experiment Could Help Us Colonize Other Planets," *National Geographic*, May 7, 2017, www.nationalgeographic.com/science/article/ascension-island-terraformed-biology-evolution-conservation.

8   W. B. Turrill, *Pioneer Plant Geography: The Phytogeographical Researches of Sir Joseph Dalton Hooker*, Springer (1953), www.springer.com/gp/book/9789401766975.

9   "Secrets of the Garden," *National Geographic*, accessed August 26, 2021, www.nationalgeographic.com/travel/slideshow/sponsor-content-royal-botanic-gardens-kew-london-england-united-.

10   Fieseler, "Mysterious Island Experiment Could Help Us Colonize Other Planets."

11   "The Size of the World Population Over the Last 12,000 Years," World Population Growth, Our World in Data, accessed August 15, 2021, https://ourworldindata.org/world-population-growth.

12   "Global Primary Energy Consumption by Source," Global Energy Consumption, Our World in Data, accessed August 15, 2021, https://ourworldindata.org/energy-production-consumption.

13   Pierre Friedlingstein, Michael O'Sullivan, Matthew W. Jones et al., "Global Carbon Budget 2020," Earth System Science Data, December 11, 2020, https://essd.copernicus.org/articles/12/3269/2020/#abstract.

14   Klaus Schwab, *Stakeholder Capitalism: A Global Economy that Works for Progress, People and Planet* (New Jersey: Wiley, 2021), xiii.

15   Ibid.

16   Thin Lei Win, "We Can't Tackle the Climate Change Crisis without Changing Construction. Here's Why," World Economic Forum, January 4, 2021, www.weforum.org/agenda/2021/01/planet-warming-emissions-buildings-construction-climate-goals-risk.

17   "Sharing an Equitable and Sustainable Digital Future," Infosys, 2021, www.infosys.com/sustainability/documents/infosys-esg-report-2020-21.pdf.

18   Brian C. Lines et al., "Overcoming Resistance to Change
      in Engineering and Construction," *International Journal of
      Project Management*, January 2015, www.researchgate.net/
      publication/271448451_Overcoming_resistance_to_change_in_
      engineering_and_construction_Change_management_factors_for_
      owner_organizations.

19   Michael G. Jacobides and Martin Reeves, "Adapt Your Business to
      the New Reality," *Harvard Business Review*, Sept.–Oct. 2020, https://
      hbr.org/2020/09/adapt-your-business-to-the-new-reality.

20   Ed O'Boyle, "4 Things Gen Z and Millennials Expect From
      Their Workplace," *Gallup*, March 30, 2021, www.gallup.com/
      workplace/336275/things-gen-millennials-expect-workplace.aspx.

21   Karianne Gomez, Tiffany Mawhinney, and Kimberly Betts,
      "Welcome to Generation Z," Deloitte, accessed August 26,
      2021, www2.deloitte.com/content/dam/Deloitte/us/Documents/
      consumer-business/welcome-to-gen-z.pdf.

22   Andrew Bloomenthal and Margaret James, "Capacity Management,"
      Investopedia, December 30, 2020, www.investopedia.com/terms/c/
      capacity-management.asp.

23   "Take Action for the Sustainable Development Goals," Sustainable
      Development, United Nations, accessed August 16, 2021, https://
      www.un.org/sustainabledevelopment/sustainable-development-
      goals/.

24   "Welcome to GRI," Global Reporting Initiative, accessed August 16,
      2021, https://www.globalreporting.org/.

25   MoneyShow, "Socially-Responsible Investing: Earn Better Returns
      From Good Companies," *Forbes*, August 16, 2017, https://www.
      forbes.com/sites/moneyshow/2017/08/16/socially-responsible-
      investing-earn-better-returns-from-good-companies/?sh=
      649e6da7623d.

26   "The Paris Agreement," United Nations Framework Convention
      on Climate Change, accessed August 16, 2021, https://unfccc.int/
      process-and-meetings/the-paris-agreement/the-paris-agreement.

27   Corey Glickman and Jeff Kavanaugh, "Attract Talent and Conserve Resources with Smart Spaces," Infosys, August 2019, www.infosys.com/about/knowledge-institute/insights/documents/attract-talent-conserve.pdf.

28   "Infosys Collaborates with RXR Realty to Develop a Smart Office Platform Running on Microsoft Azure for Safe Return to Work," Infosys, May 13, 2021, www.infosys.com/newsroom/press-releases/2021/develop-smart-office-platform.html.

29   Jairo da Costa Junior, Jan Carel Diehl, and Dirk Snelders, "A Framework for a Systems Design Approach to Complex Societal Problems," *Design Science* 5, e2, January 17, 2019, www.cambridge.org/core/journals/design-science/article/framework-for-a-systems-design-approach-to-complex-societal-problems/058568678B9FF25E6653EE53925838F8.

30   Bloomenthal and James, "Capacity Management."

31   "The Digital Disruptions for Sustainability (D^2S Agenda)," Sustainability in the Digital Age, March 2, 2020, https://drive.google.com/file/d/1kYfAXcFi2zl7jgor7Zp1I2x30ywNFkCh/view.

32   Robert G. Eccles and Svetlana Klimenko, "The Investor Revolution," *Harvard Business Review*, May 2020, https://hbr.org/2019/05/the-investor-revolution.

CHAPTER 2

1   "Bhutan Country Profile," BBC, February 14, 2018, www.bbc.com/news/world-south-asia-12480707.

2   Tshering Denkar, "Food on Wheels—First of its kind in Bhutan," *Daily Bhutan*, March 4, 2020, www.dailybhutan.com/article/food-on-wheels-first-of-its-kind-in-bhutan.

3   Mary Kay Magistad, "Bhutan's Tough Tobacco Laws," *The World*, April 19, 2011, www.pri.org/stories/2011-04-19/bhutans-tough-tobacco-laws.

4   Chris Dwyer, "Bhutan's Dark Sense of Humour," Travel, BBC, February 28, 2017, www.bbc.com/travel/article/20170223-bhutans-dark-sense-of-humour.

5   "Bhutan—The Last Place," Frontline World, PBS, May 2002, www.pbs.org/frontlineworld/stories/bhutan/interview.html.

6   "Gross National Happiness," Berkshire Publishing Group, 2012, www.ciis.edu/PCC/PCC%20Documents/PCC%20PDFs/Gross-National-Happiness-Allison-1.pdf.

7   "International Day of Happiness, 20 March," Department of Economic and Social Affairs, United Nations, accessed August 27, 2021, www.un.org/development/desa/dspd/international-days/international-day-of-happiness.html.

8   "The Permanent Mission of the Kingdom of Bhutan to the United Nations in New York," Ministry of Foreign Affairs Royal Kingdom of Bhutan, accessed August 27, 2021, www.mfa.gov.bt/pmbny/?page_id=124.

9   "Article 9: Principles of State Policy," Bhutan's Constitution of 2008, www.constituteproject.org/constitution/Bhutan_2008.pdf?lang=en.

10 Soo Youn, "Visit the World's Only Carbon-Negative Country," *National Geographic*, October 17, 2017, www.nationalgeographic.com/travel/article/carbon-negative-country-sustainability.

11 "CO2 Emissions (kg per PPP $ of GDP)," World Bank Open Data, The World Bank, accessed July 24, 2021, https://data.worldbank.org/indicator/EN.ATM.CO2E.PP.GD.

12 Emmanuelle Dotezac, "Investors Now Looking at Private Equity Through ESG Lens," IQ-EQ, May 19, 2021, https://iqeq.com/insights/investors-now-looking-private-equity-through-esg-lens.

13 Larry Fink, "Larry Fink's 2021 letter to CEOs," BlackRock, accessed August 27, 2021, www.blackrock.com/corporate/investor-relations/larry-fink-ceo-letter.

14 "The Global ESG Benchmark for Real Assets," Global Real Estate Sustainability Benchmark (GRESB), accessed August 27, 2021, https://gresb.com/.

15   "Disclosing Through CDP: The Business Benefits," Climate
      Disclosure Project (CDP), accessed August 27, 2021,
      https://6fefcbb86e61af1b2fc4-c70d8ead6ced550b4d987d7c03fcdd1d.
      ssl.cf3.rackcdn.com/comfy/cms/files/files/000/004/718/original/
      CDP_Disclosure_brochure_2021.pdf.

16   Corey Glickman and Jeff Kavanaugh, "Attract Talent and Conserve
      Resources With Smart Spaces," Infosys, August 2019, www.infosys.
      com/about/knowledge-institute/insights/documents/attract-talent-
      conserve.pdf.

17   "The State of Disclosure 2017: An Analysis of the Effectiveness of
      Sustainability Disclosure in SEC Filings," Sustainability Accounting
      Standards Board (SASB), 2017, www.sasb.org/wp-content/
      uploads/2017/12/2017State-of-Disclosure-Report-web.pdf.

18   Valeska V. Geldres-Weiss, Nicolás Gambetta, Nathaniel P. Massa,
      and Skania L. Geldres-Weiss, "Materiality Matrix Use in Aligning
      and Determining a Firm's Sustainable Business Model Archetype
      and Triple Bottom Line Impact on Stakeholders," *Sustainability* 13,
      January 20, 2021, www.mdpi.com/2071-1050/13/3/1065/pdf.

19   "2018 Global Sustainable Investment Review," Global Sustainable
      Investment Alliance, March 2019, www.gsi-alliance.org/wp-content/
      uploads/2019/03/GSIR_Review2018.3.28.pdf.

20   Leslie P. Norton, "These Are the 100 Most Sustainable Companies
      in America," Barron's, February 7, 2020, www.barrons.com/articles/
      the-100-most-sustainable-companies-51581095228.

21   Shuli Ren, "The World's Largest Pension Fund Has Cooled on
      ESG. Should You?," Bloomberg, May 5, 2021, www.bloomberg.com/
      opinion/articles/2021-05-05/the-world-s-largest-pension-fund-has-
      cooled-on-esg-should-you.

22   Bert Van Hoof, "Data-Driven Work Spaces: IoT and AI Expand
      the Promise of Smart Buildings," *Harvard Business Review*,
      September 24, 2018, https://azure.microsoft.com/mediahandler/
      files/resourcefiles/create-smart-spaces-with-azure-digital-twins/
      Harvard_Business_Review_Data_Driven_Work_Spaces_EN_US.pdf.

23   Michele Pelino and Andrew Hewitt, "Extend IoT Smart Building Solutions to Transform the Workplace," Forrester, May 12, 2020, www.forrester.com/report/Extend+IoT+Smart+Building+Solutions+ To+Transform+The+Workplace/RES132901.

24   "A Surprising Way to Cut Real Estate Costs," JLL, September 25, 2016, www.us.jll.com/en/trends-and-insights/workplace/a-surprising-way-to-cut-real-estate-costs.

25   John Elkington, "25 Years Ago I Coined the Phrase 'Triple Bottom Line.' Here's Why It's Time to Rethink It.," *Harvard Business Review*, June 25, 2018, https://hbr.org/2018/06/25-years-ago-i-coined-the-phrase-triple-bottom-line-heres-why-im-giving-up-on-it.

26   Ibid.

27   "Transforming Our World: The 2030 Agenda for Sustainable Development," Department of Economic and Social Affairs, Sustainable Development, United Nations, accessed August 30, 2021, https://sdgs.un.org/2030agenda.

28   John Mackey and Raj Sisodia, *Conscious Capitalism: Liberating the Heroic Spirit of Business*, Harvard Business Review Press, January 7, 2014.

29   "Ping An Builds China-Specific ESG Smart Rating System to Promote Responsible Investment in China," press release, PRNewswire, June 22, 2020, www.prnewswire.com/news-releases/ping-an-builds-china-specific-esg-smart-rating-system-to-promote-responsible-investment-in-china-301081066.html.

30   Chenxi Yu, Shiqing Cui, Zhuo Qi, and Shasha Gu, "Application of Ping An CN-ESG Data and Framework in Quantitative Investment Strategy," Ping An, January 2021, https://group.pingan.com/resource/pingan/ESG/Report/pingan-cn-esg-data-and-framework-in-quantitative-investment-strategy.pdfo.

31   Max Jarrett, personal interview with industry expert, July 26, 2021.

32   Stephen Ferguson, "Apollo 13: The First Digital Twin," Siemens, April 14, 2020, https://blogs.sw.siemens.com/simcenter/apollo-13-the-first-digital-twin/.

33   Tim Smith, "Asset Valuation," Investopedia, March 16, 2020, www.
     investopedia.com/terms/a/assetvaluation.asp.

34   Gayle Brager, "Benefits of Improving Occupant Comfort and Well-
     being in Buildings," LafargeHolcim, 2013, https://src.lafargeholcim-
     foundation.org/dnl/93603859-d59e-498a-b056-405d16e39171/F13_
     OrangeWS_Brager.pdf.

35   Francesco Bonaccurso, "Harnessing Sustainability to Drive Value
     from Your IT Investment," Consulting, Infosys, March 11, 2021,
     www.infosysconsultinginsights.com/2021/03/11/sustainability-to-
     drive-it-investment-value/.

36   "Greenhouse Gases at EPA," United States Environmental
     Protection Agency, accessed August 27, 2021, www.epa.gov/
     greeningepa/greenhouse-gases-epa.

37   National Academies of Sciences, Engineering, and Medicine,
     Accelerating Decarbonization of the US Energy System (The
     National Academies Press, 2021), https://books.google.com/
     books/about/Accelerating_Decarbonization_of_the_U_S.
     html?id=DD8yzgEACAAJ&source=kp_book_description.

38   "Lean Manufacturing and the Environment: Research on
     Advanced Manufacturing Systems and the Environment and
     Recommendations for Leveraging Better Environmental
     Performance," United States Environmental Protection Agency,
     October 2003, www.epa.gov/sites/default/files/2016-11/documents/
     lean_environment_report.pdf.

39   Win, "We Can't Tackle the Climate Change Crisis without Changing
     Construction. Here's Why."

40   "WRI Leads Zero Carbon Buildings for All Initiative Launched at UN
     Climate Action Summit," press release, World Resources Institute,
     September 23, 2019, www.wri.org/news/release-wri-leads-zero-
     carbon-buildings-all-initiative-launched-un-climate-action-summit.

41   Diana Budds, "How Do Buildings Contribute to Climate Change?"
     Curbed, September 19, 2019, https://archive.curbed.com/2019/9/19/
     20874234/buildings-carbon-emissions-climate-change.

42 "What is LEED?," United States Green Building Council (USGBC), accessed August 27, 2021, www.usgbc.org/help/what-leed.

43 Louise Mozingo and Ed Arens, "Quantifying the Comprehensive Greenhouse Gas Co-Benefits of Green Buildings," Center for the Built Environment, University of California Berkley, October 24, 2014, https://escholarship.org/uc/item/935461rm#author.

44 "Sharing an Equitable and Sustainable Digital Future," Infosys, 2021, www.infosys.com/sustainability/documents/infosys-esg-report-2020-21.pdf.

45 "Decarbonization: The Race to Zero Emissions," Morgan Stanley, November 25, 2019, www.morganstanley.com/ideas/investing-in-decarbonization.

46 Joseph E. Aldy and Gianfranco Gianfrate, "Future-Proof Your Climate Strategy: Smart Companies Are Putting Their Own Price on Carbon," *Harvard Business Review*, May–June 2019, https://hbr.org/2019/05/future-proof-your-climate-strategy.

47 "Emissions Trading in Practice: A Handbook on Design and Implementation," International Carbon Action Partnership, accessed August 30, 2021, https://icapcarbonaction.com/en/?option=com_attach&task=download&id=745.

48 Cecilia Pera, "Carbon Offsetting: A Short Guide," ClimateSeed, December 16, 2020, https://climateseed.com/blog/carbon-offsetting-a-short-guide.

49 National Academies of Sciences, Engineering, and Medicine, *Accelerating Decarbonization of the US Energy System* (The National Academies Press, 2021), www.nap.edu/catalog/25932/accelerating-decarbonization-of-the-us-energy-system.

50 "The Ten Principles of the UN Global Compact," United Nations Global Compact, accessed August 19, 2021, https://www.unglobalcompact.org/what-is-gc/mission/principles/principle-6.

51 "The UN Global Compact Ten Principles and the Sustainable Development Goals: Connecting, Crucially," United Nations Global Compact, June 2016, www.unglobalcompact.org/library/4281.

52   "Principle 6: Labour," United Nations Global Compact, accessed
      September 1, 2021, www.unglobalcompact.org/what-is-gc/mission/
      principles/principle-6.

53   Amit Kapoor and Bibek Debroy, "GDP Is Not a Measure of Human
      Well-Being," *Harvard Business Review*, October 4, 2019, https://hbr.
      org/2019/10/gdp-is-not-a-measure-of-human-well-being.

54   Michael O'Leary and Warren Valdmanis, "An ESG Reckoning Is
      Coming," *Harvard Business Review*, March 4, 2021, https://hbr.
      org/2021/03/an-esg-reckoning-is-coming.

55   Jim Fong, "An Early Outlook of a Millennial-led Economy in
      2030," November 8, 2019. https://upcea.edu/an-early-outlook-of-a-
      millennial-led-economy-in-2030.

56   David Rogers Tilley, "National Metabolism and Communications
      Technology Development in the United States, 1790–
      2000," *Environment and History* 12, no. 2, May 2006, www.
      environmentandsociety.org/node/3263.

57   Win,"We Can't Tackle the Climate Change Crisis without Changing
      Construction. Here's Why."

58   World Resources Institute, "WRI Leads Zero Carbon Buildings for
      All Initiative Launched at UN Climate Action Summit," September
      23, 2019, https://www.wri.org/news/release-wri-leads-zero-carbon-
      buildings-all-initiative-launched-un-climate-action-summit.

CHAPTER 3

1   Sayed Hemeda and Alghreeb Sonbol, "Sustainability Problems of
      the Giza Pyramids," *Heritage Science* 8, no. 8, January 30, 2020,
      https://heritagesciencejournal.springeropen.com/articles/10.1186/
      s40494-020-0356-9.

2   Brad Smithfield, "The Great Pyramid of Giza Was Once Covered in
      Highly Polished White Limestone, Before It Was Removed to Build
      Mosques and Fortresses," *The Vintage News*, September 6, 2016,

www.thevintagenews.com/2016/09/06/the-great-pyramid-of-giza-was-once-covered-in-highly-polished-white-limestone-before-it-was-removed-to-build-mosques-and-fortresses/.

3 "EGYPT: Administrative Division," City Population, accessed August 31, 2021, www.citypopulation.de/en/egypt/admin/.

4 Wael Fahmi and Keith Sutton, "Cairo's Contested Garbage: Sustainable Solid Waste Management and the Zabaleen's Right to the City," *Sustainability* 2, June 18, 2010, www.mdpi.com/2071-1050/2/6/1765#cite.

5 "King of the Rubbish Heap: Cairo's Zabbaleen Trash Collectors Recycle to Stay On Top," RT Documentary Channel, February 12, 2019, https://rtd.rt.com/stories/zabbaleen-cairos--rubbish-collectors-21st-century-change/.

6 Alex Gray, "Germany Recycles More Than Any Other Country," World Economic Forum, December 18, 2017, www.weforum.org/agenda/2017/12/germany-recycles-more-than-any-other-country/.

7 RT Documentary Channel, "King of the Rubbish Heap: Cairo's Zabbaleen Trash Collectors Recycle to Stay On Top."

8 "One third of your life is spent at work," Gettysburg College, accessed August 19, 2021, www.gettysburg.edu/news/stories?id=79db7b34-630c-4f49-ad32-4ab9ea48e72b.

9 Hannah Furlong, "Keurig's K-Cups Inch Closer to Being 100% Recyclable," Sustainable Brands, September 22, 2015, https://sustainablebrands.com/read/chemistry-materials-packaging/keurig-s-k-cups-inch-closer-to-being00-recyclable.

10 "The Amount of K-Cups That Have Been Trashed in Landfills Could Wrap Around the Planet 10 Times," The Story of Stuff Project, accessed August 19, 2021, https://action.storyofstuff.org/sign/amount-k-cups-have-been-thrown-landfills-could-wrap-around-planet-over-11-times.

11 "Towards A Circular Economy: Business Rationale for An Accelerated Transition," Ellen MacArthur Foundation, December 9, 2015, https://emf.thirdlight.com/link/ip2fho5h21it-6nvypm/@/preview/1?o.

12   Wasim Salama, "Design of Concrete Buildings for Disassembly: An Explorative Review," ScienceDirect, April 1,2017, www.sciencedirect.com/science/article/pii/S2212609016301741.

13   Ellen MacArthur Foundation, "Towards A Circular Economy: Business Rationale for An Accelerated Transition."

14   "Industrial Symbiosis: Realising the Circular Economy," Eco-innovation Action Plan, European Commission, January 27, 2014, https://ec.europa.eu/environment/ecoap/about-eco-innovation/experts-interviews/20140127_industrial-symbiosis-realising-the-circular-economy_en.

15   Peter Yeung, "The Country Rejecting Throwaway Culture," Future Planet, January 28, 2021, www.bbc.com/future/article/20210128-right-to-repair-how-the-french-are-fighting-avoidable-waste.

16   Vanessa Forti et al., "The Global E-waste Monitor 2020," 2020, http://ewastemonitor.info/wp-content/uploads/2020/12/GEM_2020_def_dec_2020-1.pdf.

17   Patricia Megale Coelho, Blanca Corona, Roland ten Klooster, and Ernst Worrell, "Sustainability of Reusable Packaging—Current Situation and Trends," *Resources, Conservation & Recycling: X*, April 2020, www.researchgate.net/publication/340865737_Sustainability_of_reusable_packaging_-_Current_situation_and_trends.

18   S Ramachandran and Jeff Kavanaugh, "Being Resilient: Transformation in the Automotive Industry," Infosys Knowledge Institute, June 2020, www.infosys.com/iki/insights/transformation-automotive-industry.html.

19   Pamela Largue, "EVs—a $46 Trillion Market Opportunity Between Now and 2050," Smart Energy International, June 10, 2021, www.smart-energy.com/industry-sectors/electric-vehicles/evs-a-46-trillion-market-opportunity-between-now-and-2050/.

20   "Raising Ambitions: A New Roadmap for the Automotive Circular Economy," Circular Cars Initiative, World Economic Forum, December 2020, http://www3.weforum.org/docs/WEF_Raising_Ambitions_2020.pdf.

21   Colin McKerracher, Aleksandra O'Donovan, Nick Albanese et al., "Electric Vehicle Outlook 2021," BloombergNEF, 2021, https:// about.bnef.com/electric-vehicle-outlook/.

22   Asad Farid, Nick Anderson, and Jamie Rosser, "Battery Adoption at the Tipping Point," Berenberg Thematics, February 10, 2016, www. bacanoralithium.com/pdfs/Berenburg_lithium_report_Feb2016.pdf.

23   Vinod Venkateswaran, Suraj Nair, and S Ramachandran, "An Ecosystem Approach for EV Adoption," Infosys Knowledge Institute, Infosys, May 2021, www.infosys.com/iki/insights/ ecosystem-approach-ev-adoption.html.

24   Jennifer Nastu, "Partner with Suppliers for Sustainability, Efficiency, Cost Savings," Environment + Energy Leader, March 11, 2021, www.environmentalleader.com/2021/03/partner-with- suppliers-for-sustainability-efficiency-cost-savings/.

25   "Sparkling Jewels, Opaque Supply Chains: Jewelry Companies, Changing Sourcing Practices, and COVID-19," Human Rights Watch, November 24, 2020, www.hrw.org/report/2020/11/24/ sparkling-jewels-opaque-supply-chains/jewelry-companies- changing-sourcing#.

26   "Sustainable Materials Management Basics," United States Environmental Protection Agency, accessed August 19, 2021, www. epa.gov/smm/sustainable-materials-management-basics.

27   "Managing, Reusing, and Recycling Used Oil," United States Environmental Protection Agency, accessed August 19, 2021, www. epa.gov/recycle/managing-reusing-and-recycling-used-oil.

28   "Cell Phone Recycling," Wastecare Corporation, accessed August 19, 2021, www.wastecare.com/Articles/Cell_Phone_Recycling.htm.

29   "Recycle Your Cell Phone. It's an Easy Call Fact Sheet," United States Environmental Protection Agency, 2008, https://nepis.epa. gov/Exe/ZyNET.exe/P1001FNV.TXT?ZyActionD=ZyDocument& Client=EPA&Index=2006+Thru+2010&Docs=&Query=&Time= &EndTime=&SearchMethod=1&TocRestrict=n&Toc=&TocEntry= &QField=&QFieldYear=&QFieldMonth=&QFieldDay=&IntQField

Op=0&ExtQFieldOp=0&XmlQuery=&File=D%3A%5Czyfiles%5
CIndex%20Data%5C06thru10%5CTxt%5C00000004%5CP1001
FNV.txt&User=ANONYMOUS&Password=anonymous&Sort
Method=h%7C-&MaximumDocuments=1&FuzzyDegree=0&Image
Quality=r75g8/r75g8/x150y150g16/i425&Display=hpfr&DefSeekPage=
x&SearchBack=ZyActionL&Back=ZyActionS&BackDesc=Results%20
page&MaximumPages=1&ZyEntry=1&SeekPage=x&ZyPURL.

30   Varun Mishra, "Global Refurbished Smartphone Market Declines 1%
     in 2019," Counterpoint, June 10, 2020, www.counterpointresearch.
     com/global-refurbished-smartphone-market-declines-1-2019/.

31   "IDC Forecasts Worldwide Market for Used Smartphones to Reach
     351.6 Million Units with a Market Value of $65 Billion in 2024,"
     International Data Corporation, January 7, 2021, www.idc.com/
     getdoc.jsp?containerId=prUS47258521.

32   "'Power by the Hour': Can Paying Only for Performance Redefine
     How Products Are Sold and Serviced?," University of Pennsylvania,
     Wharton, February 21, 2007, https://knowledge.wharton.upenn.
     edu/article/power-by-the-hour-can-paying-only-for-performance-
     redefine-how-products-are-sold-and-serviced/.

33   Carlos Galera-Zarco and José Antonio Campos, "Exploring
     Servitization in Industrial Construction: A Sustainable Approach,"
     Sustainability 13, no. 14, July 17, 2021, www.mdpi.com/2071-
     1050/13/14/8002/pdf.

34   "Blockchain Explained," Investopedia, accessed August 15, 2021.
     www.investopedia.com/terms/b/blockchain.asp.

35   "Cryptocurrency Money Laundering Risks and How to Avoid
     Them," Elliptic, February 26, 2021, www.elliptic.co/blog/
     cryptocurrency-money-laundering-risks-and-how-to-avoid-them.

36   "Revolutionizing Logistics and Transportation through Blockchain,"
     Infosys, 2020, www.infosys.com/services/digital-interaction/
     documents/revolutionizing-logistics-transportation-blockchain.pdf.

37   Nicholas Nhede, "BP and Infosys Partner on Managed Energy-
     as-a-Service Offering in India," Smart Energy International, April

29, 2021, www.smart-energy.com/industry-sectors/energy-grid-management/bp-and-infosys-partner-on-managed-energy-as-a-service-offering-in-india/.

38   Matthew Bandyk, "2020 Outlook: Utilities Will Be Pushed to Further Embrace Distributed Energy Resources," Utility Dive, January 17, 2021, www.utilitydive.com/news/2020-outlook-utilities-will-be-pushed-to-further-embrace-distributed-energ/569613.

39   Kelsey Horowitz et al., "An Overview of Distributed Energy Resource (DER) Interconnection: Current Practices and Emerging Solutions," National Renewable Energy Laboratory, US DOE, April 2019, www.nrel.gov/docs/fy19osti/72102.pdf.

40   "Distributed System Implementation Plan," Con Edison, June 20, 2020, www.coned.com/-/media/files/coned/documents/our-energy-future/our-energy-projects/distributed-system-implementation-plan.pdf.

41   "Voices of Experience: Insights into Advanced Distribution Management Systems," Office of Electricity Delivery and Energy Reliability, United States Department of Energy, February 2015, www.energy.gov/sites/prod/files/2015/02/f19/Voices%20of%20Experience%20-%20Advanced%20Distribution%20Management%20Systems%20February%202015.pdf.

42   "Utility's Power Lines Caused Huge 2019 California Wildfire," Associated Press News, July 16, 2020, https://apnews.com/article/3d35a822b32a447b665281d0bb2e8fd2.

43   "Smart Grid System Report: 2018 Report to Congress," United States Department of Energy, November 2018, www.energy.gov/sites/prod/files/2019/02/f59/Smart%20Grid%20System%20Report%20November%202018_1.pdf.

44   Jayant Sathaye, Larry Dale, Peter Larsen et al., "Estimating Risk to California Energy Infrastructure from Projected Climate Change," Ernest Orlando Lawrence Berkeley National Laboratory, June 2011, https://www.osti.gov/servlets/purl/1026811.

45   "Transforming the Power Grid with Autonomous Robots," Infosys, accessed August 31, 2021, www.infosys.com/navigate-your-next/ documents/autonomous-robots.pdf.

46   "Make Energy While the Sun Shines: How We Made Our Hyderabad Campus 100% Solar—Powered," Infosys, accessed August 31, 2021, www.infosys.com/about/corporate-responsibility/environmental/ energy/energy-sun-shines.html.

47   "How Much Energy is Consumed in US Buildings?" US Energy Information Administration, May 3, 2021, www.eia.gov/tools/faqs/ faq.php?id=86&t=1.

48   Ellen MacArthur and Frans van Houten, "3 Shifts Can Scale the Circular Economy—Triggering a More Resilient, Prosperous System," Platform for Accelerating the Circular Economy, World Economic Forum, February 11, 2021, www.weforum.org/ agenda/2021/02/3-shifts-can-scale-the-circular-economy-ellen-macarthur-frans-van-houten/.

49   Ryan Finlay, "They Used To Last Years," *Medium*, October 23, 2015, https://ryanfinlay.medium.com/they-used-to-last-50-years-c3383ff28a8e.

50   Amanda Capritto, "Impossible Burger vs. Beef: Which is Better for the Environment?," CNET, October 28, 2019, www.cnet.com/health/ nutrition/is-fake-meat-really-better-for-the-environment/.

51   Jared Wolf, "Better Brands: Is Beyond Meat Sustainable?" *Sustainable Review*, January 29, 2021, https://sustainablereview.com/ is-beyond-meat-sustainable/.

52   Krista Tukiainen, "Financing Waste Management, Resource Efficiency and Circular Economy in the Green Bond Market," Climate Bonds Initiative, May 7, 2020, www.climatebonds.net/files/ reports/markets_waste_resource_efficiency_briefing_2020.pdf.

53   Ibid.

54   "Green Bond Principles," International Capital Market Association, June 2021, www.icmagroup.org/assets/documents/Sustainable-finance/2021-updates/Green-Bond-Principles-June-2021-140621.pdf.

55   Thomas Singer, "Business Transformation and the Circular
      Economy," The Conference Board, accessed August 19, 2021, www.
      stern.nyu.edu/sites/default/files/assets/documents/TCB-Business-
      Transformation-and-the-Circular-Economy-RR.PDF.

56   Sarah Murray, "Measuring What Matters: The Scramble to Set
      Standards for Sustainable Business," *Financial Times*, May 13, 2021,
      www.ft.com/content/92915630-c110-4364-86ee-0f6f018cba90.

CHAPTER 4

1   "Aristotle & Happiness," Pursuit of Happiness, https://www.pursuit-
      of-happiness.org/history-of-happiness/aristotle.

2   Richard Kraut, "Aristotle's Ethics," *The Stanford Encyclopedia
      of Philosophy*, June 15, 2018, https://plato.stanford.edu/entries/
      aristotle-ethics/.

3   Klepeis NE, Nelson WC, Ott WR et al., "The National Human
      Activity Pattern Survey (NHAPS): A Resource for Assessing
      Exposure to Environmental Pollutants," *Journal of Exposure Analysis
      and Environmental Epidemiology* 11, no. 3, May–June 2001, 231–252,
      https://pubmed.ncbi.nlm.nih.gov/11477521/.

4   "68% of the world population projected to live in urban areas by
      2050, says UN," Department of Economic and Social Affairs, United
      Nations, May 16, 2018, www.un.org/development/desa/en/news/
      population/2018-revision-of-world-urbanization-prospects.html.

5   Franco Vazza and Alberto Feletti, "The Quantitative Comparison
      Between the Neuronal Network and the Cosmic Web," *Frontiers
      in Physics* 8, November 2020, www.frontiersin.org/articles/10.3389/
      fphy.2020.525731/full.

6   Carl Zimmer, "100 Trillion Connections: New Efforts Probe and
      Map the Brain's Detailed Architecture," *Scientific American*,
      January 2011, www.scientificamerican.com/article/100-trillion-
      connections/.

7   Ann Sussman and Justin B Hollander, *Cognitive Architecture: Designing for How We Respond to the Built Environment* (United Kingdom: Routledge, 2014).

8   Jason Till, Jennifer Hiley, Guy Faithfull et al., "Service Blueprinting: The 'Rosetta Stone' of Digital Transformation," Infosys, October 2019, www.infosysconsultinginsights.com/wp-content/uploads/2019/10/service-blueprinting_pov_infosys-consulting.pdf.

9   "The Meaning of 'Form Follows Function,'" ThoughtCo, accessed September 7, 2021, www.thoughtco.com/form-follows-function-177237.

10   "Form Follows Function," Guggenheim, accessed September 1, 2021, www.guggenheim.org/teaching-materials/the-architecture-of-the-solomon-r-guggenheim-museum/form-follows-function.

11   Kendra Cherry, "The Basics of Human Factors Psychology: Maximizing Human Capabilities," Verywell Mind, December 14, 2020, www.verywellmind.com/what-is-human-factors-psychology-2794905.

12   Steven Shorrock, "Human Factors and Ergonomics: Looking Back to Look Forward," Humanistic Systems, February 25, 2018, https://humanisticsystems.com/2018/02/25/human-factors-and-ergonomics-looking-back-to-look-forward/.

13   Frans Osinga, *Science, Strategy and War: The Strategic Theory of John Boyd* (The Netherlands: Eburon Academic Publishers, 2005).

14   Neil Perkin, "Agile Business is More About Maneuverability Than Speed," *Medium*, August 18, 2017, https://medium.com/building-the-agile-business/agile-business-is-more-about-manoeuvrability-than-speed-c4de10980d33.

15   "Backgrounder on the Three Mile Island Accident," United State Nuclear Regulatory Commission, accessed August 19, 2021, www.nrc.gov/reading-rm/doc-collections/fact-sheets/3mile-isle.html.

16   Patrick Sisson, "The ADA at 25," Curbed, July 23, 2015, https://archive.curbed.com/2015/7/23/9937976/how-the-americans-with-disabilities-act-transformed-architecture.

17 Ibid.

18 "Affleck House," Frank Lloyd Wright Foundation, accessed August 19, 2021, https://franklloydwright.org/site/affleck-house/.

19 Jeff Kavanaugh, *Consulting Essentials: The Art and Science of People, Facts, and Frameworks* (Texas: Lioncrest Publishing, 2018), 209–211.

20 Sumedha M. Joshi, "The Sick Building Syndrome." *Indian Journal of Occupational and Environmental Medicine* 12, no. 2, 2008, www.ncbi.nlm.nih.gov/pmc/articles/PMC2796751/.

21 Martin W. Liddament, "A Guide to Energy Efficient Ventilation," AIVC, International Energy Agency, March, 1996, www.aivc.org/sites/default/files/members_area/medias/pdf/Guides/GU03%20GUIDE%20TO%20ENERGY%20EFFICIENT%20VENTILATION.pdf.

22 Rajesh Varrier et al, "Drive Change from Within," Infosys Knowledge Institute, March 2020, https://www.infosys.com/services/microsoft-cloud-business/insights/documents/workplace-transformation-research-study.pdf.

23 Abraham H. Maslow, "A Theory of Human Motivation," *Psychological Review*, 1943, https://psychclassics.yorku.ca/Maslow/motivation.htm.

24 Abraham H. Maslow, *Motivation and Personality* (New York: Harper & Row Publishers, 1954).

25 "One Third of Your Life is Spent at Work," Gettysburg College, accessed August 19, 2021, www.gettysburg.edu/news/stories?id=79db7b34-630c-4f49-ad32-4ab9ea48e72b.

26 "WELL v2 Concepts and Features," WELL, accessed August 19, 2021, https://v2.wellcertified.com/wellv2/en/concepts.

27 Peter Hustinx, "Privacy by Design: Delivering the Promises," *Identity in the Information Society* 3, 253–255, May 7, 2010, https://link.springer.com/article/10.1007%2Fs12394-010-0061-z.

28 Ann Cavoukian, "Privacy by Design: The 7 Foundational Principles," Information and Privacy Commissioner of Ontario, January 2011, www.ipc.on.ca/wp-content/uploads/Resources/7foundationalprinciples.pdf.

29   "Volume of Data Collected by Smart Buildings Worldwide
      from 2010 to 2020," *Statista*, May 13, 2016, www.statista.com/
      statistics/631151/worldwide-data-collected-by-smart-buildings/.

30   "Coronavirus: DOD Response," United State Department of
      Defense, accessed August 19, 2021, www.defense.gov/Explore/
      Spotlight/Coronavirus-DOD-Response/.

31   Jeff Kavanaugh and Rafee Tarafdar, *The Live Enterprise: Create
      a Continuously Evolving and Learning Organization* (New York:
      McGraw-Hill Education, 2021).

CHAPTER 5

1   "Wide Awake on the Sea of Tranquility," NASA, July 9, 2014, www.
      nasa.gov/exploration/home/19jul_seaoftranquillity.html.

2   William B. Bonvillian, Richard Van Atta, and Patrick Windham,
      The DARPA Model for Transformative Technologies (Open Book
      Publishers, 2019), https://library.oapen.org/bitstream/id/fb06e944-
      3ab5-4c38-b4a7-0a8f7078809c/9781783747931.pdf.

3   Paul Baran, "On Distributed Communications: I. Introduction
      to Distributed Communications Networks," Rand Corporation,
      August 1964, www.rand.org/content/dam/rand/pubs/research_
      memoranda/2006/RM3420.pdf.

4   Guy Raz, "'Lo' And Behold: A Communication Revolution,"
      NPR, October 29, 2009, www.npr.org/templates/story/story.
      php?storyId=114280698.

5   Jeremy Bernstein, "Erwin Schrödinger: Austrian Physicist,"
      Encyclopedia Britannica, accessed August 8, 2021, www.britannica.
      com/science/wave-mechanics.

6   Olivier Rieppel, "The 'Law of Superposition'." In *Evolutionary
      Theory and the Creation Controversy* (Springer, 2011), 111–133,
      https://link.springer.com/chapter/10.1007/978-3-642-14896-
      5_6.

7   Oliver Heaviside, *Electromagnetic Waves* (Taylor & Francis, 1889), www.google.com/books/edition/Electromagnetic_Waves/ 4pM3AAAAMAAJ?hl=en&gbpv=0.

8   "James Clerk Maxwell: A Force for Physics," Physics World, December 1, 2006, https://physicsworld.com/a/james-clerk-maxwell-a-force-for-physics.

9   Bruce Hunt, "Oliver Heaviside: A First-Rate Oddity," *Physics Today* 65, no. 11, 48–54, November 1, 2012, https://physicstoday.scitation. org/doi/10.1063/PT.3.1788.

10   Aditya, "Availability vs. Reliability vs. Durability vs. Resiliency vs. Fault Tolerance," *Medium*, April 23, 2020, https://sprinkle-twinkles. medium.com/availability-vs-reliability-vs-durability-vs-resiliency-dfead8c92c58.

11   Ron Miller, "Satya Nadella Looks to the Future with Edge Computing," TechCrunch, October 8, 2019, https://techcrunch.com/2019/10/08/ satya-nadella-looks-to-the-future-with-edge-computing.

12   Abhijit Sunil, "Predictions 2020: Edge Computing Makes The Leap," Forrester, November 4, 2019, https://go.forrester.com/blogs/ predictions-2020-edge-computing/.

13   Gloria Omale, "Gartner Survey Reveals Two-Thirds of Organizations Intend to Deploy 5G by 2020," Gartner, December 18, 2018, https://www.gartner.com/en/newsroom/press-releases/2018-12-18-gartner-survey-reveals-two-thirds-of-organizations-in.

14   "Technological Convergence: Regulatory, Digital Privacy, and Data Security Issues," EveryCRSReport.com, May 30, 2019, https://www. everycrsreport.com/reports/R45746.html.

15   Jeff Kavanaugh and Rafee Tarafdar, *The Live Enterprise: Create a Continuously Evolving and Learning Organization* (New York: McGraw-Hill Education, 2021).

16   "Introducing Krti 4.0—the Next Generation AI Platform for Operational Excellence," Infosys, accessed August 24, 2021, www. infosys.com/engineering-services/documents/next-generation-ai-platform.pdf.

17   Phil Christensen, Bentley Systems, personal interview with industry expert, July 7, 2020.

18   Marc Andreesen, "Why Software Is Eating The World," *The Wall Street Journal*, August 20, 2011, www.wsj.com/articles/SB10001424053 111903480904576512250915629460.

19   David P. Reed, "Reed's Law," Fx Solver, accessed August 1, 2021, www.fxsolver.com/browse/formulas/Reed%27s+Law.

20   David P. Reed, "The Law of the Pack," *Harvard Business Review*, February 2001, https://hbr.org/2001/02/the-law-of-the-pack.

21   "Guide to Building the Case for Deep Energy Retrofits," Rocky Mountain Institute, September 2012, https://rmi.org/wp-content/uploads/2017/04/Pathways-to-Zero_Bldg-Case-for-Deep-Retrofits_Report_2012.pdf.

22   "World Green Building Trends 2018 Smart Market Report," World Green Building Council, November 13, 2018, https://www.worldgbc.org/news-media/world-green-building-trends-2018-smartmarket-report-publication.

23   Stephen Del Percio, "Good News, Bad News for LEED in Two Recent Studies," Smart Cities Dive, accessed September 2, 2021, www.smartcitiesdive.com/ex/sustainablecitiescollective/good-news-bad-news-leed-two-recent-studies/7721/.

24   John Nye, "How Quick Is the Energy Payback with Smart Building Automation?" 75F, July 19, 2018, www.75f.io/blog/how-quick-is-the-energy-payback-with-smart-building-automation.

25   "Rule of Thumb," United States Environmental Protection Agency, March 2016, www.epa.gov/sites/default/files/2016-03/documents/table_rules_of_thumb.pdf .

CHAPTER 6

1   Derrick Nunnally, "The Man Blamed for the Fall of Tacoma's Galloping Gertie," *The Olympian*, October 31, 2015, www.theolympian.com/news/local/article42065382.html.

2   Grady Hillhouse, "Why the Tacoma Narrows Bridge Collapsed," Practical Engineering, March 9, 2019, https://practical.engineering/blog/2019/3/9/why-the-tacoma-narrows-bridge-collapsed.

3   Lauren Gold, "Cornell Expert in Group Behavior Shows Why London's Millennium Pedestrian Bridge Was Not Built for People," *Cornell Chronicle*, November 2, 2005, https://news.cornell.edu/stories/2005/11/explaining-why-millennium-bridge-wobbled.

4   Steven H. Strogatz, Daniel M. Abrams, Allan McRobie, Bruno Eckhardt, and Edward Ott, "Crowd Synchrony on the Millennium Bridge," *Nature* 438, 43–44, November 2, 2005, www.nature.com/articles/438043a.

5   Josh Ridley, personal interview with industry expert, June 2, 2020.

6   "Roadmap for the Integrated Design Process," Greenspace, NCR, Inc, accessed August 25, 2021, www.greenspacencr.org/events/IDProadmap.pdf.

7   Salman Azhar, "Building Information Modeling (BIM): Trends, Benefits, Risks, and Challenges for the AEC Industry," ASCE Library, June 15, 2011, https://ascelibrary.org/doi/10.1061/%28ASCE%29LM.1943-5630.0000127.

8   ThoughtWire, "The Evolution of Building Management Systems: From Limited Control to a Fully Integrated Digital Twin," IoT For All, July 31, 2020, www.iotforall.com/evolution-building-management-systems.

9   Josh Ridley, personal interview with industry expert, June 2, 2020.

10   John Uri, "50 Years Ago: Apollo 13 Crew Returns Safely to Earth," NASA, April 17, 2020, www.nasa.gov/feature/50-years-ago-apollo-13-crew-returns-safely-to-earth.

11   Scott Rechler, personal interview with industry expert, June 3, 2020.

12   "Data Driven Companies Will Deliver Service Focused Real Estate," Property Funds World, July 16, 2021, www.propertyfundsworld.com/2021/07/16/303614/data-driven-companies-will-deliver-service-focused-real-estate.

13   Raja Rajeshwari Chandrasekharan, Shweta Nayak, Dylan Cosper, "Infosys Return to Workplace—Building Safe, Nurturing and

Resilient Workplaces," Infosys Knowledge Institute, May 2020, www.infosys.com/iki/insights/return-workplace-safe.html.

14 Alfonso Velosa, "Prepare for the Impact of Digital Twins," Gartner, September 18, 2017, www.gartner.com/smarterwithgartner/prepare-for-the-impact-of-digital-twins.

15 Xingxing Zhang et al., "Digital Twin for Accelerating Sustainability in Positive Energy District: A Review of Simulation Tools and Applications," Frontiers in Sustainable Cities, June 21, 2021, www.frontiersin.org/articles/10.3389/frsc.2021.663269/full.

16 Tommaso Spanevello, "Digital Twins: Accelerating the Digital Transformation in the Rail Sector," Global Railway Review, July 1, 2021, www.globalrailwayreview.com/article/120887/digital-twins-rail.

17 Ron Miller, "Satya Nadella Looks to the Future with Edge Computing," TechCrunch, October 8, 2019, https://techcrunch.com/2019/10/08/satya-nadella-looks-to-the-future-with-edge-computing.

18 Izabela Rojek et al., "Digital Twins in Product Lifecycle for Sustainability in Manufacturing and Maintenance," MDPI, December 23, 2020, www.mdpi.com/2076-3417/11/1/31.

19 Rithika Hannah Messiahdas, "Augmented Reality & Virtual Reality is Now a Reality For Enterprise," Infosys, 2019, www.infosys.com/services/microsoft-cloud-business/insights/documents/augmented-virtual-reality-enterprises.pdf.

20 "Facts and Figures about Materials, Waste and Recycling," US Environmental Protection Agency, accessed August 1, 2021, www.epa.gov/facts-and-figures-about-materials-waste-and-recycling/containers-and-packaging-product-specific-data.

21 Magali A. Delmas, "How to Boost Recycling: Reward Consumers with Discounts, Deals and Social Connections," The Conversation, 2019, https://theconversation.com/how-to-boost-recycling-reward-consumers-with-discounts-deals-and-social-connections-124389.

22 Phil Christensen, personal interview with industry expert, July 7, 2020.

23 Stefano Centomo, Nicola Dall'Ora, and Franco Fummi, "The Design of a Digital-Twin for Predictive Maintenance," 2020 25th IEEE International Conference on Emerging Technologies and Factory Automation, 2020, pp. 1781–1788, https://ieeexplore.ieee.org/document/9212071.

24 Kosmas Alexopoulos, Nikolaos Nikolakis, and George Chryssolouris, "Digital Twin-Driven Supervised Machine Learning for the Development of Artificial Intelligence Applications in Manufacturing," International Journal of Computer Integrated Manufacturing, 33:5, 429–439, DOI: 10.1080/0951192X.2020.1747642, April 8, 2020, www.tandfonline.com/doi/full/10.1080/095119 2X.2020.1747642.

25 Dean Hopkins, personal interview with industry expert, June 12, 2020.

26 Louise Wright & Stuart Davidson, "How to Tell the Difference between a Model and a Digital Twin," Advanced Modeling and Simulation in Engineering Sciences 7, March 11, 2020, https://amses-journal.springeropen.com/articles/10.1186/s40323-020-00147-4.

CHAPTER 7

1 Ursula Hartenberger, "Why Buildings Matter," The Guardian, July 1, 2011, www.theguardian.com/sustainable-business/sustainable-building.

2 Robert Siegel & Melissa Block, "Blair Steps Down, Takes Up Mideast Peace," NPR, June 27, 2007, www.npr.org/transcripts/11478169?storyId=11478169.

3 "Churchill and the Commons Chamber," UK Parliament, accessed August 2, 2021, www.parliament.uk/about/living-heritage/building/palace/architecture/palacestructure/churchill.

4 Susan Lund, Anu Madgavkar, James Manyika et al., "The Future of Work after COVID-19," McKinsey, February 18, 2021, www.mckinsey.com/featured-insights/future-of-work/the-future-of-work-after-COVID-19.

5   Win, "We Can't Tackle the Climate Change Crisis without Changing
     Construction. Here's Why."

6   Josh Ridley, personal interview with industry expert, June 2, 2020.

7   Rimes Mortimer, personal interview with industry expert, June 9,
     2020.

8   Josh Ridley, personal interview with industry expert, June 2, 2020.

9   Celine Herweijer, Benjamin Combes, Antonia Gawel et al.,
     "Unlocking Technology for the Global Goals," World Economic
     Forum, January 2020, http://www3.weforum.org/docs/Unlocking_
     Technology_for_the_Global_Goals.pdf.

10   Amy C. Edmondson, "Wicked-Problem Solvers: Lessons from
     Successful Cross-Industry Teams," *Harvard Business Review*, June
     2016, https://hbr.org/2016/06/wicked-problem-solvers.

11   Gregg D. Ander, "Daylighting," Whole Building Design Guide,
     September 15, 2016, www.wbdg.org/resources/daylighting.

12   "Ventilation and Air Quality in Offices: Fact Sheet," United States
     Environmental Protection Agency, accessed August 25, 2021,
     www.epa.gov/sites/default/files/2014-08/documents/ventilation_
     factsheet.pdf.

13   Juan Pedro Tomás, "Infosys Collaborates with RxR Realty to
     Develop a Smart Office Platform," In-Building Tech, May 17, 2021,
     https://inbuildingtech.com/smart-buildings/infosys-collaborates-
     with-rxr-realty-to-develop-a-smart-office-platform/.

14   "The Deloitte Global Millennial Survey 2020," Deloitte, January
     2020, https://www2.deloitte.com/content/dam/Deloitte/global/
     Documents/About-Deloitte/deloitte-2020-millennial-survey.pdf.

15   "Gartner Forecasts 51% of Global Knowledge Workers Will Be
     Remote by the End of 2021," press release, Gartner, June 22, 2021,
     www.gartner.com/en/newsroom/press-releases/2021-06-22-gartner-
     forecasts-51-percent-of-global-knowledge-workers-will-be-remote-
     by-2021.

16   Janet Pogue McLaurin and Tim Pittman, "Across the Globe,
     Workers Want a Hybrid Work Model," Gensler, accessed September

8, 2021, www.gensler.com/blog/across-the-globe-workers-want-a-hybrid-work-model.

17   Reza Alaghehband, "Keeping Pace with the Smart Building Evolution," Engineered Systems, April 21, 2021, www.esmagazine. com/articles/101408-keeping-pace-with-the-smart-building-evolution.

18   "Work-at-Home After COVID-19—Our Forecast," Global Workplace Analytics, accessed September 8, 2021, https:// globalworkplaceanalytics.com/work-at-home-after-COVID-19-our-forecast.

19   Lisette van Doorn, Amanprit Arnold, and Elizabeth Rapoport, "In the Age of Cities: The Impact of Urbanisation on House Prices and Affordability." In *Hot Property* (Springer, 2019), 3–13, https://link. springer.com/chapter/10.1007/978-3-030-11674-3_1.

20   Kelsey Miller, "The Triple Bottom Line: What It Is & Why It's Important," Harvard Business School, December 8, 2020, https:// online.hbs.edu/blog/post/what-is-the-triple-bottom-line.

21   "68% of the World Population Projected to Live in Urban Areas by 2050, Says UN," Department of Economic and Social Affairs, United Nations, May 16, 2018, www.un.org/development/desa/en/news/ population/2018-revision-of-world-urbanization-prospects.html.

22   Benjamin Goldstein, Dimitrios Gounaridis, and Joshua P. Newell, "The Carbon Footprint of Household Energy Use in the United States," Proceedings of the National Academy of Sciences of the United States of America, August 11, 2020, www.pnas.org/ content/117/32/19122.

23   Scott Sedam, "The Home Building Technology Revolution, Part III: The Missing Link," ProBuilder, March 11, 2021, www.probuilder. com/home-building-technology-revolution-part-iii-missing-link.

24   Anna Hensel, "The Coronavirus Is Accelerating Foot Locker's Plans to Move Its Stores Out of Malls," Modern Retail, May 22, 2020, www.modernretail.co/retail/the-coronavirus-is-accelerating-foot-lockers-plans-to-move-its-stores-out-of-malls/.

25 "Smart Stadium Market—Growth, Trends, COVID-19 Impact, and Forecasts (2021–2026)," Mordor Intelligence, 2020, www.mordorintelligence.com/industry-reports/smart-stadium-market.

26 "Thrive in the New Normal," WorxWell, accessed September 8, 2021, https://worxwell.com/.

27 "Infosys Collaborates with RXR Realty to Develop a Smart Office Platform Running on Microsoft Azure for Safe Return to Work," press release, Infosys, May 13, 2021, www.infosys.com/newsroom/press-releases/2021/develop-smart-office-platform.html.

28 "2019 United States Manufacturing Facts," National Association of Manufacturers, accessed September 5, 2021, www.nam.org/state-manufacturing-data/2019-united-states-manufacturing-facts/.

29 "Sources of Greenhouse Gas Emissions," United States Environmental Protection Agency, accessed August 25, 2021, www.epa.gov/ghgemissions/sources-greenhouse-gas-emissions#commercial-and-residential.

30 "Annual Energy Outlook 2021: Emissions," p. 3, United States Energy Information Agency, February 3, 2021, www.eia.gov/outlooks/aeo/pdf/08%20AEO2021%20Emissions.pdf.

31 Ibid, 5.

32 S Ramachandran, Samad Masood, and Nampuraja Enose, "Industry 4.0 Maturity Index at Infosys—A Case Study," Infosys, September 2019, www.infosys.com/iki/insights/industry-maturity.html.

33 Günther Schuh, Reiner Anderl, Jürgen Gausemeier, Michael ten Hompel, and Wolfgang Wahlster, "Industrie 4.0 Maturity Index," acatech—National Academy of Science and Engineering, 2017, www.acatech.de/wp-content/uploads/2018/03/acatech_STUDIE_Maturity_Index_eng_WEB.pdf.

34 "Top 50 Smart City Governments," Eden Strategy Institute, accessed August 25, 2021, www.smartcitygovt.com/202021-publication.

35 Brian Buntz, "The World's 5 Smartest Cities," IoT World Today, May 18, 2016, www.iotworldtoday.com/2016/05/18/world-s-5-smartest-cities/.

36   Jacob Corvidae, Chiara dalla Chiesa, Robert Denda et al., "Net Zero Carbon Cities: An Integrated Approach," January 11, 2021, www. weforum.org/reports/net-zero-carbon-cities-an-integrated-approach.

37   Gordon Feller, personal email interview with industry expert, June 8, 2020.

38   Andrew J. Hawkins, "Kansas City Just Installed Free Public WI-FI and Dozens of 'Smart' Streetlights," The Verge, May 9, 2016, www. theverge.com/2016/5/9/11640558/kansas-city-free-public-wifi-smart-streetlights-google-sprint-cisco.

39   "What is City Possible," City Possible, accessed September 8, 2021, https://citypossible.com/about/#textwithmap.

40   SMC Labs, San Mateo County, accessed September 7, 2021, https://smclabs.io/about-us/.

41   "Urbanization: Expanding Opportunities, but Deeper Divides," Department of Economic and Social Affairs, United Nations, February 21, 2020, www.un.org/development/desa/en/news/social/urbanization-expanding-opportunities-but-deeper-divides.html.

42   Skip Descant, "Phoenix Partnership Promises to Further Regional Smart Cities Work," Government Technology, October 1, 2018, www.govtech.com/products/phoenix-partnership-promises-to-further-regional-smart-cities-work.html.

43   "Bowman Helping Phoenix Become a Top Tech-Driven 'Smart Region'," Arizona State University, July 18, 2020, https://sustainability-innovation.asu.edu/news/archive/bowman-helping-phoenix-become-a-top-tech-driven-smart-region/.

44   Diana Bowman, personal email interview with academic expert, March 12, 2021.

45   "Metro21: Smart Cities Institute," Carnegie Mellon University, accessed September 8, 2021, www.cmu.edu/metro21/about/index. html.

46   "Smart City Challenge," United States Department of Transportation, December 29, 2016, www.transportation.gov/sites/dot.gov/files/docs/Smart%20City%20Challenge%20Lessons%20Learned.pdf.

47 "City of Pittsburgh Proposal, Beyond Traffic: The Smart City Challenge," United States Department of Transportation, February 4, 2016, www.transportation.gov/sites/dot.gov/files/docs/Pittsburgh%20Vision%20Narrative.pdf.

48 "World Urbanization Prospects 2018: Highlights," p. 7, United Nations, Department of Economic and Social Affairs, Population Division, 2019, https://population.un.org/wup/Publications/Files/WUP2018-Highlights.pdf.

49 "Report on the Environment," United States Environmental Protection Agency, accessed August 26, 2021, www.epa.gov/report-environment/indoor-air-quality.

CHAPTER 8

1 Rossella Lorenzi, "Rome's Oldest Aqueduct," *Archaeology*, January 2018, www.archaeology.org/issues/281-1801/features/6178-rome-aqua-appia-aqueduct.

2 Richard Bruschi, "The Ancient Roman Road, a Timeless Engineering Feat," History of Yesterday, October 17, 2020, https://historyofyesterday.com/the-ancient-roman-road-a-timeless-engineering-feat-f09538ea24d7.

3 Artemis Zafari, "The Water System of Ancient Rome," Engineering Rome, December 6, 2019, http://engineeringrome.org/the-water-system-of-ancient-rome/.

4 Giovanni De Feo, Andreas N. Angelakis, Georgios P. Antoniou et al., "Historical and Technical Notes on Aqueducts from Prehistoric to Medieval Times," *Water* 5, 1996–2025, November 28, 2013, www.mdpi.com/2073-4441/5/4/1996/htm.

5 Nick Orsi, "The Engineering Behind the Via Appia," Engineering Rome, 2013, http://engineeringrome.org/the-engineering-behind-the-via-appia/.

6 Bruschi, "The Ancient Roman Road, a Timeless Engineering Feat."

7   "Eavesdrop, Fiasco, and 8 More Words with Surprising Origins,"
    Merriam-Webster, July 20, 2021, www.merriam-webster.com/words-
    at-play/top-10-words-with-remarkable-origins-vol-1/fiasco.

8   "Sharing an Equitable and Sustainable Digital Future," Infosys,
    2021, www.infosys.com/sustainability/documents/infosys-esg-
    report-2020-21.pdf.

9   Saskia Feast, "Deeds Not Words: The Growth Of Climate Action in
    the Corporate World," Natural Capital Partners, accessed August
    26, 2021, https://assets.naturalcapitalpartners.com/downloads/
    Deeds_Not_Words_-_The_Growth_Of_Climate_Action_In_The_
    Corporate_World.pdf.

10 Bernhard Fietz and Edeltraud Günther, "Changing Organizational
    Culture to Establish Sustainability," *Controlling & Management
    Review* 65, 32–40, April 8, 2021, https://link.springer.com/
    article/10.1007/s12176-021-0379-4.

11 Dickon Pinner, "Decarbonizing Industry will Take Time and
    Money—But Here's How to Get a Head Start," McKinsey
    Sustainability, McKinsey, December 14, 2018, www.mckinsey.com/
    business-functions/sustainability/our-insights/sustainability-blog/
    decarbonizing-industry-will-take-time-and-money-but-heres-how-
    to-get-a-head-start.

12 Spyros Sakellariadis, personal interview with industry expert, May
    27, 2020.

13 Dave Bartlett, "The Top Ten Ways We Waste Energy And Water In
    Buildings," Breaking Energy, July 26, 2011, https://breakingenergy.
    com/2011/07/26/the-top-ten-ways-we-waste-energy-and-water-in-
    buildings/.

14 Win, "We Can't Tackle the Climate Change Crisis without Changing
    Construction. Here's Why."

15 Corey Glickman and Jeff Kavanaugh, "Attract Talent and Conserve
    Resources with Smart Spaces," Infosys, August 2019, https://www.
    infosys.com/about/knowledge-institute/insights/documents/attract-
    talent-conserve.pdf.

16   Mike Greenberg, "Arete: The Spirit of Excellence," Mythology
      Source, June 30, 2020, https://mythologysource.com/arete-greek-
      goddess.

17   Henry George Liddell and Robert Scott, *An Intermediate Greek-
      English Lexicon: Founded Upon the Seventh Edition of Liddell and Scott's
      Greek-English Lexicon* (Benediction Classics, 2010).

18   Stephen Miller, *Arete: Greek Sports from Ancient Sources* (California:
      University of California Press, 2004), 149–152.

19   Chris Irwin, "How Comfy are your Building's Occupants? Part 1," J2
      Innovations, February 25, 2020, www.j2inn.com/blog/how-comfy-
      are-your-buildings-occupants-part-1.

20   "Chapter 1: General Principles," Planning, Design and Construction
      Guidelines, University of New Hampshire, accessed August 26,
      2021, www.unh.edu/facilities/chapter-1-general-principles.

21   Ann Cavoukian and Mark Dixon, "Privacy and Security by Design:
      An Enterprise Architecture Approach," Information and Privacy
      Commissioner, September 2013, www.ipc.on.ca/wp-content/
      uploads/Resources/pbd-privacy-and-security-by-design-oracle.pdf.

22   Scott Rose, Oliver Borchert, Stu Mitchell, and Sean Connelly, "NIST
      Special Publication 800-207: Zero Trust Architecture," National
      Institute of Standards and Technology, August 2020, https://
      nvlpubs.nist.gov/nistpubs/SpecialPublications/NIST.SP.800-207.pdf.

23   Kevin Casey, "Hybrid Cloud by the Numbers, 2020: 10 Stats to See,"
      The Enterprisers Project, July 27, 2020, https://enterprisersproject.
      com/article/2020/7/hybrid-cloud-10-statistics.

24   "The Paris Agreement: What is the Paris Agreement?" United
      Nations Framework Convention on Climate Change (UNFCCC),
      accessed September 3, 2021, https://unfccc.int/process-and-
      meetings/the-paris-agreement/the-paris-agreement.

25   "Paris Agreement Under the United Nations Framework
      Convention on Climate Change (Paris Agreement)," December 12,
      2015, https://unfccc.int/sites/default/files/english_paris_
      agreement.pdf.

26 George Serafeim, "Social-Impact Efforts That Create Real Value," *Harvard Business Review*, September–October 2020, https://hbr.org/2020/09/social-impact-efforts-that-create-real-value.

27 Alberto Carrillo Pineda, Heidi Huusko, Cynthia Cummis, and Alexander Farsan, "Understand the Methods for Science-based Climate Action," Science Based Targets, February 25, 2021, https://sciencebasedtargets.org/news/understand-science-based-targets-methods-climate-action/.

28 Ibid.

29 "Science-Based Target Setting Manual," Science Based Targets, April 2020, https://sciencebasedtargets.org/resources/legacy/2017/04/SBTi-manual.pdf.

30 Ibid.

31 Serafeim, "Social-Impact Efforts That Create Real Value."

32 Joe Kennedy, "How Induced Innovation Lowers the Cost of a Carbon Tax," Information Technology and Innovation Foundation, June 2018, https://www2.itif.org/2018-carbon-tax-report.pdf.

33 Alan McGill, Richard Gledhill, Malcolm Preston, Liz Logan, and Kathy Nieland, "Carbon Disclosure Project 2010: Global 500 Report," Circle of Blue, 2010, www.circleofblue.org/wp-content/uploads/2010/11/CDP-2010-G500.pdf.

34 "Alphabet, Citigroup and Walmart Named Among Global Leaders on Corporate Climate Action in CDP Climate A List," Climate Disclosure Project, January 20, 2020, www.cdp.net/en/articles/media/alphabet-citigroup-and-walmart-named-among-global-leaders-on-corporate-climate-action-in-cdp-climate-a-list.

35 "SBTi Criteria and Recommendations," Science Based Targets, April 2021, https://sciencebasedtargets.org/resources/files/SBTi-criteria.pdf.

36 Ibid.

37 "Buildings Life Cycle Assessment (LCA)," MIT Concrete Sustainability Hub, accessed September 9, 2021, https://cshub.mit.edu/buildings/lca.

38   "Quantifying Building Life Cycle Environmental Impacts," MIT
     Concrete Sustainability Hub, November 27, 2016, https://cshub.mit.
     edu/sites/default/files/documents/Building%20LCA_Final.pdf.

39   Hans-Jochen Luhmann, Sabine Balk, and Hans Dembowski,
     "Appropriate Carbon Prices," Development and Cooperation, May
     20, 2020, www.dandc.eu/en/article/why-carbon-emissions-pricing-
     and-carbon-shadow-pricing-both-make-sense.

40   Luc Hillege, "Environmental Cost Indicator (ECI)—Overview,"
     Ecochain, June 13, 2019, https://ecochain.com/knowledge/
     environmental-cost-indicator-eci/.

41   Aashish Sharma, Abhishek Saxena, Muneesh Sethi et al., "Life
     Cycle Assessment of Buildings: A Review," Elsevier, September 2,
     2010, www.researchgate.net/publication/227421373_Life_cycle_
     assessment_of_buildings_A_review.

42   Spyros Sakellariadis, personal interview with industry expert, May
     27, 2020.

43   Jeff Kavanaugh and Rafee Tarafdar, *The Live Enterprise: Create
     a Continuously Evolving and Learning Organization* (New York:
     McGraw-Hill Education, 2021).

44   Jeffrey Hiatt, *A Model for Change in Business, Government and our
     Community* (Colorado: Prosci Learning Center Publications, 2006).

45   "Principle 6: Labour," United Nations Global Compact, accessed
     September 1, 2021, https://www.unglobalcompact.org/what-is-gc/
     mission/principles/principle-6.

46   Ibid.

47   "Global Nonresidential Green Buildings Market Report (2021 to 2030)—
     COVID-19 Growth and Change," press release, *Global News Wire*,
     May 28, 2021, www.globenewswire.com/en/news-release/2021/05/28/
     2238060/28124/en/Global-Nonresidential-Green-Buildings-Market-
     Report-2021-to-2030-COVID-19-Growth-and-Change.html.

48   Jeff Kavanaugh and Rafee Tarafdar, *The Live Enterprise: Create
     a Continuously Evolving and Learning Organization* (New York:
     McGraw-Hill Education, 2021).

49 "Lao Tzu," BBC World Service, accessed September 9, 2021, www. bbc.co.uk/worldservice/learningenglish/movingwords/shortlist/ laotzu.shtml.

EPILOGUE

1 "UN Report Finds COVID-19 is Reversing Decades of Progress on Poverty, Healthcare and Education," Department of Economic and Social Affairs, United Nations, July 7, 2020, https://www.un.org/ development/desa/en/news/sustainable/sustainable-development-goals-report-2020.html.

2 "Financing for Sustainable Development Report 2021," Inter-agency Task Force on Financing for Development, Development Finance, United Nations, accessed August 2, 2021, https:// developmentfinance.un.org/fsdr2021.

3 Schwab, *Stakeholder Capitalism*, p. xiii.

4 Timothy Goodson, "Global Energy Review 2021," International Energy Agency, 2021, https://iea.blob.core.windows.net/assets/ d0031107-401d-4a2f-a48b-9eed19457335/GlobalEnergyReview2021.pdf.

5 "Report on the Environment," United States Environmental Protection Agency, accessed August 26, 2021, www.epa.gov/report-environment/indoor-air-quality.

6 Kim Fausing, "Climate Emergency: How Our Cities can Inspire Change," World Economic Forum, January 17, 2020, www.weforum. org/agenda/2020/01/smart-and-the-city-working-title/.

7 "World Urbanization Prospects 2018: Highlights," p. 7, United Nations, Department of Economic and Social Affairs, Population Division, 2019, https://population.un.org/wup/Publications/Files/ WUP2018-Highlights.pdf.

8 "The Sustainable Development Goals Report 2020," United Nations, July 7, 2020, https://unstats.un.org/sdgs/report/2020/The-Sustainable-Development-Goals-Report-2020.pdf.

9   "Financing for Sustainable Development Report 2021," Inter-agency Task Force on Financing for Development, Department of Finance, United Nations, 2021, https://developmentfinance.un.org/sites/developmentfinance.un.org/files/FSDR_2021.pdf.

10 "Global Smart Cities Industry," ReportLinker, May 2021, www.reportlinker.com/p05485940/Global-Smart-Cities-Industry.html?utm_source=GNW.

11 "Estimating the Size of the Commercial Real Estate Market in the US," Nareit, July 2019, www.reit.com/data-research/research/nareit-research/estimating-size-commercial-real-estate-market-us.

12 Reshma Singh, Monto Mani, and Swapnil Joshi, "Decarbonize, Democratize, and Digitalize India's Built Environment: A Transformative 2050 Vision for Wellness and Resilience," Infosys, 2021.

13 Winston Churchill, "Their Finest Hour," International Churchill Society, June 18, 1940, https://winstonchurchill.org/resources/speeches/1940-the-finest-hour/their-finest-hour.

14 Cheryl L. Mansfield, "STS-135: The Final Voyage," NASA, July 27, 2011, www.nasa.gov/mission_pages/shuttle/shuttlemissions/sts135/launch/sts-135_mission-overview.html.

15 Marina Koren, "Sunrise, Sunset, Sunrise, Sunset, Sunrise...," *The Atlantic*, September 15, 2015, www.theatlantic.com/notes/2015/09/sun-international-space-station/405463/.

16 "International Space Station Facts and Figures," NASA, Sep 7, 2021, www.nasa.gov/feature/facts-and-figures.

17 Johannes Kemppanen, "More than SCE to AUX—Apollo 12 Lightning Strike Incident: A Look 50 Years On," NASA, February 24, 2021, https://history.nasa.gov/afj/ap12fj/a12-lightningstrike.html.

18 NASA Johnson Space Center, "Apollo 12 Spacecraft Commentary," p. 14, NASA Johnson Space Center Mission Transcript History Portal, November 24, 1969, https://historycollection.jsc.nasa.gov/JSCHistoryPortal/history/mission_trans/AS12_PAO.PDF.

19 "NASA Johnson Space Center Oral History Project: Edited Oral History Transcript," NASA, January 26, 2000, https://

historycollection.jsc.nasa.gov/JSCHistoryPortal/history/oral_
histories/AaronJW/AaronJW_1-26-00.htm.

20   Enric Sala, "Now or Never for Saving Our Natural World," Project
Syndicate, March 9, 2020, www.project-syndicate.org/commentary/
global-deal-nature-biodiversity-by-enric-sala-2020-03.

INDEX

Page numbers in *italics* indicate figures and tables.

ABOUT THE AUTHORS

Corey Glickman is Vice President at Infosys and leads their sustainability and design business, delivering smart space initiatives for clients globally. Corey is a member of both the World Economic Forum Pioneer Cities group and the MIT Technology Review Board and is a faculty expert at Singularity University. The American Institute of Graphic Arts named Corey one of the one hundred most influential designers of the decade.

Jeff Kavanaugh is Vice President and Head of the Infosys Knowledge Institute, the research and thought leadership arm of Infosys, a leading tech and consulting company. Jeff is an adjunct professor at the Jindal School of Management at the University of Texas at Dallas and author of the books The Live Enterprise and Consulting Essentials. Jeff has been published in Harvard Business Review and other leading business publications.

Made in United States
Orlando, FL
30 November 2022

25259746R00214